Stillness in Motion in the Seventeenth-Century Theatre

Art forms begin in a collaboration of stillness and motion, and throughout history the categories of the still and the moving gain value according to the cultural weight given to the permanent, the stable and the elapsing, the ephemeral. In the seventeenth century, emerging practices, such as print, collecting, and performance, influence early modern discourse of stillness and motion – a discourse always articulated by metaphors of gender.

Stillness in Motion in the Seventeenth-Century Theatre provides a comprehensive examination of this aesthetic theory. The author investigates this aesthetic history as a form of artistic creation, as a form of philosophical investigation, as a way of representing and manipulating ideas about gender, and also as a way of acknowledging, reinforcing and making a critique of social values for the still and moving, the permanent and elapsing. Creating an experiential argument for scholarly attention to performance, this book suggests that without knowing *how* performance creates meaning in reception, our understanding of a century where much of the political, theatrical, and social action occurred between audiences and in public spaces is blunted. The focus on performance and reception offers theories on the practice of reading and the frequent use of theatrical techniques employed by authors to evoke the sensations of live performance. The author also examines the practice of collecting and the give and take of reception in the context of theories of gift exchange.

The book's analysis covers the entire seventeenth century with chapters on the work of Ben Jonson, John Milton, the pamphletheatre, Aphra Behn, John Vanbrugh, and Jeremy Collier and will be of interest to scholars in the areas of literary and performance studies.

P.A. Skantze is an independent scholar and director working in Rome. Currently a fellow at the Italian Academy at Columbia University, she was a Fulbright senior research fellow in 2002 investigating transnational identity in theatre festivals across the European Union.

Routledge studies in Renaissance literature and culture

Stillness in Motion in the Seventeenth-Century Theatre

P.A. Skantze

Routledge
Taylor & Francis Group

LONDON AND NEW YORK

First published 2003
by Routledge
11 New Fetter Lane, London EC4P 4EE

Simultaneously published in the USA and Canada
by Routledge
29 West 35th Street, New York, NY 10001

Routledge is an imprint of the Taylor & Francis Group

© 2003 P.A. Skantze

Typeset in Sabon by
Rosemount Typing Services, Thornhill, Dumfriesshire
Printed and bound in Great Britain by
Antony Rowe Ltd, Chippenham, Wiltshire

British Library Cataloguing in Publication Data
A catalogue record for this book is available
from the British Library

Library of Congress Cataloging in Publication Data
Skantze, P. A., 1957–
    Stillness in motion in the seventeenth century theatre / P.A. Skantze
        p. cm. – (Routledge studies in Renaissance literature and culture)
    Includes bibliographical references and index.
    1. English drama–17th century–History and criticism. 2. Drama–Technique.
    3. Theater–England–History–17th century. 4. Quietude in literature. I. Title.
    II. Series.

PR678.T35 S58 2003
822'.409–dc21
                                                                2002037046
ISBN 0–415–28668–9

HotSpur: . . . in his ear I'll hollow "Mortimer!"
         Nay, I'll have a starling shall be taught to speak
         Nothing but "Mortimer," and give it to him
         To keep his anger still in motion.
Worcester: Hear you, cousin, a word . . .
                                    (I Henry IV, I. iii. 221–5)

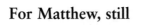
For Matthew, still

Contents

Acknowledgments

This book has had its own moving journey with three principal stops, Columbia University, the University of Michigan at Ann Arbor, and Rome, Italy. My inspiration began in classes at Columbia with Carolyn Heilbrun and Nancy Miller, and continued outside those classes in discussions with Sue Heath and Lucy Reinhardt. Just when my affection for the novel was beginning to be superseded by my preference for performance and theatre, I heard the siren call of John Milton in the voice of Margaret Ferguson. As the director of my dissertation, Margie brought to bear all her talents as a teacher: acute insights, generosity, and patience when the project seemed to expand beyond the boundaries of all reason. She remains a model for scholarship and teaching. Jean Howard's arrival at Columbia was a boon to many of us; her clarity correcting my confusion and the wealth of knowledge she brought to the process made my work richer. Julie Stone Peters granted me the gift of an inability to read and work in the seventeenth century without seeing the effects of print culture everywhere. Sue Winnet offered friendship and a passionate interest in thinking about teaching and writing. Susan Manning was a model for me of the independent scholar working in the academy; her pursuit of her work on dance in the midst of a very textual world showed me the way with my own performance work. Mike Seidel and Martin Meisel, two scholars and gentlemen, cheered my time at Columbia with jokes about Restoration theatre only a specialist could love or understand. Martin's classes in European drama still provide me with a foundation for thinking about contemporary issues of identity, tradition, and nationality in European performance.

I am grateful to many people at the University of Michigan, Ann Arbor. From the first pleasure of being welcomed and supported by Enoch Brater and our delight at being able to talk "theatre," through all the classes and the many, many students who offered themselves as sacrifice to my experiments in using music, dance, scene production, and film clips to show them "how" Shakespeare, Behn, and Milton (!) made theatre work. Parts of this book came into being across the table on Sunday nights when

Patsy Yaeger and I dined on ideas and the joy of thinking in sound. Patsy made me believe in myself in the worst moments of adjusting to academic life and her belief in me sustains me now as an independent scholar. Val Traub arrived at Ann Arbor just in time to challenge me constantly with just the right probing questions and to champion clarity where there was only the suggestion of connected ideas. Her support and her largesse have never waned. Linda Gregerson by her poetry, by her love of ideas and the way they can be expressed always made me want to write about performance more vividly. Michigan profited by the arrival of Carroll Smith-Rosenberg and Alvia Golden and I profit from their sustaining friendship. Carroll read parts of the manuscript and encouraged interdisciplinary thinking, and Alvia encouraged laughter and perspective. Many friends supported me by laughter and over red wine, Suzanne Raitt, Arlene Keizer, Anita Norich, and Liz Barnes, while dinners at Nick and Elena Delbanco's gave solace on cold Michigan nights.

Students at Michigan also deserve thanks, too many will go unnamed. Gina Bloom became a colleague and a friend and together we developed ways of teaching performance; her work on the voice helped me to think in sound. I thank Troy Gordon and Andrew Sofer and Flagg Miller. Gillian Knoll from the first moment she appeared in my office demanded that I teach her everything I knew, and much I didn't, about Shakespeare. As she makes her own career as a scholar, I am grateful to have been so much prodded and praised by her.

Some people have supported me by the work they do and how they do it: Joe Roach, Peggy Phelan, and John Russsell Brown form a very particular triumvirate of scholars and friends whose work in performance and whose advice and encouragement inspire me.

As an independent scholar my circle of influence includes many friends outside the Academy whose intellectual and cultural curiosity makes me more adventurous. I thank Roya Kowsary who provides a model of independent intellectual spirit in her examining, questioning, theorizing elegantly and then laughing, and I am grateful for her model of friendship. I thank Laura Flanders for her friendship and her commitment to change a world sometimes frozen in its own inability to act and Elizabeth Streb for the work she makes and the way she makes it 'go.' While I was writing my dissertation I benefited from the extraordinary company of Vincent Virga and James McCourt, and hope to continue to do so for the time remaining. I thank Larry Osgood, Currie and the independent scholars in PSI. In Rome, grazie to Julio Velasco, Pierre-Yves Pogrom, Sara Antonelli, Berringer Fifield, and Jeffery Blanchard.

Since the gift always moves and since it sometimes moves anonymously, I acknowledge here all who have been a part of this book's moving toward publication. I am grateful to the two anonymous readers for Routledge and hope I have accomplished the major part of what they urged me to do to make the book as good as it could be. Talia Rodgers supported my project in the beginning on its arrival at Routledge; Rosie Waters moved it along through its initial readers' reports, and Joe Whiting found it a home in this series. I thank them all.

I thank my father for his support of me in every sense, but most especially for his pleasure in my successes, which made them seem sweeter. I thank my mother for her support and also her own love of the dramatic, of the theatrical, a love that fostered my own. My sister wrestles daily with the practical difficulties of creating performance, of keeping the spirit moving when outside support might be weak. I am blessed in her company both as a sibling and as a performer and artist. The end of the production of this book took place in between visits to Vanderbilt hospital where my brother was recuperating from an accident. In some sense the arguments for motion became all the more apt as a wish for his recovery, as a promise of Larr once again in motion. Throughout my life it has been his voice finding wonder in what I do and what I have accomplished which I borrowed and will borrow to keep on. This book came into being through the power of hearing "Red, that's sensational," over and over again.

The final thank you cannot be effusive or sustained enough to convey the joy of the gratitude. It is to Matthew that I dedicate this book; if the reader finds felicitous sentences, apt language, a measured flow between one paragraph and another, such moments occur because Matthew listened to me read the book chapter by chapter, making emendations or asking me to explain more clearly which allowed me to articulate the ideas fully. The pleasure of his company grows "the more by reaping," and I know that "age" will not wither nor custom "stale" such "infinite variety" as his.

Part of the Prologue appears in P.A. Skantze "Making It Up: Improvisation as Cultural Exchange between Shakespeare and Italy," in Michele Marrapodi (ed.) *Shakespeare and Intertextuality* (Rome: Bulzoni Editore, 2000; reprint forthcoming Manchester University Press) and is reproduced here with permission of Manchester University Press.

Introduction

Lovers and madmen have such seething brains
Such shaping fantasies that apprehend
More than cool reason ever comprehends

The forms of things unknown, the poet's pen
Turns them to shapes, and gives to airy nothing
A local habitation and a name.
    A Midsummer Night's Dream, V. i. 4–6, 16–18

The woods

Almost as oft-cited as Prospero's retiring wand speech, these lines from *A Midsummer Night's Dream* with the happy dyads of lovers and madmen, of apprehension and comprehension, and the mixed collusion of the daily, "a name," married to the undefinable, "airy nothing," produce a concentrated meditation on the quality of reception between maker and receiver. Apprehension receives in the wake of the production of images: the horses of the imagination following the cart of shaping fantasies. But the common sense of the word apprehension also includes in its meanings a worrying, an uncertainty, an instinct often fearful. Only madmen and lovers, according to this famous couplet, use apprehension as a divining rod, finding water where the mind perceives dry ground. Comprehension, even in the sound of its saying, circles and settles. Its coolness contrasts with the necessary heat in a word like "seethe."

These four lines of Shakespeare suggest a parable of learning by the senses. Comprehension brings with it the comfort of full knowledge, complete in itself – an end in seeking. While apprehension, by contrast, partakes in microcosmic wonder, expanding always at the almost not seen borders of a fantasy. The eyes strain, the ears open, the heart pounds in the effort, the mouth pants in anticipation, it is a sensuously participatory phenomenon never completed. And yet both words are poachers, their roots prehensile (to take); thus the plethora of words about capturing used for knowledge, to grasp something, to 'get it.' Apprehension takes coming and going; lovers and madmen can be apprehended for 'their own good,' locked up till the "shaping fantasies" fade.

Somewhere here at the crux of apprehension and comprehension, at the intersection of the mad and the loved, lies the aesthetic pleasure and power of representing, implying, and reordering stillness and motion in theatrical performance. A collaborative pleasure and power made by writers, readers, players, and audiences as they move between the aural, usually communal, worlds of performance and live exchange to those intimate exchanges sometimes communal, in the world made by print.[1] In *A Midsummer Night's Dream* those who apprehend are transformed in their learning by the trickery of pageant makers and illusionists. Comprehenders never enter the woods. Though both forms of knowing are corporeal, only apprehending seems to break over the whole body, a reacquainting of the porous self with its "somatic" knowing (Melrose 1994). Shakespeare combines the verbs at the end of the lines in an almost aphoristic analogy for sensuous knowing occurring in the presence of a performed, peopled experience and intellectual learning gained by pouring over a comprehensible text. Neither word is ever very far from the other; but the participation of the bodies doing the comprehending and the apprehending differ according to circumstance, place, and duration.

The logic of theatrical narrative, its action in the present and its obligation to make a past world through which the audience might apprehend present and future, is carried through these lines spoken by Theseus, the Duke, in *A Midsummer Night's Dream*. Clearly the ruler need not tell us – the audience – about the particularities of lovers and madwomen, we have seen the fancies shaped before us. Yet the pressures of a staged representation of communal life requires Theseus as ruler to create language to reconfigure what has happened, to remind and to reorder for the memory of the participants and to explain for those in the audience who might depend upon his summaries and definition. No point in telling a person who has apprehended meaning what it means. Yet when the apprehender full of the physical feel of discovery finds herself no longer alone, how does she tell what has changed, how to tell how, *how* to show *how*?

It is my contention that in order to understand the seething and the cool in the larger ambit of the seventeenth-century theatre one must believe (or be open to being convinced) that the theatre offers something that print cannot. When literary historians have traveled back in time with a magnifying glass in hand, the shape of what they have found has been predetermined not simply by presentist, patriarchal, or Freudian notions, to name but a few scholarly habits, but also by the habit of looking for authors. Even those whose most pertinent queries investigate and question the existence of an 'author' generally search the absences for something fundamentally made from a literary scholar's tutored preference for print. But the shape of the transition occurring in the seventeenth century is a shape perceived only if one also looks for bodies in a room or in a courtyard or in a marketplace; bodies that are listening, watching, and responding to bodies on a stage, in a masque, giving a sermon, or reading a pamphlet. To be sure authors are here too, but they are a combined product of the imagination, of the delivery of the words, of the interpretation by makers and receivers alike, and sometimes of the memory of their own particular authorial bodies at their own particular theatres where their plays are being performed.

As an author I wish for a critical form something like a pop-up book where every time the words seem to sink the bodies into the sea of the abstract, a bit of paper would jump up out of the text and make Blackfriars Theatre into three-dimensional space, setting before us the close proximity of audience to thrust stage, for example. Though I would hope for such animation, what I describe is not a longing for an accompanying CDRom. Language must evoke the heat and smell of bodies: a screen between the spit of the player and the audience being sprayed would protect one from the physical consequences of live performance and a flat, colored, moving picture would be set at a scale too small to account for the mimetic and the anti-mimetic in the human shapes. Instead I will attempt to remind us often about the materiality of the world of performance *and* the world of reading, which is more tangible in this period than we sometimes credit.

For speculation about the effect of performance, the evidence must be drawn in inventive ways from the trace texts (records of playgoing, antitheatrical tracts) historians of theatre generally use.[2] Let me pause here to remind all of us as readers and writers of fixed texts that the state of performance is motion, even if the motion consists solely of an actor's respiration. The motion of theatrical exchange, not simply the external one of the bodies on the stage, or the motion of the sound of voices in the air, or even the silent motion of time passing can happen in pauses or through gestures. Motion can beget motion: an audience member can be moved – to tears, to laughter, to anger. Sometimes in improvisatory performances such an exchange between an audience member and player can become for a moment the principle give and take of the piece, as the audience takes up what Susan Bennett calls "the productive role of any theatre audience" (1990: 1).

In his most recent work, *Author's Pen and Actor's Voice*, Robert Weimann intervenes to suggest how scholars of early modern theatre and Shakespeare can benefit from work in contemporary theories of performance. Weimann seeks to "establish a new nexus for doubleness and diversity in the purpose of playing [and] the function of representation . . . There is a significant correlation between multiplicity in the purpose of playing and fluidity in the employment of theatrical space" (2000: 12). Citing performance critics, specifically feminist critics, Weimann sees similar patterns in the manner of representation theorized: "As far as certain sixteenth-century performance practices stubbornly resisted the reduction of the real and the representational into one [an attribute of performance Peggy Phelan theorizes in *Unmarked*] they, including Elizabethan performers' voices and bodies, continued to penetrate the boundary between the signs of life on-stage and those off-stage" (14). Multiplicity and fluidity in the space of performance and its reception cause a fluctuation according to Weimann between "'goose-quills' and 'common players,'" "between forms of theatre in motion" (18).

As for goose-quills, scholars of drama have often been tricked by the false promise of the playtext as well as critical essays on drama; because a piece of writing that resembles literature exists, the act of deconstruction or theoretical analysis can undermine any animate possibility of production. The act of writing about writing further encourages this forgetting, this neglect of the moments on stage when a body cannot enter unless it opens a door. Similarly a gesture may create a change in the space of the stage between one spoken line and another. "But," as dance scholar Susan Leigh Foster suggests:

> A kind of stirring . . . connects past and present bodies. This affiliation based on a kind of kinesthetic empathy between living and dead but imagined bodies enjoys no primal status outside the world of writing. It possesses no organic authority, it offers no ultimate validation for sentiment, but is redolent with physical vitality and embraces a concern for beings that live and have lived. Once the historian's body recognizes value and meaning in kinesthesia it cannot disanimate the physical action of past bodies it has begun to sense.
>
> (1995: 7)

Foster's insistence on the value and meaning of kinesthesia is a contemporary version of what I describe as Aphra Behn's *pedagogy of motion*, a supposition that the body learns with the mind, and indeed that often behavior, that bodily thing, only changes when the senses too are educated (See Prologue). Stephen Greenblatt's literary desire, "I begin with the desire to speak with the dead," becomes for the performance scholar a sensuous longing to perceive those "dead but imagined bodies" Foster elegizes (1988). More than to speak with the dead, an act conceivably done with eyes closed, mind open, one wants to give room to the movements of once living actors, of once living audiences whose breath, whose smell, whose voices, whose shapes, whose ages, and whose social positions all inhabited the space marked out for theatrical play.

To inflate the spaces so deceptively short in the text as well as the exchange at live performance, one must rely partly on what Mark Franko has termed "subjective reminiscence" (1993: 152). Franko develops the theory of how one practices this work of memory in his Introduction to *Acting on the Past*:

When the historian, archival inscriptions in hand, revisits the deserted site of display, the vivid presence of the performance is long gone. It is then that memory passes through theory by virtue of cultural necessity and the historian's interpretation becomes the prosthesis of an imaginary performative practice, returning theory to its etymological roots in vision and speculation.

(2000: 1)

This unfolding of the fan of the text into a dimensional space and time is coupled with an historical understanding of the conditions of performance and of reading in the seventeenth century. While text and performance studies have offered valuable insights into the history of performance and the critical treatment of the printed play as a work of poetry or fiction, the authors I consider in this study evidence more complicated borrowings between forms considered indebted to the oral or to the printed.

The history of the scholarship that concerns itself with the gulf between the two forms of production (print and performance) provides too easy an encampment on either side for those who value one form of production above the other. Adam Fox in his excellent history of oral and literate culture between 1500 and 1700 writes that "the boundaries between speech and text, hearing and reading, were thoroughly permeable and constantly shifting so that the dichotomy is difficult to identify and impossible to sustain" (2000: 39).[3] I specifically examine print as a material object rather than as "text" because I am convinced that the hands holding the pages, the ears hearing the words, the book upon the shelf help us to understand the physical nature of a relation between reader and author, between words and the implied performance of the dramatic work. Though much exciting criticism has been generated by Barthes' elegant suggestions about reading the world as a text, I want to reclaim the specificity of print for a period where the book was not such an ubiquitous object – except for the Bible necessary to the home – and the book of a play a relatively new material thing.[4]

Thus this study sets out to imagine the space beyond the stage as well as to animate the performance possibilities on it. Though the last decades have seen an increase in work on early modern performance and the body, the predominant method of investigation, the way one is encouraged to think about the body, continues to be textual. As Susan Foster argues, when scholars use the term "performative," they often employ the work of Judith Butler, and the implication of Butler's work based initially on speech-act theory is that one is looking for a script rather than gestures, sounds, physical exchange that convey meaning (see Foster 1998). While accounting for bodies performing and receiving might seem an effort disconcertingly speculative to all of us who have been trained to rely on text, and to believe that that reliance provides "firm" evidence, without this effort to reanimate kinesthetic exchange in time and space, our understanding of the relation of readers to playtext, audience to performed work, remains static.

Stillness in Motion as a title for and subject of my investigations suggests an interchange, an ongoing fluctuation occurring in seventeenth-century theatre and in society. Speaking of the effects on a culture of exchanges between language and meaning Maurice Merleau-Ponty reminds us that when new ideas emerge in language and meaning, those ideas are not wholly new, rather "it is clear that the principle has been previously present in the culture as an obsession or anticipation, and that the act of consciousness which lays it down as an explicit signification is never without residue" (1964: 41). The transition between oral and printed modes of production in the seventeenth century resembles Merleau-Ponty's hypothesis that language "sometimes remains a long time pregnant with transformations which are to come"; even activities which have fallen into "disuse continue to lead a diminished life in the language" while "the place of those which are to replace them is sometimes already marked out – even if only in the form of a gap, a need, or a tendency" (41).

The value placed upon different modes of production according to stillness and motion changes throughout the century, but does so gradually and erratically in a manner not unlike that of the changes in language that Merleau-Ponty theorizes. There is an "obsession or anticipation" present in the ongoing play between the still and the moving and every act "of consciousness" which articulates this play is "never without residue" (41). The means by which authors and audience attribute value offers evidence of outmoded philosophies, those "leading a diminished life" in the language of theatre and reception, as well as signaling "a gap, a need, or a tendency" yet to be fully incorporated into the theatre by those who make and watch it. For example, when Ben Jonson describes the value of printed poetry, of being in print, he resurrects traces of an old conversation about the value of stillness as a higher, more refined state over the messy daily quality of those things that move, that require constant motion in response to their own mutabilities.

Forms of production of print and performance are not considered directly under the categories of the moving and the still. Rather traces of the obsession of comparing (a philosophical, social, aesthetic obsession), and in comparing evaluating the value of the still and moving, appear as a residue in Jonson's articulation of value for new media, new forms of communication and artistic production. Thus I am arguing for the importance of the implicit exploration of stillness and motion as a preoccupation of this changing century; both the anticipation of forms of communication to come and the residues of value for communications past underlie the practical and aesthetic considerations of performance, of print, of reception.[5]

Finally, *Stillness in Motion* makes an argument for taking the seventeenth century as a whole. From Jonson to Collier, from pamphlet writers in the Interregnum to Restoration playwrights, performance history, early modern cultural history can no longer be artificially broken at the boundary of 1642–60. Recent work by such scholars as Nigel Smith, Susan Wiseman, Sharon Achinstein, and Lois Potter as well as other cultural histories of print and of reading make it clear that the influence on the practices of reception in the years when "theatres were closed" help us to understand cultural practices in the century as a whole. In the following sections I introduce factors in the history of the aesthetic uses of stillness and motion which will recur throughout the book: theatre production and reception, printed production and reception work in the interchange between the still and the moving; the use of gender as a conception used for giving and taking away value for modes of production; and gift-exchange theory as a method for understanding the still and the moving in audience reception of performance and of print.

Stages

Let us imagine a scenario for a spectator's experience at a five-act play, allowing those seventeenth-century audience members who often came and went at will during the performance to roam without our following them. Arriving before the play begins, the spectator might stand or sit, surrounded by other audience members and perhaps conversing with companions. In an indoor theatre, music from a trio of musicians is audible just at the back of the spectator's attention, loud enough to anticipate the beginning of the play but not to drown out conversation. At the outdoor theatre, the play's opening is heralded by three blasts of a trumpet, followed, usually, by the actor calling the spectators to attention by speaking the preface to the play.[6] At indoor and outdoor theatres, most prefaces worked by gathering the spectators into an audience, first by the sight of a single figure onstage speaking in rhymed verse, and, second, with verse that generally alluded to local gossip and topical occurrences, political, royal, or international. As the player recited the lines loaded with thinly veiled references, the audience by its response could take on the role of momentary *cognoscenti*, in the know and letting each other and the player understand that they were in the know by their responses.

The play begins to the fanfare of the last couplet of the Preface – remember how the rhythm of couplets at the close of prefaces and scenes guide the audience's ear through the tattoo of a finale, how within its closed pronouncement is often embedded a transition hinting at the coming action of the following act. (I'll tell him yet of Angelo's request/And fit his mind to death, for his soul's rest. *Measure for Measure*, II. iv. 185–6.) Each act will entail multiple bodies, multiple characters who will become familiar perhaps only over time. The temporal play of exchange in performance of these dramas depends upon that time; five acts can leave room enough for the losing, the lost and the found. In many performances of a play in this period in the interludes between acts there was music or juggling or clowning. Like a stretching and yawning, these intermezzi allowed space between the playing; the pressure was not upon retaining the "tension" or catching and keeping an audience's attention. Instead the potential give and take between audience and actor allowed for pauses, for the attention to stray and return. As John Russell Brown has argued, this theatre played to an audience sharing the responsibility for a performance, part of the making and the thing made (1999).[7]

Books

The potential for exchange in this space beyond the stage reminds us as well to be skeptical of the static assumptions about readerly space. Writing about visual and textual reception in *Painting and Experience in Fifteenth-Century Italy* Michael Baxandall describes the "public mind" not as "a blank tablet on which the painter's representations of a story or person could impress themselves" but as an "active institution of interior visualization with which every painter had to get along" (1972: 45). The encounter of beholder and painting created a "marriage between the painting and the beholder's visualizing activity on the same matter" (45). As evidence for the active visualizing mind Baxandall cites at length *Zardino de Oration* (Garden of Prayer), a 1454 devotional text "written for young girls" who are to move through the passion story by fixing "the places and people in your mind: a city, for example, which will be the city of Jerusalem – taking for this purpose a city that is well known to you" (46). Having furnished herself with setting and familiar characters, she is to proceed through the Passion story with these visual aids, pausing until she sees and feels the experience of each narrative segment of the story. This conduct book assumes the reader to have a costume box and scenery stored in the imagination which the reader slips into place to produce the story in time and invented space, pausing, changing scenes, and progressing through the story.

Certainly fifteenth-century Italian reading habits, particularly a religious exercise with a reader presumed to be a young girl, cannot be imported whole to account for the reception of a seventeenth-century play/prose reader. Yet an assumption of a reader's active participation in creating the drama prompts Thomas Dekker and Thomas Middleton to anticipate in their Prologue to *The Roaring Girl* that their audience, knowing the "real" Moll Frith and having heard of the forthcoming play about her, will have created her character for themselves before seeing the play. The authors try to preempt the comparisons and evaluations of "each one" who "comes/and brings a play in's head with him." ["up he summes,/What he would of a Roaring Girl have writ/If that he findes not here, he mewes at it."] We can assume then that when a reader comes to a scene in a drama where the italics read "Exit, pursued by a bear," the reader would supply imagined motion and sound, would 'see' a bear lumbering behind the actor running.[8] Neither bear nor actor in the temporal economy of performance work like pop-up figures: the bear enters, is seen first by the audience, then a bit belatedly by Antigonus, who then runs to exit, each action provoking the following one.

Most plays printed in octavo texts (even in duodecimo) run to about one hundred pages. The text removed from the shelf is light in the hand, a 'slight' volume. Picking up a book to 'play,' a reader enters into the interchange between stillness with motion, noting the textual apparatus supplied by the printer which reminds the reader how the work is performed on stage. In a printed play the absence of scenery, actors, voices, and gestures is highlighted by the directions, actions, and songs all printed in italics. These graphic aids spur the reader to remember either the play itself, which he/she might have seen, or to remember other performances and 'stage' the play in the mind according to a mix of present text and lingering memory of the play performed.

Depending on how quickly the reader read, whether she or he might have read aloud, she or he might sit with the whole play for an hour and a half to two hours. The Chorus to *Romeo and Juliet* estimates its audience will spend a like amount of time seeing the play in "our two hours traffic upon the stage," a playing time for this tragedy inconceivable and unachievable by modern players (the modern playing time is approximately three and one-half hours).[9] This study dwells at the seventeenth-century intersection of two hours and two hours: the reader's two hours spent apprehending a text through eyes or ears in private or small company and the spectator's two hours spent apprehending similar words/text as traffic across a wooden floor, traffic made through the bodies of actors and the sounds of voices. This intersection was often traversed by the same bodies, who would attend play performances as well as read playtexts.[10]

Although readers were experiencing the social and cultural changes brought by the invention of the printing press far earlier than the seventeenth century, I choose to begin my examination of the growing interdependence upon and friction between the printed form of a play and its performed production with the work of Ben Jonson. Jonson, now an iconic figure of author in studies of print culture, orchestrates his own printed works as a monument, preserved with attention to future shelves where the works will appear under the heading "poetry." Yet in his work he also shows a melancholy recognition of the inaptness of monuments, the danger that the frozen evidence of power risks losing its power to move an audience.

While manuscript production and scribal traces offer scholars a fascinating map on which to locate early modern readers and writers in the late fifteenth and sixteenth centuries, in the seventeenth century in England it is my contention that the printed text becomes figured as a repository to 'keep' knowledge in, a container increasingly categorized under labels like "dramatic literature," "poetry," and "fiction," to name a few.[11] Shelves of labeled books offer a tangible possibility of preserving consistent and organized structures of value: a library might display (1) ancient works in the original language; (2) newer forms of investigation in the "sciences"; (3) carefully chosen contemporary works in English, Italian, or French. On what shelves the form of print derived from a performed play might appear depended upon a changing attitude about the play in print as it transformed from the earlier understanding of a playtext as the performed work's "memorial" to the custom in place by 1700 of regarding drama in print as "dramatic literature" (a category that suppresses the mourning metaphor for the performance lost). Such changes did not occur overnight or become rigid any more than did the reception of the audiences for performance or of the audiences for the book.[12] Most spectators had the aural ability to follow and judge the soliloquies, conceits and betrayals of a *Romeo and Juliet* within its two hours' traffic.

While *Stillness in Motion* explores the fluctuations of the reception of printed works and the authorial strategies employed to make print move, at the beginning of the seventeenth century in England many seeking to enhance the status of print figured it predominantly as a still mode of production, not wandering, contained, not ephemeral. Therefore my discussions of print assume a recognition of this dominant, though by no means sole, attribution of the aesthetic of stillness to the book in print. Having figured the printed work as still, however, the writers and receivers had then to contend with the public circulation of the book. The conception and production of writing, figured by many authors in terms of gestation and birth, forms the private life of authorial creation. The anxious metaphors of parent–writer to child–text make up the domestic authorial scene, but extending this metaphor, one might say true anxiety for many writers of works in print begins when the little one learns to walk. Playwrights whose works 'walk away' when performed share with authors whose works are sold and distributed anxieties about movement, permanence, and interpretation. Though the author of the printed work relies on the setting of type to record his/her work with some degree of fixity, in order to be read, the commodity of the book must circulate, it must move from printer to stall, from stall to reader.[13] Despite the relatively solid artifact of a book, movement can endanger an author's idea even as it makes possible the public life of the work. "Publishing in print multiplies the opportunity for misinterpretation," Richard Wollman asserts in an essay on John Donne and manuscript culture: when Donne restricts the movement (circulation) of his work by keeping it in manuscript, he retains "some measure of authorial control" (1993: 88).

The simultaneous vulnerability to circulation and dependence upon it extended beyond literary and theatrical creations. Mobility informed vital cultural activities of seventeenth-century England. Trade, exploration, travel, scientific quests pursued by pen and post all depended upon the mobility of ships, of humans, of letters. What was brought home from the moving adventure of trade and exploration were consumable goods, put in circulation, but sometimes exhibited as part of a collection, either as a novelty in a household or as a sign of status and micro-empire (the domestic reproducing the far-flung empire). Objects of trade, commodities, easiest managed when 'transportable,' move, usually, because someone else carries them. However, ambulatory commodities that can walk away require restraints; thus chains shackle animals to be sold or shackle human trade to its inhuman purveyor. The tension – moral, spatial, economic – of the freely moving and the closely kept influenced the activities of the social world as surely as the friction created by the moving and the still made possible the performed one.

Gender, the stage, and the book

> Performance of course destabilizes the poetic procedure of dismemberment by preserving the actor's body as stubbornly whole.
> (Note in the playbill for *She Who Once Was the Helmet Maker's Beautiful Wife*)

From the design of anatomical texts, the writing of travel narratives, to the publication of "scientific discourse," virtually every emanation of printed production in the early modern period carries within it the signs of gender used as terms for evaluation. The territory mapped by the playwrights as authors in print engages as well in the debate about the value of the theatre and performance and renders that debate in metaphors of and suppositions about gender. Like the opposition of print and performance – still and moving, absence and presence – the binary of gender, while potentially malleable in practice, retains a stubborn reductive quality when used as a conception of value for fixity and motion.

The cues the culture gives for the 'feminine' nature of ephemerality, of motion uncontained and the 'masculine' nature of a fixed truth in print, of authorship as a means of circumscribing territory, tell a false tale in a world where even imaginative analogies can crossdress. For example, the blank page of paper is often likened to a passive object, the 'feminine' body, that awaits the marks of a master's hand, and yet the same text once produced and printed becomes evidence of masculine authority. Were such metaphors simply linguistic flourishes to aid the lonely author in giving life to his/her task, the implicit gender would be a matter of aesthetic play. I am suggesting in this book, however, that representations of gender are indivisible from the social use of print, the cultural weight assigned to various media and, ultimately, the production of meaning implicit in how such media are employed. Language used to assign gender to print, to performance, and to collectible objects, as well as to the activities of collecting, reading, and watching a performance serves to articulate a growing cultural interest in the preservability of knowledge in print and concomitantly the distrust of oral forms whose 'uncollectability' figured as flighty and unstable.[14]

When I first began the research for this book, the fields of print and feminist studies tended to intersect across the discipline of history. Early modernists trained in new historicism and in feminism saw the clear indications of values placed upon writing, reading, publishing, and performing, values resolutely dressed in the costumes of gender: masculine-masculine, feminine-feminine, feminine-masculine, masculine-feminine. Yet the subtleties of costume, drapery hiding the hilt of a sword, breeches below a petticoat, often went undetected. In the early years of feminist criticism, the examination of how attributions of gender indicated cultural judgments and buttressed cultural affiliations was necessarily sacrificed to the need to delineate the blatant sexism of much criticism. In broad strokes then the story of print and gender ran thus, as print lost some of its decadence conferred by its vulgar circulation, its public nature, in the late sixteenth century in England and became more and more a manly, respectable endeavor, the ephemeral productions of theatrical performance escaped into the past under the sign of the unpreserved – that is, the inconsequential. Paradoxically, the unperserved was associated with the corporeal and feminine because bound by the temporal demands of the daily world.

The degree to which these historical biases still form the basis for scholarly investigations can be obscured when a critical work uses all the 'correct' theoretical language of gender – even work supposedly immune from the historical tendency to separate the performed from the textual. As Susan Foster argues in an essay vital to feminist scholars who study kinetic forms of production:

> If performance as assimilated into cultural studies pursues the individual sometimes at the expense of the social, it also encapsulates an unexamined appropriation of the physical (read feminine) by the textual (read masculine). Both the corporeal and the feminine, as I have tried to show, share attributes of instability, ephemerality, and unknowability, whereas the textual, *even in its deconstructed versions*, maintain a solidity and rationality that aligns with the masculine.
>
> (1998: 27)

Stillness in Motion charts a very messy and gradual development of a set of values articulated through gender for the still and the moving, the preservable and the unpreservable, the printed and the performed. These values are yet so firmly embedded in the academic training in the Humanities that the challenge for writer and reader alike is to confront the unacknowledged residues of such training. Assessments of work made according to disciplinary models gravitate toward a preference for the convenient marker of thing – book, article, text – which everyone can 'see' (read) to the inconvenient ephemeral – performance, lecture, coalition – which must be reconstructed and regarded rather than broken down and measured.[15] In undertaking textual analysis one is trained in the skills of argument, defined in its earliest usage as "proof, evidence, manifestation, token," as well as in its extended definition appropriate to the longer scholarly work, "a connected series of statements or reasons intended to establish a position (and, hence, to refute the opposite)" (Oxford English Dictionary). Yet, performed (and printed) works can employ motion to make proof, give to evidence a corporeality manifested in the transferal between audience and performers. Whether one's strengths or one's preferences instinctually alight upon the printed or the performed, however, one cannot romanticize the goodness of one form over the oppressiveness of the other. The seventeenth-century writers who were engaged in creating printed and performed works considered in this book use the power of stillness to startle the receiver into recognition combining it with the power of motion to show every possibility for the mutation and transformation of ideas, to give only one example of the potential combinations. Such dexterity demands a critical "choreography," to use Foster's challenging term, to represent the intricate dance in the aesthetic of stillness and motion in the media of print and performance.

Giving and taking – the stage and the book

> If art "degenerates" when it moves (i.e., when it allows itself to be moved, to enter a stream of time that denies the logic of the symbolic, of the economy, and in so doing installs an ethics of giving) then this "degeneration" and this movement are the most beautiful gifts of the time of dance, a time that changes places, bodies, ideas and times.
>
> (Lepecki 1996: 107)

One area of investigation in this study echoes Roger Chartier's question: "How are we to understand the ways in which the form that transmits a text to its readers or hearers constrains [and I might add frees] the production of meaning?" (1995: 1). The form in its *reception* is mysterious and difficult to account for – whether it is a performed ephemeral moment outdoors for a large audience, a smaller half-lit theatre with boxes and pit, a room or a square where a reader entertains a group by reading, or a quiet chair in which the book plays itself out in the hands of a single reader. Because often readers are also writers, we have much more documentation and scholarly speculation about readers and their responses to the written word than we have spectators and their response to the performed work. Seeking to account for the receiving bodies in audiences and rooms, one finds the language for study itself provides certain convenient deceptions. The word "audience" falsely suggests a unity able to be theorized and carted about; even the verb conjugations continue the ruse of the singular, "the audience *is* enjoying the performance tonight."

In the early 1960s reader-response theory posited a theory of reception for literature in which the reader became an active participant.[16] Suddenly one saw the hands holding the book, and how interdependent author and reader are as the author solicits and creates his/her readers and the reader responds by creating the scenes in his/her imagination. But the intricacies of reception are more manageable in theory than in practice. And in terms of performance and the quite different terms of print, what occurs for the spectator/auditor/reader not only is intangible, but it mutates as fast as one can read the word "mutate."

All manner of things can effect reception – time, space, sound, distance, weariness. How often has the joyously read novel, upon later rereading become a formula-ridden production. Happily, the opposite applies as when one rediscovers a once shunned book and in it finds the pleasures hidden by the reader's youth suddenly opened to the reader in her or his middle age. Reception of a performance is even more difficult to encapsulate, particularly because one has to have been at many performances to understand the nature of the sense of the air being 'full' when an audience is attending, receiving, and returning the performers' energy. And of course there are many degrees in between full and empty, reception can be heightened or muted by the response of those around one.[17]

To address the intangible, as well as the ample but unquantifiable experience of receiving and responding in performance, I offer theories of gift exchange to help us understand the interactions occurring at the theatre, as well as those that can occur in a private room.[18] This exchange between maker and receiver is often figured in a playwright's work, in actors' memoirs, and in audience members' recollections as an experience of give and take between performers and spectators. One might well suggest that Aristotle's treatise on catharsis is an early theory of gift exchange. Because to be the maker of, the recipient of catharsis is to undergo a change which can be a gift: a gift of re-awakened understanding, a gift of fit humility in the face of arrogance, a gift offered to the community delineating the tragic wages of greed, anger, and deception.

Thus theories of gift exchange supply the inextinguishable component of motion in an audience's relation to the stage, in an auditor's relation to the sound of the book, and in the reader's re-creation of the printed page as experience. For, as Lewis Hyde notes in *The Gift: Imagination and the Erotic Life of Property*, the principle attribute of a thing *made* gift is motion, "the gift must always move" (1979: 4). A gift in motion touches points in a circle of exchange; since a gift must remain in motion to keep the circle of exchange active, when one gift is received another must be sent on while the original gift is transformed in reception and gives increase. Think of the unfettered reciprocity of a persuaded public audience – bodies standing near the stage taking meaning (at different times and in varying intensities) from the words of the play, the sound of the actor's voice, and the gestural language of silence. The spectators in turn give by their own reception back to the performers and potentially the playwright present at the theatre. The audience's return gift takes many forms, it can be the unusual hush and stillness which paradoxically signal the audience's body moved in its emotions, it can be the outbreak of laughter or the hiss of fury, or it can be the simple but none the less eagerly sought sense that the audience has become a participating body in the work. The audience is made community in that moment and presents itself to the actors as an audience attending.[19]

John Webster in his "Character of An Excellent Actor" writes of a theatrical exchange where the actor "by a full and significant action of the body . . . charms our attention: sit in a full theatre and you will think you see so many lines drawn from the circumference of so many ears, while the actor is the centre."[20] Webster offers a lovely mix of the power of the collaboration in the still and the moving when employed in exchange. The actor by "action" creates a bond through those lines (the lines he says and the lines he draws) which draw the audience together, bound in their attention, yet bound by a motion (a seventeenth-century noun for an actor). As importantly, we read the impressions left by a man, Webster, who wrote for the theatre at the theatre, observing the audience becoming a conjoined entity.

Though repeatedly examined by critics for clues about monetary exchange and anxiety, early modern works for theatre also give ample evidence of an acceptance of the *in*calculable, the world made by exchange which cannot be measured. What can occur at the theatre, in the space and time between money paid and experience had, is a kind of secular *trans*ubstantation where the traveling gift does not go from Priest to God to wafer, but from performers to audience and back. The language of giving and sacrifice is embedded in Judeo-Christian tradition, and it remained a topic of contention between Anglican and Roman in the early modern period. Anthony Dawson writing of performance exchange notes Richard Hooker's vital transformation of the magic trick of Roman Catholic Eucharist into an action that happens not in "the sacrament, but in the worthy receiver" (1996: 37). Dawson's formulation can be understood to have some force in an exchange occurring within the 'worthy spectator' as well. At church a believer and skeptic is not externally marked; the sacraments may be received with faith or inwardly scorned and rejected. In a performance, beyond standard monetary exchange of money paid to see the play, an unquantifiable exchange might occur or might not depending on the offering and receiving bodies in the space; at the theatre too the bodies will not always be externally marked, though generally it is easy to see who is 'taken' with the performance.

Two features of the drama, its orality, "the fact that it is performed rather than read and has its origin in spontaneous ritual," and its intrinsically participatory nature that can induce motion in the spectator when watching and hearing the play make its circulation analogous to artistic gift exchange as Lewis Hyde has defined it (Peters 1990: 210, n. 10).[21] Gifts intended for traditional gift exchange in circulation are often items such as food stuffs which perish in the process of the giving ("The gift is the property that perishes" (Hyde 1979: 8). Although dramatic literature puts some stop to the perishing of performance – the record of the text circulates yet doesn't perish – the play in performance circulates only by repeated productions whose fame resides mostly in post-performance word of mouth. Since the "gift must always move" to remain in the circle of exchange, though it can be transformed, it cannot be hoarded or kept. The audience can choose to receive the play as a gift, moving it toward each other and the players; on the other hand, a lack of reception can arrest the cycle. The language for failure suggests the stilling of motion – a "dud," gone "flat," a "flop." A playwright, reluctantly or not, participates in a complicated version of a perishing cycle, "giving" the actors their parts, "giving" the play to the company, receiving the company's interpretation on viewing the production. The remuneration of actors, actresses, playwrights, and companies has rarely historically compensated either for the effort or the time of crafting a performance.

One can easily sense when a gift exchange is transformed into a commercial transaction. In fact, in performance the amount of money paid for a ticket becomes a cause for complaint in direct proportion to the sense a spectator has that it wasn't worth it – the calculation ushers in a recognition of something gone awry.[22] But the desire to keep, to hold, to have occurs in the context of a system of gifts that must move. Thus practices like collecting – books, objects of rare value, varieties of mineral substances – and putting text into print exist sometimes as checks upon the moments of give and take in reception and exchange. In fact, as Marcel Mauss, Jacques Derrida, and Pierre Bourdieu insist, the pressures of gift exchange are not always those of delight. In participating in a cycle of giving and taking a person might feel obligation as well as gratitude or resentment/displeasure upon the reception of a gift. The giving might be an act of free will or a manipulative offering designed to elicit an exorbitant return.[23] Giving and taking are the initial catalysts in the practice of collecting. However, collecting as an adventure of finding, valuing, and cataloguing necessarily takes on the questions of keeping and preserving (holding still), and of the difficulties of managing a collection. The personally relished collection may not offer enough satisfaction without the opportunity for display, and yet display includes the risk – like that of being in print – of the shame of comparison to another, the judging of one's own collection in the context of another collector's potentially more precious and more exotic array.

While desires noble and petty certainly infiltrate the activities above mentioned, at the heart of artistic endeavor (which, as the forms of production change throughout time, must contend with questions of reception, offering, collecting, and display) is the preoccupation of creating an aesthetic work which will last forever while offering its power and vision over and over again, without growing stale. Like Cleopatra the art of representation and crafted language seeks a timeless stability, "age cannot wither it," but neither can it be lifeless in its repeated display, for then might "custom stale its infinite variety." And like *Antony and Cleopatra* the work of performed art moves temporally through its story conveying motion and the passage of time, while it freezes moments of aural and spectacular beauty to remind the spectator of the aesthetic pleasures and power of the still and the moving.

The space of exchange takes shape between author and imagined audience, as well as between author, actors, and audience present at the performance. Each author discussed in this book uses different strategies to beguile his or her audience, reader, and spectator. Authorial conceptions of how such strategies might influence the audience give us clues to the changing values of orally presented and textually received knowledge. To give a brief overview of the authors considered here: Ben Jonson, whose relation to his imagined theatre audience often seems one of scourge, uses the stage as a corrective to the too susceptible and thus effeminate spectator (while confirming his readers in their superiority) by shaming the audience with tricks of withholding and revelation. Yet (there is always a "yet" with Jonson) his own *tour de force* depends upon the performance it criticizes. Jonson is caught by his need to show his skeptical opinions about showing. John Milton, whose authorial purpose early in his career is to convert the lukewarm believer by education of the senses, uses the devices of performance contained by the somewhat more fixed nature of print to craft a writing which affects its readers as sensibly, as physically, as the "sacred drama" he reads in the Bible.

In the Interregnum Milton and Richard Overton use the form of the pamphlet, in all its ephemerality, to display the drama of the present revolutionary moment as one so physically imagined in the text that the readers might find their own likenesses acting out a part in the nation's drama. Aphra Behn, woman poet and designer of theatrical innovations, creates for her spectators a *pedagogy of motion*, a temporal learning more lasting than the argued syllogism which convinces the reason but not the senses. If for Jonson effeminate audiences could be corrected by being duped, and for Milton persuasion might find its form in the body of a chaste "Lady," Jeremy Collier in his position as critic of the stage ends the century by reading the dramatic works and the theatrical space in which they play as compromised by socially dangerous freedoms embodied in the too oral female characters on stage. His "reform" of the stage, which is a reform meant to control an audience's reception (at times specifically the women in the audience), begins in replenishing manly vigor and power on the stage by silencing the female characters. The women's silence, according to Collier, will 'naturally' initiate a return to a static, instructive form of classical drama.

Staging this book

> Theatre is completely ephemeral, it's there and then, it's gone. There are no souvenirs except what is left in your mind and in your feelings. The most intense, the most compelling experiences simply disappear into the ether. That's why I love it so – because you can trust it.
>
> (Ruth Malaszech, principal actor, *Mabou Mines*)

As will be clear by now, within the history of the distinctions made about performance and the printed text, the surface binaries actually signal the ongoing history of the aesthetic uses of stillness and motion: (1) as a form of artistic creation and production; (2) as a form of philosophical investigation; (3) as a way of representing and manipulating ideas about gender; (4) as a way of acknowledging and reinforcing or making a critique of social values for the still and the moving, the permanent and the elapsing, the closely held and the freely given. The practice of attributing value to the moving and the still engaged in by philosophers, artists, and critics has carried with it political, cultural, and social repercussions. Throughout this book I seek to show the collaboration rather than the binary opposition of motion and stillness but in this last introductory moment I separate them to suggest how powerful are their implications for Western thought. As Homi Bhabha has suggested, colonial discourse is dependent upon "the concept of 'fixity' in the ideological construction of otherness"(1997: 18). Though Bhabha goes on to note the paradox of the chaotic in the representation of stereotype, for a moment I want to remain with this "concept of 'fixity.'"

Stillness in Motion considers the seventeenth century a period that saw the rise of the 'container,' spaces architectural and printed which provided new forms of structure to display their contents.[24] In England, scientists and philosophers, influenced by European concepts of collection, organization, and display of knowledge, created dictionaries, encyclopedias, and museums and cabinets of curiosities as the century turned toward the eighteenth. The colonial pursuits of the century furthered this world of display by providing the plunder which would become the collector's wonders. As Paula Findlen writes, "in a sense, the creation of the museum was an attempt to manage the empirical explosion of materials that wider dissemination of ancient texts, increased travel, voyages of discovery and more systematic forms of communication and exchange had produced" (1994: 3).

More and more cultural trust was placed in that which could be proven from the retrievable printed evidence – proving to the reader how an intricate narrative worked on the pages or to the judges how a law was based on written precedent – as against the forms of production which kept changing and moving only to eventually disappear. In fact, possibly the "two-sex" theory which changed the notions of gender in the seventeenth century may have arisen to some extent from this growing habit of organizing data into columns – thing and not thing, male and female – as well as from the scientific examination of gender as a biological difference (see Laquer 1992: 10).

While I invoke (and momentarily freeze) such fixed columns to reiterate how the cultural distrust of motion and reliance upon concepts of fixity impede our study of performance, I hope the reader will note the tyranny of fixity when it offers a single notion of gender or race or class. I confess to the desire to understand more flexible ideas of a collaboration of the comforts of fixity – the rest in periodic certainty, the establishment of shared goals – with the necessary rigors of change that might demand of the audience, the reader or the citizen a re-evaluation of what she or he held to be stable. Such understanding might aid not only in undoing the scarcity model of rigid classifications, but also result in a more fluid practice of theory and the teaching of drama.

In this book I have used a mix of voices, moving from the conventional scholarly to the less conventional form of a written re-creation of the possibilities of performance. The presence of these voices signals not only an attempt to understand how to write about performance that is still in process, but also evidences an attempt to create a way of writing about theatre, about audience, and about history that can move across the plane of analysis to display and evoke the "somatic intelligence" at work in the making and receiving of moving art.

The necessity of traversing disciplines when thinking about performance does not forgive any of the oversimplification I may have produced. Humility is the lot of anyone trying to bridge the false gaps – forged most often by methodological differences – between art history, architecture, and performance, to give one example. To examine seventeenth-century performance in isolation from seventeeth-century literature, art, politics, and social history would seem unforgivably narrow. Yet the calls for interdisciplinary projects and the academic conferences on the interdisciplinary have not yet devised a method by which the academy is at ease when it comes to the written production of the interdisciplinary. To write across categories is to risk asking of one's reader a kind of flexibility not built into a system where the categories of disciplines – and those of methodology – have historically shaped the reader's immediate responses. With the suggestions I have made here I hope to enlarge the much too restricted ambit to which theatre studies has often been relegated, but these suggestions are necessarily general. If the reader wants to pursue an inquiry further, the experts cited in notes will offer more nuanced and elaborate details than I can give here.

Borrowing from the period about which I write, I begin each chapter with a paragraph entitled "The Argument." In seventeenth-century texts the argument often served as a map for those who might want to plot where they are in the story while following out *how* the story is being told. Sometimes the argument spoiled the surprise – "Britomarte tricked by the false Duessa" – and sometimes not – "Eve tempted by the serpent." Though it is not the way of scholarly texts to have such summaries set off from the chapter, I do so in part to draw attention to how much the scholarly habit of asking, "what is the argument," or the slightly more hostile, "what is your methodology," can forestall the discovery possible when performance and its effects are at the center of the purpose of the chapter.[25] In her *A Semiotics of the Dramatic Text*, Susan Melrose calls for a way of writing about performance which would start to "look, in this practice, like the variously recorded traces of a full-scale action toward a theatre production . . . which might be our only way to approach what I call elsewhere theatre's 'multi-modal heteroglossia and praxia'" (1994: 64). Melrose goes on to acknowledge that an "authored" text such as hers cannot create such polyphony – though it makes possible a way of conceiving of one that might.

Neither can this text provide that multivocality: still, the work of the chapters is not the work of evidence and proof so much as animation and discovery. Though Melrose's layered and challenging argument for a way of writing about performance addresses contemporary work, it is my contention that as performance historians, though we may not be able to 'see' the original performance before us, we must think in sound, in the polyphony of rehearsal, anecdote, historical fact, conjecture, and immediate reception. The argument at the heading of the chapter offers the basic chord structure on which the chapter will improvise. This is of course a music contingent on participation and in many places the musician is thoroughly dependent upon the generosity of her auditors.

Prologue
Making sense

Heaven give thee moving graces!
Measure for Measure, II. ii

In the midst of the seventeenth century Thomas Hobbes published *Leviathan* beginning his discussion "Of Man" with "Of Sense," and his discussion of sense with motion. Using the term "pressing" for the external action of an object upon the senses, he gives a picture of "man" worked upon by outward weights: "Neither in us that are pressed, are they anything else, but divers motions; (for motion, produceth nothing but motion)" (1996: 10). In his second chapter, "Of Imagination," Hobbes contrasts stillness with motion, "that when a thing lies still, unless somewhat els stirre it, it will lye still for ever, is a truth no man doubts of . . . when a thing is in motion, it will eternally be in motion" (10–11). For Hobbes, as for thinkers before and after him, motion, experienced as pressure, awakened the senses to ideas engendered by the objects around the moved body. Interpreting the consequences of the effects of motion required an accounting of the sensual reception and perception of both motion and stillness, a pair never far from each other in early modern philosophical investigations about the world of ideas, aural, written, and performed.[1]

According to Hobbes, motion cannot be separated from the senses, and it is here that the investigation of the uses of stillness and motion on the early modern stage begins. In studies of performance, theorists have drafted and redrafted models of kinesthetic history, kinesthetic reception and production, acknowledging in their efforts the need for a theory that can evoke motion vividly enough to give us the ability to comprehend the performed world in motion. Anyone who looks to the world of performance in the seventeenth century must acknowledge with the pressed-upon Hobbes that one is studying a culture whose theories and practices assume the perceived world to be created kinetically, in a balance between the moving and the still. Our task then may be one of apprehension rather than comprehension, which will not surprise my readers.

Theories that posit the rigorous separation of the reception of the mind – primary and superior – from the pressing of the senses – intuitive and fuzzy – had just begun to influence an understanding of the making and reception of art through the first half of the seventeenth century.[2] Although the technological changes of our own day tend to widen the separation between body and mind in so far as they make ever more possible interactions where bodies need not be in the same room to communicate, to apprehend the theatrical experience of the early modern spectator one must experiment with 'thinking through the body.' To experiment with thinking through the body is not to fit a captious physical habit over a largely analytical, intellectual process but to conceive of sensuous reception as an inseparable 'way' of discerning. If a spectator receives the performance through the senses, pressed upon by the motion of actions, of sounds, of music made by the performers, then his or her 'thinking,' interpretation of meaning, must be more capaciously conceived of by scholars than as a simply cerebral act. Bruce Smith's description of oratory applies to our understanding of performance reception: "Oratory represents, in its purest form, the proposition that *all* human speech is a form of persuasion . . . Words like *per-motio*, (literally 'through-movement') register a sense of oratory as bodily exertion" (1999: 248). Bodily exertion is not just a component of the speaker's delivery; the movement by which the speech is conveyed travels through the bodies of the listeners who are moved as they are persuaded.

In "Rhetorical *Ductus* or Moving Through Composition," Mary Carruthers explains that in early modern theories of rhetoric "*ductus* is the movement within and through" a rhetorical performance, in fact *ductus* "insists upon movement, the con*duct* of a thinking and feeling mind on its *way* through a composition" (2001: 101). Rhetoric and performance are inseparable in this period and Carruthers aids us in conceiving of motion in the making and receiving of spoken language. Rhetoricians, like actors, study how to make a "direct and easy path" for their audiences depending on whether the speaker wants an audience to "just step along with no obstacles" or "to work a bit, to look beneath or through [the] words to another agenda" the speaker might have (103). Like live performance, the "principles of rhetorical craft apply to situations," and "movement within and through" a literary piece is performed, as it is with music and dance. Carruthers fashions a picture of the world of speaking, hearing, and responding as one mediated through the senses, through motion.

We are aided in an effort to understand how sensuous reception works by recent work in the history of science and the history of perception. Many critics now counter the traditional scholarly narrative in which the seventeenth century ushered in the categorical, binary thinking of the eighteenth century. Work in the history of science suggests the theories of the body as "intellect," as discerning instrument, lingered well into the second half of the seventeenth century. In "What is the Histories and Theories of Perception the History of?", Stephen Straker discusses John Yolton's contributions to the studies of perception. Yolton argues "that we have been engaged in a systematic misunderstanding of seventeenth- and eighteenth-century texts about perception and cognition . . . [such texts] are not advancing a representation theory in which 'ideas' stand in for objects perceived . . . rather, they endorse a theory of *direct perception* whereby the perceiver is immediately cognitively acquainted with things perceived" Straker 1985: 269, emphasis added).[3]

For the spectator at the early modern theatre, the process of cognition posited here suggests a sensuous unfolding as well as a temporal one. While the reception of print and the way in which that reception will change the time of receiving and understanding is an essential part of the cultural history of the seventeenth century, early modern theatre reception occurs in this world of immediate cognition rather than delayed understanding. While Susan Stewart's meditation on reading and narrative comes from a nineteenth-century conception of reader and book in *On Longing*, her explanation of written and oral time is useful here: "While oral verbal art unfolds in time, written verbal art unfolds in time and space; the book offers a concrete physical textuality, an 'all-at-onceness' of boundaries which the oral performance allows to elide into the surrounding context of the situation . . . the book denies us a transcendent simultaneity; we must unfold the pages in time" (1993: 8). Of course in early modern performance, oral art unfolds in space and through bodies as well, and the book can become part of a performance not at all concrete as we will see, but the influence of delay, the *gradual* loss of "transcendent simultaneity" occurs in the one hundred years this book examines. Thus to investigate early modern ideas about perception and reception of performance and print, and in this way create performance theory for early modern theatre, we would do well to take up Yolton's challenge: "If we could understand how physical movements, as well as physical objects, become meaningful, we might be able to give up the talk of causal interactions between mind and matter"(Straker 1985: 273, n. 39).

The search for the manner in which seventeenth-century performance works begins here with the assumption that sensual apprehension occurs in the wake of movement: that is, in its immediate aftermath, as if the movement was an originary vessel cutting through the air and leaving behind waves that lifted and plunged the receiver. This image reverberates in the province of sound, described as moving in waves, but also makes room for the kinetic consequences of movements made by the actors and perceived by the audience. So, someone begins to speak or read aloud, or a player thrusts another aside and moves even further back upon the stage; each shifting of the air shared by bodies instigates minute reactions in the imperceptible shift Yolton posits as not causal, the "immediate" moment at which "perception is cognition"(269). If we allow the sensuously made to be intellectually effective, then our interpretation of performances and performed texts must be guided by traces different than those diagrammed in textual, historical, or philosophical analysis. Not only must we bring the audience into the imagined theatre, but we must use a method of understanding performance as if by Braille, noting in touch and 'feel' the raised moments of effect and exchange and manipulation made by writer and players and remade and returned by the audience in participation.

By virtue of the shifts and changes in theories of perception, cognition, and production, early modern culture of the seventeenth century can best be apprehended through a transition. A transition between (a) the reception of the performance and the printed book heard and read as a production perceived directly through the senses and (b) the beginnings of a separation between ideas and the objects that stand in for them. According to early modern theories of cognition, all forms of persuasion and communication would need to make an impression upon the senses. Bruce Smith contributes to our understanding of reception by causing us to "hear" early modern culture in *The Acoustic World of Early Modern England*; Smith quotes Steven Feld who "argues for the existential force of hearing in the shaping of cultures. The relationship of people to places, [Feld] proposes is existential: 'as place is sensed, senses are placed; as place makes sense, sense makes place'" (1999: 47). Since the senses tend to be called into play immediately in the presence of the addresser and the addressee, then, not surprisingly, those authors who are writing for the stage create through the kinetic language of bodies, sounds performed for the body receiving and responding in motion. As important, however, is that those who are writing for the stage *and* the book seek as well to make the language press upon the senses of the absent reader, configuring their work to imaginatively shorten the distance between the words and a body speaking them.

The writers of this book seek to move their audience (sometimes to move it to become still), to change the recipient by the contact he or she has with the performed and printed world before them. One author this book does not take up directly, Shakespeare, produces in his work exemplary instances of reflection upon the press of words, of speaking and the consequences for the bodies acted upon/pressed upon in the reception of the performance. Shakespeare's plays follow Hobbes' rule of motion in that the moving language "produceth," has as its product, motion. In *Measure for Measure* Shakespeare creates a story in which the entire play rests upon the counterbalance of stillness – rigid authority, vows of chastity, sentences of death – and motion – mercy, fertility and procreation, acquittal and life.[4] The title of the play itself suggests many themes running through this book, acts of exchange, of giving, of sacrifice, of a world in motion poised precariously upon the preposition "for."

When makers of theatre create 'meta-sensual,' meta-theatrical moments to stage 'how' performance works, they portray the interaction between speaking, moving bodies on stage experiencing a similar kinetic effect to the one happening in the receiving and responding bodies offstage. Consider scene ii of Act II. As Isabella enters into this scene, the audience watches her demonstrate the powers of speech and gesture, of sensible and sensuous reasoning that we may realize the breeding nature of senses (ours included) in contact one with another. Having tried at first to appeal to Angelo's function – his office as temporary Duke – which proves "too cold," Isabella becomes moved in her own speech and thereby moves Angelo. At line 43, prodded by Lucio, our onstage pragmatist, who tells her she is "too cold," Isabella reluctantly begins again to "sue" to Angelo for her brother's life. Hers is a performance where even a reader "hears" the improvisatory nature of the supposedly "fixed" words.

All improvisation has that uncanny (productive) panic: no matter how set one's speech, until one begins speaking nothing happens nor can anything happen without the actor's action. It is the nature of the Shakespearean world to endlessly reproduce these moments of pressure as if the pressure were happening anew, at the moment of performance or of hearing/seeing.[5] This immediacy is furthered when Shakespeare includes the audience in the tension by having characters on stage who respond to the character improvising as if they too understood the stakes of 'making it up.' Angelo's burgeoning lust is the end of the sensual story of the Act through which we see Isabella as an author of a moving 'text' in the air. Isabella's purpose is to teach toward the salvation of her brother, but her improvised lesson to Angelo produces a kinetic jumble of symbols, which, perceived by the listener, cannot but alter him.

After Lucio's second jibe of "too cold," Isabella begins to travel through the topography of performed sense beginning with the oral: "too late? Why no; I that do speak a word/May call it again"(ll. 59–60). While actors might choose to speak these lines ruminatively or urgently, the sound of Isabella's voice attracts all those around her to attend to the nature of sound and its potential reprieve. The embedded echo remains, "call" may mean retract but it also may be called again, "mercy, mercy, mercy." Remember the Duchess in *Richard II* who defies sense and political logic, taking the risk of the comically illogical by remaining on her knees before Bolingbroke, now King, in supplication. Her perseverance is performed to provoke not rational response, but the forgiveness granted from the assaulted senses (eye, ear) of the King who realizes the Lady really will stay on her knees until she knows her son is safe. So Isabella touches the sense of Angelo – whose "snow broth" blood must be made to run a bit more freely – metaphorically piling up objects before him as evidence, punctuated by a truncated line in the motion of verse:

> . . . Well, believe this,
> No ceremony that to great ones 'longs,
> Not the King's crown, nor the deputed sword,
> The marshal's truncheon, nor the judge's robe,
> Become them with one half so good a grace
> As mercy does.
>
> (ll. 60–5)

Imagine the sound of Isabella's voice, her breathing as she walks out onto the plank she creates for herself in the line, "believe this." She must develop an argument in crescendo, and she does, styling the arrangement of props of state, of power in order to dismantle them by mercy. Her credo, "believe this" constructs the manly order of authority of King, knight, marshal, and judge to uncloak them here and find the costume wanting unless filled by a body performing mercy. Her approach is an arrogant one to be sure, but I suspect a role the actor's body inhabits by either mimicking Angelo's arrogance or filling the words with the urgency of building a desperate argument.

Isabella uses theatrically pressing tricks to unhook Angelo's too much certainty from his too sudden authority and make him again feeling man, man with compassion. Her language mimics the tumble of Italian jugglers. She offers Angelo a virtuoso performed instance of understanding in which Angelo plays the imaginative lead: "If he had been as you and you as he,/You would have slipped like him, but he, like you,/Would not have been so stern" (ll. 66–8). Not merely a tug at the power of substitution that is the centerpiece of this play – bodies for other bodies, measure for measure – the words tumble over themselves and, in the feat of their imagining, seek to bypass the expected "no," with the chutes and ladders of "like." Saying the words out loud reminds the reader how quickly the syllables slide by and make what looks like truth. Lucio, when he commends this move, understands the juggler's prowess as power. He further commends Isabella's potentially improvised gestures since the language suggests she might place her hand on the sleeve of Angelo imagined to be a brother, "ay touch him, there's the vein." Though "vein" can be glossed as style, what Lucio understands as a man at once sensually aware and sluggish in his acuity by too much of that same reliance, is that the veins, the blood, the very combustion which later in the century will come to be known as circulation, carries the conviction through the body and changes the motion that might have stagnated in the denial of mercy.

Angelo acknowledges Isabella's efforts by suggesting she "but waste[s]" her words. In doing so, he raises the stakes and the pitch of Isabella's performed persuasion (a lovely moment of Angelo's misrecognition of the power of theatre, generosity and mercy, since all spoken things are naturally "wasted," dispersed). She moves on to the Heavenly judge and ends her reminder of His mercy with a direct appeal for Angelo to apprehend the power of mercy rather than comprehending the rightness of justice. "Think on that" she begins with Angelo's hitherto favorite organ for the exercise of power and continues that "mercy will breathe within your lips/Like a man new made" (ll. 79–81).[6] This contest of Isabella's pleading for her brother's life and Angelo's deluded delineation of himself as the Law that condemns equally without favor heats up; the asides spoken by the conduits of the action for the audience – Lucio and the Provost – sound like those of spectators at a game to the death. Toward the end of the scene, Lucio multiplies his encouraging asides as Isabella ends her escalating aria of analogy from tyrants to giants to apes to angels laughed into mortality, by returning Angelo to himself, or more precisely by suggesting he recall not simply "mercy, mercy, mercy," but revelation of self to self. Self knowledge begins with supplication to the senses, "go to your bosom/knock there, and ask your heart what it doth know/That's like my brother's fault . . ." (ll. 139–41).

"If," Isabella reasons, Angelo's heart "confess/a natural guiltiness" then the recognition by one sense bars the condemnation by another: "Let it not sound a thought upon your tongue/Against my brother's life" (ll. 141–4). Finally, Angelo surrenders to the apprehension growing within him. His first sign of surrender comes in an aside, coupled as it is with the dangers of duplicity always lurking in the *sotto voce* on the stage. He acknowledges the change in him; he is moved in the wake of Isabella's words, the press of her body's urgency, the language directed at his senses making an iconography, a gallery of speaking pictures, where Angelo might perceive and learn mercy and self knowledge.[7] And he ties his tongue up on the word "sense," wondering at the fruitful properties of sensuous address and reception: "She speaks, and 'tis such sense that my sense breeds with it" (ll. 144–5). Of course the problem with Angelo's lumpen recognition is that he will immediately transfer this instance of cognition to "country matters." But his perception still resonates for a book seeking to offer a series of chapters on speaking, sense, and the breeding of sensuous responses that make understanding, that persuade – that make sense.

Breeding ideas, recognitions, reminders, revelations are all the fruitful progeny of the creation of stories in motion. Stillness, motion's inseparable partner in the necessary rest and aesthetic play of stopping, co-creates the space of the exchange that speaks sense to the senses. In a work considering the play of stillness and motion in the early modern theatre, the many associations clinging to this foundational pair bring us into discussions of gender and the 'natural' state of the feminine (wandering) and the masculine (steady) as well as into discussions of value for forms of artistic production. At the intersection of narratives of gender and the value of the printed word are the cultural assumptions made about print and stillness, the containable and the manageable, and performance and motion, the wandering and the wanton. But the binaries the world learns to make would undo the subtleties, the anxieties, the inventive crossing of forms actually at work in the creation of both plays and books. We lose much when we treat one as an *experience* and the other as an *object*.

Eighteenth-century theories of sense perception and later theories of phenomenology articulate their suppositions across the relation of object to subject.[8] While the duet of seeing and knowing occurs when an object shown to a receiving subject is perceived by the senses, an argument made (usually assumed to be made in print) to the receiving subject does not proceed through the senses but rather directs itself to the mind. I err upon the side of gross oversimplification only to point out one technological confusion I think present – or perhaps more precisely absent – in thinking about the early modern world of perception. While there is much to say and much has been said about the image and the reception of the image in the wake of the Reformation, what seems as crucial to me in thinking about early modern receivers of readings, print, and performances is that the "object" that is perceived through the senses is not an object *per se*. What I mean is that the book, while becoming certainly a more familiar object over the course of the sixteenth and seventeenth centuries, is for many readers something to be animated or something heard, or something experienced as something like a performance.[9]

An author whose project is to stimulate the senses and thereby affect and perhaps persuade appeals to the palate of the senses to create impressions that might move through the air to the ear or to the ear and eye of listener/spectator to be reassembled with the aid of the senses receiving. There are traces in the works of the authors I discuss in *Stillness in Motion* where they seem to be "thinking in sound," following Kristin Linklater's description, the sound of the words made in the body release the meaning. In fact, this theory of the mixture of sensual reception in reading as well as in performance can be 'heard' in a quote from John of Salisbury's *Metalogicon*: "fundamentally letters are shapes indicating voices. Hence they represent things which they bring to mind through the windows of the eyes. Frequently they speak voicelessly the utterances of the absent" (quoted in Clanchy 1993: 253). The 'code' of learning by the senses, I would argue, is very different than the code we work with now, that of the separation of mind and body in the receiving process. Many in early modern studies do try to remember the moving bodies by invoking the word "body" or by studying the unmoving parts of the idea of a "body" analyzed. Yet I would argue such textual analysis of texts elides the task of the scholar of "kinesthetic history," to quote Susan Foster, which is to imagine a world that cannot think without the body (or more accurately bod*ies* as Susan Melrose suggests), the senses, those organs of perception more multiple than two. Within this notion is the understanding that early modern writers can often frustrate scholars looking for recorded theories of such perception precisely because such writers would not analytically refer to a method of thinking that would require they imagine the senses and intellect as separate receptors.[10] In *The Order of Things* Michel Foucault taught us to look back in time for the minute space made when one conventional set of ideas imagined as a grid has another slightly different grid placed upon it, and to investigate how the slippage between the two grids opens the new space for questions about assumed and ingrained behavior. So in the seventeenth century one can begin to chart a course for theories of intellectual perception and learning that is gradually separating itself from the field of the senses. This transition, as I suggested above, between one kind of thinking and another makes for a rich conjunction in the work of playwrights/authors discussed in this book, who address the senses as immediate receptors while also beginning to experiment with the delay in reception offered by print. This introduction of a temporal dimension of delay and reflection would eventually change notions of reception of the printed and the performed.

1 Permanently moving

Ben Jonson and the design of a lasting performance

THE ARGUMENT

Ben Jonson articulates his pursuit of literary renown made in and through print. In his careful attention to the publication of his writing, Jonson demonstrates the tensions at work near the beginning of the seventeenth century between renown in print and renown in playing. Jonson looks both backwards and forwards, using his poetry and his plays to revere (and amend) the ancients as well as to collect and scrutinize new ideas in circulation among his contemporaries. As a collector, Jonson pursues his craft with an attention to distinguishing those things worthy of display on stage, while he uses delay to manipulate the power of the author as an expert showman. In *Epicoene; or, the Silent Woman* the allied practices of collecting/showing and devising/performing are represented through a controlled demonstration of motion and stillness communicated through the signs of gender. In this play, the "secret" for Jonson operates as a correction for an audience too wedded to theatrical illusion as well as a gift offered to a reading audience not participating in the temporal unfolding of the theatrical performance. In *The Gypsies Metamorphosed*, Jonson is again at work as collector, but this time within a form, the masque, whose very nature is to combine stillness and motion in performance. Yet, here in this masque, as to a lesser extent in Jonson's plays for public theatre, the text for performance bears traces of Jonson's wistful desire to lay claim to both the power of the performed piece and the longevity of the printed poetry and to have that claim last, embedded somehow in the very language left in print.

Collecting, timing, and display

The culture of collecting exhibits instances of the interchange between the permanent and the performed: a group of objects collected, enumerated and shelved, remain unknown unless shown, demonstrated, or paraded before an admiring public. While power and recognition depend upon display, the efficacy of display depends upon timing. The collector must educate the spectator about an object's rarity, often by a progression of less exquisite, less perfect samples until the "palate" is trained to appreciate the subtleties of the verifiably unique. Like the Renaissance collectors Paula Findlen describes in *Possessing Nature: Museums, Collecting and Scientific Culture in Early Modern Italy*, Ben Jonson participated in the cultural appetite for erudition and exhibition: "through the possession of objects" [in Jonson's case ideas and words displayed as if part of a collection of objects] collectors "physically acquired knowledge, and through their display . . . symbolically acquired the honor and reputation that all men of learning cultivated" (1994: 3).

According to Marjorie Swann, author of *Curiosities and Texts: the Culture of Collecting in Early Modern England*, writing itself reflected the practice of collecting in the seventeenth century, having a "*collector*-function during the early modern era" (2001: 152). Swann suggests Jonson "could innovatively construct author-functions which were conceived as activities of collecting and cataloguing" (152). If in his "1616 folio *Workes*, Jonson becomes the collector of his own texts, removing them from their earlier contexts of use-value and recontextualizing them within a printed book," he continues his work of cataloguing on the stage as well (149).

Small differences in modes of display on the part of various collectors serve to stage a collection for an audience, from whom the collectors seek to elicit responses of awe and wonder.[1] For example, to place a large amphibious animal under glass at the level of a beholder's waist offers a different relation, evokes a different first response, than would the same animal if suspended from the ceiling. As in the theatre, so in these halls of wonder: sixteenth-century libraries and cabinets of curiosities generally provided a communal space for the practice of "show and admire." For example, reports from John Dee's library depict men in conversation, responding, asking questions, and comparing as part of the process of being spectators to a display of richness and rarity.[2]

In the venues in which Ben Jonson collected and displayed—the theatre and the Court—he was accustomed to seeing his work played, often to active spectators. He could watch audiences respond, and he might know the satisfaction, however infrequent, of hearing laughter or sighs of wonder.[3] The practitioner of theatre whose instincts are to collect and display presents evidence for the sensuous perception of his or her spectator in markedly different ways than one whose intentions are simply to communicate. While the temporal demands of live performance force playwrights to acknowledge the prerogative of motion in time's relentless passing, a playwright, director or actor can use techniques to delay or to awaken an audience's attention to time and its passing. For actors who cannot resist their own power of rhetoric, such a technique might involve slowing down the delivery so that all eyes and all ears are fixed on the speaker, often to the great frustration of the other actors and to the detriment of the play's momentum. But the playwright also has methods of adjusting speech, creating confusions in grammar and playing with accents or speeches in broken sentences that add to the sense of stopping and pausing before surrendering again to the push of time. Many playwrights in the seventeenth century indicate pauses or tableaus in their stage directions as well as actions to be taken by actors to still the movement and then set it going again.

Manipulating moments of stillness and motion on the stage, Jonson's drama of collecting took many forms: he loved neologisms, archaic words, and idiosyncratic contractions. He anatomized the follies of the society around him as well as the language the society used to enact such follies. Timothy Murray charts Jonson's course toward authorhood through his catalogues and compilations in Jonson's *The English Grammar* and *Timber; or Discoveries.* Where other authors might organize usage and then clarify, Jonson concentrates on the history of usage, Murray argues, understanding "stable semiotic meaning to derive from syntactic and orthographic order and stability – achieved by consent of the learned" (1987: 46). Murray connects Jonson's attention to history and order to the production of theatre and compares the goals of "Renaissance theatre" with Jonson's own: "Renaissance public theatre valued the transient, spectacular moment over the history of dramatic texts, authors and their ideas . . . Jonson's thought process . . . is predicated on the conservation of literary history; the recovering and ordering of lost masterpieces and their author's intentions" (47). By collecting all of Renaissance public theatre under the sign of a love of the transient, Murray neglects the play of the still and the moving within the plays of the Renaissance period. In fact, the spectacular, often placed in motion alongside invocations of the value of the permanent, was a form of dramatic language itself, as this book seeks to show. Further I would amend Murray's statement to suggest that Jonson's purpose was not simply to "conserve" literary history, in which case print and library would be enough, but to 'animate' literary history, to stage spectacles that reinforced the teachings of the lost masterpieces.

The influence of the profound effect of the technological changes in the nature of the seventeenth-century printed word has claims on our attention here, not least because it represents a crucial collaboration of stillness and motion. In recent studies of print culture, Jonson has become an exemplar of the early modern writer who fashions himself as an author. However, the give and take between old and new forms of production and reception made his task less one of jettisoning the non-printed in favor of the printed than of importing the power of the aurally received into the evolving mode of reception, the silently read (see Brady and Herendeen 1991; Chartier 1994). Because books could be bought, held, and shelved, they became participants in the intertwined worlds of the circulating and the conserved.

Richmond Barbour, correcting a common critical lapse in treating an author's career as if it all took place simultaneously, suggests we look more closely at Jonson's earliest efforts to have his works printed. Barbour finds the young Jonson's desire for printed fame includes the establishing of an intimate relation between author and reader. The ideal state of this relationship would be similar to an equally idealistic one between those men of learning congregating in libraries and museums, whose engaged passions create an atmosphere of exchange, dispute, and admiration. "Though the quartos of *Every Man Out* and *Poetaster* display firm literary aspirations, Jonson conceives their publication to serve personal relationships – speech and human presence – which must compensate for the defects of his text" (1992: 323).[4] The "defects" of the text include not only the incomprehensible – which requires the author's explaining presence – but also the inapprehensible, the lack of an immediate exchange between the body reading and the body writing.

Because writers and readers in the sixteenth and early seventeenth centuries did not conceive of the site of reading as private (i.e., one person with one book in hand) it should not surprise us that the language used to address readers suggests a corporeal relationship between author and reader.[5] Barbour aligns an instance cited in Natalie Zemon Davis' work on early modern print alongside Jonson's offer to the reader in *The Poetaster*: "Davis notes one Bernard Palissy, a potter who tells his readers, 'If you don't believe what my books say, get my address from the printer and I will give you a demonstration in my own study' . . . [and from the quarto of *Poetaster*] 'hee praies thee to think charitably of what thou hast read, till thou maist heare him speake what he hath written'" (322–3). Barbour goes on to speculate whether Jonson expects his readers to hear him at the theatre or to meet him expostulating at his favorite tavern.

Notice the temporal nature of Jonson's request; the explaining author begs his reader's generosity "till" the reader may hear the author. The temporal world of reception and of acknowledgment in print might offer the author control in that he makes the words on the page without interference from players, but the reader controls the time of reception. And the work requires charity, readerly largesse, *until* the voice of the author makes all clear. Whether Jonson promises a delayed explication or a certain tone and inflection of meaning as he "speake[s] what he hath written," Barbour by way of Davis and Jonson reminds us this is a corporeal and adjacent world of book to hand, of body holding the book to body writing it.

Jonson often compared the disquieting vicissitudes of the experience of theatrical performance to the comfort he gained by imagining the reader receiving his work in print.[6] On the title page of the late play *The New Inn* (1631) Jonson declares, "I do trust myself and my book" to the reader rather than bear "the disdain of a scornful spectator" (1692: 721).[7] Perhaps it is always easier in the imagination to hope for the generosity of the auditor/reader; Jonson's "scornful" spectator probably came from memory not imagination, the memory of hearing the spectator's scorn first hand at the playhouse. Scornful readers, however, are mercifully absent from the writer's view.

Answering hoped for readerly generosity with writerly generosity, Jonson offers with his printed text his own self. In one of the many metaphors for the relation of author to book, Jonson here acknowledges a dependence upon the reader that he would often portray as distasteful when that dependence was one of a playwright on the reception of a theatre audience. Alternating between demanding understanding as an equal and demanding protection as if a widow and an orphan ("myself and my book"), Jonson puts his trust into the hands of his reader. But Jonson also claims status through the object of the book that is himself. "Stepson to a master bricklayer, dropout from Westminster school," Jonson must represent himself to his audience without pedigree or a nod to relatives in the inner circle (Barbour 1998: 505). In "Jonson and the Motives of Print," Barbour argues that the object of "Jonson's ownership, whatever the property's value, is himself; and his book makes such possession credibly visible and therefore possible" (503). While Barbour and I differ on whether this act could be construed as a generous one as well as a self-interested one, we both see Jonson anticipating Locke in Jonson's insistence on his work as his property, his work circulating in some sense as a piece of himself.

In contrasting his reader to a spectator at his play, Jonson implies a further distinction between comprehension and apprehension. Collecting in the seventeenth century, as with print and performance, dwells at the juncture of comprehension and apprehension. Though the instinct to collect may partly be the desire to be comprehensive, to know all by possessing all, the reception the collector seeks for the collection is one of apprehension, hoping to induce in the spectator an experience of wonder and awe rather than a static, satisfied certainty.[8] To have Jonson's book and discover the essence of Jonson contained there, a reader would by logical extension comprehend his meaning. Jonson's wincing response to his spectator(s), "bearing" disdain, suggests he seeks to claim an intimacy of participation in giving and receiving, likening it to the apprehension of watching.[9] In fact, for Jonson the "gift" of himself and his book (however mitigated by his bad temper) participates in a cycle of what he hopes to be an exchange, though the circle of communal reception is less immediate than in the public theatre. Of course this dynamic of printed give and take between author and reader takes place in a commercial world, and some critics suggest Jonson reluctantly continued writing for the public stage only for financial reasons.[10] That Jonson made money from printing does not, however, erase his extra-financial desires for fellowship and understanding.

While Jonson's preoccupation with the printed self follows Foucault's definition of "the author function" (1977: 125), it bears remembering that such a term was impossible, as Roger Chartier argues, without the organizing principle of print and publishing through which scattered diverse writings transform into "unification and coherence" (1992). Further, Jonson and other poets of the century were transforming the medium of oratory and persuasive address into a printed form quickly and widely dispersed among readers and listeners. At the crux of a crucial technological transition between screen and page ourselves, late twentieth-century scholars must think backwards to when *print* was the untested, unrefined form.

As I suggested in the Introduction, one must begin with the premise that the stage offered something print did not. And that that "something" marked an absence that spurred writers to try and use the power of one medium to enhance the other. Many writers including Jonson and John Milton, I argue, agonized not simply over fame and presentation, but over the perceived limitations – a lack of animation – in the book, over how to incorporate the immediacy of spoken address into the relation of poet to reader. The enhanced power Jonson implies possible in the relation of author to reader, the intimacy of "his book/his body" entrusted to the reader, was not a flat, unmoving intimacy. Where the performed version of a work disperses among the bodies who manage the stage, change the scenes, play the music, inhabit the characters, the printed work might concentrate performed elements brought to life in the reader's imagination without mishap or "bad acting."

As the title of this book suggests, fixing words in print or objects in a collector's cabinet does not, paradoxically, signal an end to the fixer's task. Neither obscurity nor inertness will win for the fixed works the fame such meticulous crafting seeks. Since Jonson is both maker and collector he sits in the eye of this paradox. Jonson in his oft-cited remarks about his masque *Pleasure Reconciled to Virtue* describes the power of producing sensation in spectators: a "power to surprize with delight, and steale away the spectators for themselves . . . Onely the envie was, that it lasted not still, or (now it is past) cannot by imagination, much lesse description, be recovered to a part of that spirit it had in the gliding by" (Demaray 1968: 30). Jonson's formulation of the "gliding by" is normally used to acknowledge his grudging recognition of the power of performance and even more often used to suggest the grandeur of the masque. Yet I see in it an unguarded moment of wistfulness for Jonson, a wanting to make that part manifest in the "gliding by" *companion* to the fixed words that fueled the power even as it elapsed in performance.

In fact, Jonson describes the bittersweet conjunction of the still in the moving in his description. Though the work cannot "last" unless "still," made permanent by some form of memorialization, it cannot last still because what it was, was made in motion and the elapsing nature of performance results in a stillness at the end. No word is perhaps more wistful than "still" in its two meanings, "still" as in continuing and "still" as in fixed before me to see forever.[11] So too the wistfulness of the maker/collector can turn to disappointment when the audience or the collaborative parties to the making do not acknowledge the power of the performance.

In the frontispiece for *The New Inn*, a disappointed Jonson also condemns the production of that work "as it was never acted, but most negligently played by some, the King's servants, and more squeamishly beheld and censured by others, the King's subjects." As protective of his progeny print as Milton will be later on in his *Areopagitica*, Jonson sighs with relief that the play, his self and his book, is "now at last set at liberty to the readers." (Here readers are potentially not the King's subjects, another proleptic Miltonic similarity.) Crucial to our understanding of the crux of the two media Jonson works in is his "set at liberty" which implies that Jonson wants even the work in print to move, not to be fixed by bad performance *or* imprisoned again by negligent readers. Note that Jonson's language "set at liberty to the readers" confers freedom not solely from the license of the printed work to circulate, but from the right reception of free readers, as if the reading releases the work into freedom, a collaborative effort.

At the heart of Jonson's articulated purpose for his printed poetic communication is a "transaction of perfect if closed reciprocity in which to give something – a poem, a praise, a liking, a reading – is at the same moment to be getting it back (Fish 1984: 48). This "reciprocity" according to Stanley Fish simultaneously functions as "self replenishing" and "defiantly excluding" within the circumscribed parameters of the "community of the same," a community Fish claims Jonson reinforces in his address to his "author-reader" audience (48). One dynamic bridge between the keeping, at its extreme the hoarding, of collecting and the releasing of the dispersed and ephemeral, is an act of willed exchange, the bestowal of something as gift.[12]

In *The Gift: Imagination and the Erotic Life of Property* Lewis Hyde distinguishes between gift exchange and the kind of self confirming movement Fish sees in Jonson's poetry. Reciprocity is "the simplest" form of gift exchange, "two points establish a line, but a circle lies in a plane and needs at least three points" (1979: 16). "Circular giving differs from reciprocal giving": (1) in a circle "no one ever receives [the gift] from the same person, thus the "gift goes around a corner before it comes back. I have to give blindly"; (2) when a "gift . . . moves in a circle its motion is beyond the control of the personal ego . . . each donation is an act of faith" (16). Though Hyde's distinctions are made in thinking about traditional gift cycles, he imports ideas about motion and gift exchange into a discussion of artistic labor, specifically poetic labor (Ezra Pound and Walt Whitman). To return to Jonson's holy community of the two that is one – "author-reader" – the self replenishing Fish sees in the exchange seems to me to often wear thin for Jonson. In fact, this poet of withdrawal and control must be measured with the maker/collector who coins new words, who devises new theatrical tricks, who writes in *Timber or Discoveries* that "we are recreated with change" (Jonson 1927–53, v. 8: 117).

The theatre, particularly the public theatre, offers an extraordinarily complicated circle of exchange. Lest the language of gift seem too divorced from economic preoccupations of the burgeoning London and the in-debt Ben Jonson, the rhetoric of the freely given can never be completely extracted from the Judeo-Christian ideology espoused in early modern England. Post-Reformation England makes some revision upon the Roman Catholic theology of Christ's gift bestowed regardless of merit; yet, grace is conferred on those who offer themselves, their belongings in charity. Jonson often praises "donatives" and the moral virtue of the gesture of offering.[13] Perhaps not yet fully washed in grace, Jonson does as often chide the recipients to his dramatic offering since they seem not to receive and return the gift given. Yet he puts himself again and again in the precarious position of offerer.

If one insists upon the interpretation of Jonson only as a determined author who covets the laureate, even then how could he resist trying to produce the evidence of his poetic power, the display of his puissant collection of words and things, written across the bodies of those watching? But if, as I am suggesting, Jonson displays a mix of the wistful and the frustrated, then the continued offering he makes of his work – even to the less worthy public audiences or to the not quite worthy enough Court – acknowledges the paradox of wanting the sign of power in the "gliding by," while knowing that to attempt to make it means watching what must pass and watching the passing not necessarily translate into the glory and delight planned.[14] The animation of scenes from *Epicoene* and *The Gypsies Metamorphosed* in the following sections show Jonson at work on the cusp of stillness and motion, moving between both giving and the triumphant power of withholding and revelation, between the desire for intimacy and understanding with readers and the joys of collective discovery and shared satisfaction.

"A whore and so much noise"

To display is to categorize: even the simplest question about where to place an object or a scene depends upon comparison and discrimination.[15] As a collector of local customs, of linguistic anachronisms, of faults caused by inappropriate borrowings of gender by man or woman, Jonson used the stage, royal, public and private, not as a mirror to nature but rather as a set of scenes that work like diagrams. Unlike the static illustrations of the later Encyclopedias, however, the staged moment allowed for authorial intervention even more effective than a footnote.[16] Where folly was anatomized, it was also interrupted immediately by characters authorized to correct or at least arrange the multiple voices producing a portrait of a nation dangerously susceptible, though still potentially redeemable, if influenced by the wisdom of the playwright.

Jonson seems perpetually on a point between a love of the opportunity to show and teach and a disgust at having his work be paraded upon a stage where action is uncontrollable. To this end he invoked and then manipulated the seductive power of theatrical performance powerfully enough to have his audience understand his rebuke, a perverse form of seduction by performance in itself. When writing about language, Jonson, according to Timothy Murray, sought to collect and "know intimately the diverse uses of language before combating their curses and confusions"; so in his plays Jonson does not simply employ characters who pontificate, but rather creates staged illustrations of contemporary society in order to display the folly and then to display its correction (46). Though this phenomenon appears in miniature in several of Jonson's plays, it is in *Epicoene; or, the Silent Woman* that Jonson makes the most vivid allegorical reference to the power of show, the dangers of seeing without understanding, and the paradoxical consequences of withholding. And he does so quite plainly by displaying these values in categories of gender.

While in many of his plays Jonson uses the gender of the characters to comment on the nature of performance and print, in *Epicoene* Jonson invents a canny metaphor for the difference between individual reading and communal performance, the secret. Even better, he makes the secret about gender, hiding the truth even from the spectators themselves in violation of an unwritten tradition of early modern theatre where the audience usually knows at least as much as each character knows. For the reader of the 1616 Folio, and later editions of *Epicoene*, Jonson creates a private spectacle, one that can be distinguished from the spectacle set before an uninitiated audience at Blackfriars Theatre. The playgoer sits/stands expectantly in the crowd watching the "bride" be displayed, desired, decried, and finally discovered. The surprise of Epicoene's crossed, crossdressing completes the production. The spectator, accustomed to his/her role of comic audience, anticipates trouble, confusion, unveiling perhaps, but does not expect to be kept so much in the dark as to wake with Morose to the shock of the boy (actor) turned again boy. The reader, however, picks up the text, peruses all the textual apparatus – Horatian epigraph, date of publication, printer's name – turns the page and discovers the plot – as though prematurely unveiled – on the Dramatis Personae page: "Epicoene, a young gentleman suppos'd the silent woman."[17]

Secrets are erotic; they establish a bond between the holder of the secret and whomever he or she tells it to. As such, a secret also requires an audience that does not "know," an audience that suffers a kind of illiteracy, an inability to "read" the signs, the hints about the secret. Jonson establishes an erotic bond with his readers, creating in the culture of print a culture of desire. But the springing of the surprise has its own erotic pleasures as well, not the slow burn of knowing and not telling but the fast burst of recognition, surprise, and perhaps even shame filling the playhouse as the trick is unveiled.

If the gift of the secret creates a bond, like all bonds the debt can become a burden if the knowledgable audience must refrain from telling the secret when under strain. In the printed version of *Epicoene*, Jonson "raises" his readers to omniscient author status, so they enjoy two forms of erotic pleasure: the sublime joy of being in on the plot as it unfolds and, if they see the play in the theatre afterwards, a shared erotic superiority as they watch the audience members be surprised. Any number of famous scenes in *Volpone* or in *The Alchemist* portray characters empowered by the secret and their dupes, but in *Epicoene* Jonson gives the sensation of the experience to both those who know the secret and experience satisfaction and those who don't know and suddenly "feel" what it is *to be* a dupe rather than just watching one.

One possible interpretation of Jonson's choice of timing and of revelation would be to equate surprise with vulgarity: the dramatic act is more suited to those "such as have no taste," the spectators of the "loathsome stage" susceptible to gullible "supposing" (1975: 282). In such a version of the textual universe, Jonson honors the reader, his collaborator, whose full knowledge of the trick being *played* allows collusion between author and audience to plot against and dupe Morose, scorn the La Fooles and condescend to the Collegiates, all in the theatre of the reader's imagination free of groundlings and noise. However, if we complicate Jonson's fluctuating authorial positions to include the author who longs to make a participatory intimacy with the reader, telling the secret might possibly be a gift of compensation – as Barbour suggests making up for the "defects" of the text – for the reader who cannot experience the work as it is played before him or her. Though *Epicoene*, as Philip Mirabelli notes in "Silence, Wit, and Wisdom in *The Silent Woman*," "represents a radical innovation: for the first time on the English stage knowledge of a title character's true sex is withheld from the audience," the radical innovation extends beyond the stage to Jonson's (potentially manipulative) act of making the reader a collaborator (1989: 310). Thus Jonson grants print a higher honor not only or even necessarily because by its "lasting" nature it deserves such status, but because in it Jonson can bequeath a secret to his reading public. The reading public is invited to experience in the delayed revelation of Epicoene a shared frisson of power with the master of plots and revelations.

In a competing feat of connoisseurship and mastery, Jonson uses the stage in *Epicoene* to display a double secret as well as a collection of follies having to do with obstruction and control. Writers for the public theatre frequently used the resilient joke of characters who are "in the know." Standing in for the audience, all knowing characters observe the haplessness of those characters who are ignorant of the secret as they act out their roles on the stage – Malvolio capers to mind. But under Jonson's eye and hand

Epicoene doubles the duping while displaying through a series of 'mini-theatricals' the roles of spectator, audience, playwright, and critic acted out by the characters. While participatory in nature, the role of the audience in this transaction is more passive, more circumscribed than when the audience joins in the secretive play. Things are being thrown at them rather than thrown with them. Jonson manipulates motion, but his choice to stage a hidden manipulator actually restricts the amount of motion in exchange that he can employ.

As Scott Cutler Shershow suggests in his article "'The Mouth of 'hem All': Ben Jonson, authorship and the performing object," Jonson's derision of actors and acting as "motions," or mere puppets, informs his work even in the plays in which actual puppets don't appear (1994). In *Epicoene* Jonson binds the show to invisible strings, and those strings bring a blessing and a curse: more control for the playwright/puppetmaster of the show and less "room" for the characters on stage to move in an engaged exchange with the audience. In hampering this exchange Jonson's method of giving follows more closely Derrida's sense of the impossibility of the freely given than Hyde's idea of giving as a release into the unknown; Jonson's bequest of the play in performance comes with strings attached.

Jonson's constricted choreography, designed for the presentation of the silent woman, begins in Act II, scene v, of *Epicoene* where Epicoene is displayed for her would-be purchaser Morose. Morose, the uncle and impediment to Dauphine's inheritance, seeks a wife to get an heir upon and so leave his nephew penniless. Though fertility is born of the motion of generation, Jonson creates a character who seeks to breed only to hoard, to stifle the natural motion of an inheritance as it is passed on. Thus far in the progress of the play even the theatre audience knows the "silent woman" is a hoax hatched by the nephew and that Cutbeard her attendant is Dauphine's man. Epicoene's silence means that her entrance can only be one of display. The object that cannot speak but is presented impels the other characters to remark upon her, to assess her, to look at her, and to interpret her silence.

Such moments of absence, silence or emptiness performed upon the stage create their own pressure; as if the vacuum created in the performance cannot sustain itself in time, presence, noise and visible motion cyclically fill the absent place. Often such lacunae open a space for new things to be seen, or for a voluble and mobile human body – usually female – to be anatomized. Rigorous anatomizing can only take place in a woman's absence (sometimes an absence consisting of enforced silence) since, were she "present," she herself might interrupt or amend the assessment. Hyde makes an intervention in his discussion of gift exchange that bears reflecting upon here. He suggests that gifts in their motion tend to fill vacuums: "the gift moves to the place that has been the longest time empty" (1979: 23). If performance in its insistent, incessant motion has that quality of gift and exchange which puts pressure on things to return to motion, then an empty space, or a too long held stasis, will call forth the motion to fill it. Since Morose is hoarder *par excellence*, maker of unnatural silence and stillness, withholder of inheritance, his acts form a parable upon which the pressure of motion is writ. He cannot hold the world still for his pleasure, and each time he tries, he creates larger and larger vacuums for the noisy, messy world to rush in and correct with motion.

In Act I, Jonson has systematically unveiled Morose's peculiar character: we have heard report of his demand for absolute silence culminating in a description of his head in "a turbant of nightcaps." We have seen him control his servant's speech by the theatrically very funny ploy of having the unfortunate Mute answer his master's questions by "making a leg" (a seventeenth-century form of acknowledging authority consisting of extending the leg forward and folding the body over it). The audience who cannot manipulate Morose into silence have been subject to his long speeches.

Morose's role in the tiny domestic world that he controls is one of director. Each question he asks he punctuates with, "Answer me not but with your leg," and each performed answer receives approbation, "Very well done." It is important to remember how the ploy of the man who can bear no sound offers Jonson some lovely physical comedy. The stage direction in italics "makes a leg" for the minuet of Morose's demand and Mute's submission marks a space where the actor playing the servant might have taken all sorts of license. While extending his leg forward and bowing over it, Mute might also be making faces, or developing exaggerated, repetitive movements of the leg forward and back, or even executing a graceful choreographed motion in response to his master's crotchety and inhuman demands.

Into such a world "enter Epicoene." Cutbeard brings forth his "fair charge" – Epicoene the boy playing boy playing girl – bids her "unmask," and presents her to Morose (II. v. 2). The critic and possible purchaser, Morose "sounds" her out, assessing her worthiness – to see if she is 'sound' – interpreting the meaning of her meager responses, since her worth is tied to her making almost no sound. Performance remains essential for Jonson's purposes since to "not hear" Epicoene perfectly one must hear the other speakers as well as Morose; the contrast is far greater in an auditory reception than in a silent reading. Jonson emphasizes Morose's acquiring gaze, his inflated speeches, his tyrannical direction for how Epicoene will become his scripted creation, being told when and how to speak, to play scenes and in what costume she should appear. Only Morose's voice has the power to bring action and understanding into being as he interviews Mute and Cutbeard who both make their legs in response to his speech.

Morose's unnatural desire for silence and the silent obliges him to dabble in secrets. Ironically, Morose is so extravagant in his hoarding that he cannot populate his silent world to include anyone to whom he could entrust a secret. Though obsessed with doing things *in secret*, he becomes, paradoxically, a leaky vessel as soon as he gets into public because he lacks the talent of social manipulation. His first question upon greeting Cutbeard and Epicoene is to ask Mute, "is that door shut?" The question functions differently for spectator and reader: while it might enhance a sense of an imagined private space such as the reader him or herself might inhabit while reading, for the spectator it reinforces the wonderful oddness of theatrical privacy, like whispering into a microphone. So now there is only Morose, Epicoene, Cutbeard, Mute . . . and the entire audience of the Blackfriars Theatre to witness Morose's inquisition.[18] When Morose moves to turn his attention to Epicoene, he addresses the men as if they were a human curtain shielding the revelation of the silent woman, "Give aside now and leave me to examine her condition."

To Morose's questions Epicoene offers the feminine version of making a leg, she curtsies. And like Angelo in *Measure for Measure* dressed in a "little brief authority," Morose pontificates through the first fifty lines of the scene and then suddenly decides the curtsies he inspired are now "too courtless and simple." Wanting to actually hear her voice – after all, if she was simply a mute the display of her silence would be no victory for Morose – he asks if she can speak. Again like the physical give and take of making a leg, the audience is treated to the pleasures of modest repetition. A reverse Isabella who will begin to speak *after* marriage, Epicoene answers each time in demure one-liners, she speaks so softly that Morose must have her speak again.[19] It would be the actor's choice of course whether the spectator heard the first response or simply saw Epicoene's lips moving (depending on one's vantage point in a crowded theatre with box and pit). In the theatre, the sensual reception of the scene moves in the waves of sound, one harsh and loud and authoritative, the other diminutive and weak. What is being said cannot be separated from how what is being said is being performed. Morose's character is formed as much from how he sounds as from what he says.

For the reader (whether of quarto or folio) the windy speeches of Morose are bloated paragraphs punctuated by the small phrases spoken by Epicoene.[20] Also the stage direction "she speaks softly" reminds one of the reading conundrum. The reader 'hears' both her answers clearly since they are repeated in the print before him/her. If the reader reads aloud, he/she mimics the modulation of the language; the effort of reading aloud would affect the body of the reader and make demands upon the breath and capacity in ways very like the demands made upon the actor.[21]

In scenes where Epicoene must convince Morose of her silence, the absent controller Dauphine runs a potential risk. The author stand-in suffers his work to be presented to an audience, whose acceptance of the trick depends upon the veracity of the performance. If the audience (Morose) believes the play before his eyes, the hoax of the silent woman, then the author (Dauphine) will get his money. The boy actor who plays

Epicoene must convince the audience offstage as well as convince Morose, of his virtue, of his true, however unique, nature of quiet womanhood.

The scene can be envisioned as a premier, the opening of a particularly intricate play whose success depends upon a convincing presentation, an artful composition. Cutbeard – his vocation as surgeon, a barber, he who cuts, apt in this fictional scene of castration – acts as a stage manager presenting Epicoene, the work of the anonymous author Dauphine.[22] In this scene the work of art stands at the mercy, at least in the early part of the play, to the old, monied viewer. (Morose is associated with Elizabethan ways, having been less eccentric in "the Queen's time" (I. i. 172). If Dauphine's artistry in creating the silent woman fails, he will be at the mercy of the rich old man who, jealous of his nephew's youth and easy conduct, wants to guarantee Dauphine's dispossession and loss, an end to fruition and material progeny.[23]

The marriage agreement, as Morose understands it, offers an exchange of property articulated in the terms of author to literary property. Morose buys his silent woman not because she will ensure an absence of sound but because he believes he can control the text issuing from her mouth. He states the terms of the marriage deal when he calls Epicoene's silence a "wealthy dowry" and finds her poverty to his liking since he "shall have her more loving and obedient" (II. v. 88–90). To settle the deal, Morose makes the gesture of a satisfied customer; he "print[s] on those divine [one assumes divine because unspoiled by frequent speaking] lips the seal of being mine" (II. v. 84–5). As her author, the husband affixes his mark to the lady, binding her lips, impressing his work with his colophon.

Epicoene's commodity in this market *should* be another pair of closed lips, whose sealed condition reinforces Morose's authority and potential authorship until he alone provides the key to open them. Morose's colophonic peck promises no more than a perfunctory check to make sure that the lips stay his, stay closed. For Morose to attain and retain power, the property he owns can no more be open than can Dauphine's secret plan. Open lips, open secrets, open places break a seal whose waxed authority must be closed to be read, to be deciphered, to be recognized. Only the managed display of the open place in a controlled showing of power can satisfy the possessor.

Patricia Parker glosses the Renaissance definition of the secret as the "privy place" or women's privates and the process of "unfolding" secrets as an opening of the lap or "fold" of the female (1993).[24] A kind of intellectual barker advertising his sideshow, the discloser of the hidden summons the audience to see the wonder of the world he alone describes and thus owns. Jonson, as he unfolds the secret in Epicoene's lap, displays and proves his own power – erotic and theatrical – a power gained by possession of the secret and the manipulation of its revelation. Revelation, a game of power, unveils that which is subordinate, the secret "kept" associated with the female, the foreign, and the unknown. When at the end of the play Epicoene is revealed, Dauphine mimics in performance what his author manipulates by print: a power play embarrassing all who were silly enough while watching a performance to believe *only* the evidence of their senses. And Dauphine wittily upends the unfolding of the lap to open not the privy place of the female but to reveal the surprise of restorative masculinity: the characters in the play and the audience watching the play are outfoxed by a penis.

Cutbeard, in on at least part of his master's device, brags of the success of Dauphine's plot as he goes on his way to get a "silenced minister" to "marry 'em." Responding to Truewit's worry that one of the "zealous" – read loud – ministers would mar all, Cutbeard assures him he has the matter well in hand, "Cum Privilegio." An incidental moment spoken from the mouth of a subordinate character brings the printed book onto the stage.[25] The term of "cum privilegio" translated as "with authority" appeared on the printed book as a mark of license, the kind of mark Milton will rail against in *Areopagitica* as a particularly Roman Catholic sign of paternal control undoing individual Christian authority.

A confusion of authorities occurs in the conjunction of play, book, playwright, audience, character, and performance. Here the spoken sound of the printed, secular imprimatur sends filaments of allusion out to touch upon the author of the book and the play; the author of the plot on the stage; and the author who thinks he is taking public possession of his property, the silent book of his authority, the wife. Cutbeard playing 'printer's apprentice' to Dauphine takes his 'authority' from his master. Jonson furthers his authority as author when he reminds the audience of the medium of print absent from the stage by reference to the apparatus of publishing. Morose, meanwhile, continues the relation of owner to thing displayed in his supposed triumph of marriage and his virtuoso feat of collecting the rarest of things, a silent woman.

To the reader Jonson offers a narrative thread, extra information that leads to a fuller comprehension, a comprehension in exchange for an experiential apprehension of the final surprise staged in *Epicoene*. Where the spectator might have the raucous, knee slapping joy at the broadness of characters like La Foole and Daw, the reader enjoys a quiet, knowing irony when the words of the unwitting participants in the play reveal the true nature of folly, as when La Foole and Daw claim to have taken Epicoene's maidenhead – to the spectator it is implausible, to the reader it is impossible.[26] Jonson invites his literate public to join him as critics of the excesses of the stage: to be wary of the play's limitations as a spectacle to be received by the senses and to be detached from the physical participation demanded of an audience at a performance.

The desire for reliable reader/interpreters will later in the century inform John Milton's search for collaborators who are the "fit audience though few." Yet, I suggest that both Milton and Jonson, no matter how didactic their aims, seek for an intensity of experience in the reception of their printed work similar to what they may have witnessed watching audiences respond to theatrical performance. Both men attended performances, in Jonson's case for a time he learned performance by acting, in Milton's, he frequented academic shows; both knew the sensual mode of apprehension, its totality and its nuances. Even though theatre audiences might fail in right interpretation, even though the spectacle might overshadow the message, these writers persisted in creating an embodied writing, seeking to replicate in print the physical motion inherent in the immediacy of performance (see Chapters 2 and 3).[27]

At the end of *Epicoene*, talking women and fools, randomly and injudiciously consuming what is offered them, must be accused, condemned, and shamed. (It is often hard to distinguish between Jonson's tendency toward misogyny and his tendency toward misanthropy.[28]) Only particular consumption, regulated and inspired by a single author, or authority, will keep desire balanced. The frenzy of Morose's affected impotence converts itself easily into its perverse sister wantonness: he accuses Epicoene of being a true creature of the stage, a common case, "ope" to all men. Truewit encourages La Foole and Daw to speak up, making their boasts public. Morose has "married a whore and so much noise!" – which are, presumably, the same thing (V. iv. 133).[29]

All the excess clamor of persuasion and rhetoric, trumped-up performances and hyperbolic accusations set the perfect stage for the entrance of calm, reasoned, consoling logic in the person of Dauphine. Only the promise of release given by the unimplicated nephew can set the old man right. In answer to Peter Womack's rhetorical question, "How can authorial discourse be positively staged, rather than merely emanating stylistic and semantic disturbance from the wings," Jonson presents Dauphine (1986: 28). It is not a duke or a king who sets the world right at the end of this play but an ingenious author. Though Womack argues that a character who speaks for the author cannot be understood as positive, unmitigated authorial discourse, Dauphine's control of the secret in this play makes him an exceptionally good representative for Ben Jonson. One who acts as if a stage direction reads: "Enter, Author to restore order, centerstage."

Confounded by this now unperuked heroine, Truewit speaks as spectator fooled by the spectacle before him: "you have lurch'd your friends of the better half of the garland, by concealing this part of the plot!" (V. iv. 203–4). Though the stage is not draped in the lifeless bodies of Hamlet, Leontes, Gertrude, and Claudius, the decimation in this "comedy" is comparable. Everyone is outfoxed, most are humiliated, and all are silent. Jonson presents Dauphine's triumph over Morose in place of the customary wedding at the end of comedy. Like the flushed bride(groom), Dauphine can enjoy the culminating moment of this success associated with the stability of print, but the enjoyment is only fleeting. Dauphine's smooth power results in a triumph that separates him from the community, and

Jonson does not necessarily represent this separation as wholly desirable. Though Dauphine's theatrical power depends upon the progress of time and the motion of performance, perhaps his only community can now be those absent readers who unlike Truewit were co-conspirators in the plot from the beginning. Ironically, where for the theatre audience *Epicoene* may be a one-time trick, for the author who prefers readers, as for his secretive stand-in, only in the re-playing of the play can the triumph over theatrical audiences be reiterated and its pleasures prolonged.

Finally, as a collector and displayer of knowledge Jonson is also a revealer of fraud. As in his cunning use of performance to show the limits of performance, Jonson enacts a disciplining of sensuous discerning through the senses: he offers a caution about not trusting the senses that depends upon the sensuous apprehension of the surprise unveiled. Jonson's popularity in the Restoration, and particularly the popularity of *Epicoene* after 1662, may have been in part due to this proleptic construction of separating the receiver's senses from his or her reason by use of delay and distance. Thus Jonson tries on stage to undo the immediacy of learning by the senses, not tutoring in motion toward motion, but tutoring with stillness and motion combined to produce surprise and reflection.

While it may look at first like the utopian position of author to creation, Morose's obsessive desire to control the world around him is revealed by Jonson to be the unnatural impulse of a hoarder. Over and over again in philosophy, the arts, and religion, the sometimes poignant desire to hold onto that which must move, decay, elapse, brings about tragedy. The parables are many: (1) the lesson of Midas where the solidness of gold destroys living flesh and creates a collector's nightmare of the breathing beloved forever still; (2) the fate of those who hoard where rather than moving the gift of food along by feasting, they starve themselves and allow the gift itself to rot; (3) the parable of the wasted talents where the gifts are buried, unexercised and thus barren. All these suggest a world dependent on the reciprocity of making precious and letting go. Jonson presents Morose as a case of one who cannot move between the pleasures of stillness, holding on, and motion, letting go. Morose's hoarding is too extreme, too rigid and in this extremity betrays his lack of talent as a manipulator. The maintenance of his silent world, therefore, quickly collapses under the 'natural' pressure of human, noisy existence. Dauphine, and to a lesser extent his director-colleague Truewit, go about manipulation and connoisseurship with skill and precise timing. Thus Jonson suggests that like the relation of author to reader where collaborating in the secret makes the unveiling a joint pleasure; the skilled collector knows when to hold and when to show.

The Gypsies Metamorphosed

"Lord Alexas, sweet Alexas, most anything Alexas, almost most absolute Alexas . . . " A lady from a Queen's Court begs a boon in overinflated language; language so fulsome in praise it might be a parody of the language of flattery in court masquing. A supporting member of the cast in *Antony and Cleopatra*, Charmian deploys with the language of flattery slipping in a satiric "almost." As the author of the praise, she reminds Alexas, here mocked as the recipient, who has the power. The boon she wants and indeed calls forth onto the stage is the telling of her fortune by the Soothsayer in Act I, scene ii. This fortune-telling unfolding before the audience displays anticipation, witty repartee, dark foreshadowing, and disillusionment, all while the audience's eyes are drawn to the palms they cannot see, to hear the fortunes they themselves will witness come into being by the end of the play.

Hands stretched out for dubious truths and more regulated prophecies draw the eyes and bodies of the masquers and masque audience in the central scene of Ben Jonson and Inigo Jones' *The Gypsies Metamorphosed*. Of the performed forms available for Jonson's intervention, the masque offered a hybrid form of performance. Though a display dependent on great pomp and show, the courtly place of the masque offered the possibility of a presentation made by and for the learned, a possibility that might mimic the utopian relation Jonson imagined between the poet and the capable reader. Developing the masque form, a well-wrought vehicle for display and poetic propaganda, Jonson attempted to discipline the ephemeral; as a circus entertainer with his performing lions, he could show the fierce, dangerous power of visual and aural beauty while demonstrating the superior power of the hand that holds the whip. Like all performed forms, and not a few lions, the show of mastery sometimes suffered the press of the present moment when the thing tamed would do the unexpected.[30]

Yet with the aid of architect Inigo Jones, Jonson frequently succeeded in arranging his poetry in a beautiful set of "containers," be they made of proscenium enclosures or mechanical worlds that opened to emit brocaded masquers. After the single (usually) performance of a masque, Jonson could proceed to transform the spoken poetic into the printed "work," a work immediately circulated among coteries of courtly readers and eventually given pride of place as poetry in Jonson's 1616 Folio.[31] Inigo Jones, Jonson's partner in the making of many of the masques, functioned in some sense as an early modern curator. The artistic designer of Jonson's masques sought to "familiarize the English – that is, the privileged and influential minority who have access to court masques – with a vast repertory of images, forms, and styles which [were] still largely unknown to them" (Peacock 1995: 35). By means of collection, imitation, and display in the masques, Jonson and Jones developed the form of the masque to instruct the senses of their privileged audience through a harmony of poetry and idea and playfulness that proved itself lasting when heard and when read. While Jones derived architectural motifs from the Italian models, particularly Palladio, Jonson created poetic miniatures which brought the aesthetic structure into being before the attending spectator/reader, incrementally, that is, piece by piece.

Before Jonson's insistence on producing the text of the masque in print, the masque poets and the audiences participated in a form designed to be ephemeral. When finished, the performed masque was dispersed in the moment, in a celebration of power as blatant as the tradition of dissassembling elaborately constructed triumphal arches that had served their elevating and liminal purposes for the procession of occupation and triumphal return. Only the very rich and the very powerful could afford to 'waste' the labor of months, and the performance of that waste gave proof to the largesse of the ruler. In the tradition of the masque as a "donative" of "Great Princes to their people" (Jonson as quoted in Peacock 1995: 2), Jonson participated in the giving and the taking. If the masque, and masquing, was a gift from the King to his people, then Jonson's poetic construction of the narrative – anti-masque to masque – was a return gift of order and aural beauty to whomever in the audience was worthy and capable of receiving it.

When Stephen Orgel – in essence – resuscitated Ben Jonson's masques as an entire *oeuvre* deserving of critical attention, he emphasized Jonson's intent to create "serious" literature out of a form as much a "game as a show" (1969: 1).[32] For the purposes of this study the masque form is an exemplar of a complicated performed production which depends upon a collaborative, if at times fractious, exchange between stillness (emblems, scenic designs, poised pauses in dancing, the text of the masque in print) and motion (the transformation of anti-masque to masque, bodies dancing, music, and the human voice speaking and singing). The aesthetic play of masques practiced an elaborately codified theory of address to the senses; for example, bodies dancing would produce motion and potentially the spectators themselves would be moved by watching the choreographed movement. Yet virtuosity was also proven by hesitation, the dancer holding the body still, suspending for a moment the performance.[33] Beauty held in a pose offered itself as a sight to be noted, admired, appreciated and then the next motion released both dancer and spectator. The give and take of pausing and then resuming motion impressed itself on the senses of the spectators, a reception critical for an understanding of ideas conveyed corporeally.

Philosophers, writers, and artists in the seventeenth century suggested that knowledge imprinted upon the memory through the discerning senses would endure whereas fleetingly argued ideas simply left no sustained impression.[34] Francis Bacon, in a germane reminder of how the noun "print" can transform from a material thing to a verb of the senses, describes the process of learning by emblem inherent in masques.

Relegating intellectual reception to the process of comprehension and sensuous reception to the process of apprehension, Bacon suggests that "emblem . . . deduceth conceptions intellectual to images sensible, and that which is sensible more forcibly strikes the memory and is more easily printed than that which is intellectual" (as quoted in Morley 1890: xii). In Bacon's formulation we see traces of the transition from the conception of knowledge received through the senses to the conception of an intellectual process disciplining the body and its faulty sensuous reception; yet, according to Bacon, the influence of the senses renders knowledge more permanent, "more easily printed." These words embody the paradox of the necessity for stillness and motion since the mysterious and unfixed "emblem" creates for the receiving senses an image, but because of the power of the moving display, the learning gained is more fixed in the memory. According to this model, motion can create stillness, but stillness (that which is intellectual) seems to be less successful in impressing the memory, as if stillness without motion is barren.

In her treatment of the senses in *The Theatre of the Book* Julie Stone Peters quotes Jonson's preface to *Hymenaei* where she argues Jonson equates the contrast between "'sense' (or the senses) and understanding (manifest in words and matter)" and "the contrast between live performance and the printed dramatic book" (2000: 154). Peters concludes that "Jonson attempts to establish the proper use of 'outward celebration, or shew,' which must finally turn away from the senses and (like the book itself) be turned to the service of the mind . . . Right performance, then, must model itself on the asensuous book" (154–5). Yet Bacon's notion of the lasting nature of the impression made by 'seeing' emblems in performance, experiencing them sensually and thus intellectually, suggests the world of the senses and the mind were more confused than Peters' binary formulation would allow. Jonson often represents his project as one of high-minded turning from show, but in the early seventeenth century, I argue, one could not say the book itself was asensual nor the reception of that book. As importantly, Jonson remains conflicted in his desire for the rewards of sensual spectacle and those of intellectual respect; as we have seen, he associates himself with his book and in that association does not limit the quality of himself in his book only to a quality of mind removed from sensual experience, a realm he addresses in his work for readers as well as spectators.

Bacon suggests the emblems themselves do the work of transforming ("deduceth") echoing a process John Yolton (see Prologue) seeks to understand where "physical movements, as well as physical objects, become meaningful" (Straker 1985: 273, n. 39). Since in the masque emblems are often embodied by dancers, Yolton's suggestion helps us to remember that the interpretation of the masque was one where spectators deduced in the movement of the dancers allegories to order, analogies of virtue or vice, etc. Such sensory deduction takes place, Mark Franko suggests, between dancer and spectator in seventeenth-century French court ballets as active *praxis* or *theoria*. The exchange between audience and masquers demands interpretation in the dancing as well as simultaneous interpretation by the audience of the meaning of the dancing (1993: 30). In Jonson's *Hymanei*, for example, this participation worked by motion, the senses educated by the presentation and elucidation of such emblems in dance as Virtue, Strength, Sovereignty. Following Bacon this display would instill a more lasting impression (imprint) formed in the spectator's memory by means of his or her active, present interpretation.[35] The education of the senses of audience and masquers, necessarily a participatory endeavor because the learning depended upon the bodies performing and the bodies watching, was carried out through a display of antiquity (in language and character). The figures of the dancers, dressed as symbols themselves, danced in a moving gallery of pictures, pausing at times to form a larger picture. Clearly sensual understanding was multi-dimensional and cumulative, demanding lessons adapted to eye, to ear, to touch.

The Gypsies Metamorphosed (1621) does not supply the other worldly and suspended examples of 'deducing' emblems collected in a masque such as *Hymenaei*. Yet the mixed genre of masque and popular theatre in *The Gypsies Metamorphosed* allows us to see Jonson combining the tasks of dutiful poet praising the King while displaying the poet's power to give and bestow through words and acts. Inhabiting the place of prophet and sage, Jonson makes the representation of fortune-telling enact a more earthly rendition of deduction: the fortunes discovered in the marks on an aristocratic hand become the supposed mysteries on which the gypsy interpreters work.

Just as in the scene from *Antony and Cleopatra* where Charmian anticipates and longs for the Soothsayer's performance, the "site" of fortune-telling portrayed on the masque stage brings together the audience, the characters they watch, and the actors who inhabit them.[36] We all lean metaphorically and literally forward to 'see' what the fortune-teller will see as she or he holds the hand of a character in the play or a member of the court. The methods of theatrical play are sharpened: *what will be said*, a question for any theatrical performance, heightens into a prophecy, and the attendant question, *what will it mean*, initiates a participatory act on the part of the spectator while the poet/playwright reinforces, changes, makes subtle satire upon the received meaning in the language used to draw out the allusions. Fortune-telling hints at the alchemical in the masque form: though potentially dismissible as a showy sleight of hand, once heard the predictions become embedded in the memory; should the prophecy prove 'true,' the predictions appear in retrospect portentous and revelatory.

Dressed in a costume of gypsy (a costume which would mock the ragtaggle of "real" gypsy by the creation of a carefully designed negligence), the "Captain" (George Villiers, Duke of Buckingham) of the gypsies begins his soothsaying rounds, "With you, lucky bird, I begin" (l. 275).[37] The "lucky bird" is James I, who at this moment of anti-masque receives a jocular, familiar reading following a pattern well known in fortune-telling. First the Captain narrates James' habits of hunting and eating, then his wealth, then his unmarried state, not surprisingly for the audience who know James' preferences, "he is no wencher" (l. 287). But as the fortune continues it mimics the movement of the entire masque because the Captain suddenly reads "in your Jupiter's mount, what is here?/a king? a monarch?" (ll. 295–6).

The familiar, disguised play of gypsies to a regular member of the audience transforms to the recognition by Buckingham, now the true courtier, of the King. No one in the audience would 'forget' who the King is, who Buckingham is, but they could suspend the formal for the informal of pretend demanded by the narrative created in the masque. Revelation proceeds through Buckingham by way of questions posed by a fortune-teller. The question mark could function in print as an emphatic surprise with ironic possibility or it could function in performance to enhance the role Buckingham plays as a soothsayer whose predictions are discoveries not yet confirmed. Then the revelation moves out from the masquers toward the audience who shift their perception from the "gypsy" and the aristocrat to the "gypsy" and the King.

Like all masque transformations, the knowledge must be corporeally mediated and translated into dance.[38] At the moment of speech when truths are revealed, responses to revelations are passed through a dance until the physical measures have released jollity – in the case of a rustic dance – or have elevated the mind – in the case of a precise and beautiful ballet. After dancing, when the Captain returns to the King to continue predicting the future, his language changes, he makes – you will pardon the expression – a full-court press, praising the merits of the King as king, no longer telling the daily fortunes of the King as man.

In recent critical analysis of masques, the reader can be instructed in biographical, political, psychological, economical, and cultural interpretations of the poetry, but the intricacies of how the piece worked, why it was or was not considered a success in performance, are overshadowed by the textual and historical evidence. Even Roy Strong and Stephen Orgel, two of the most influential critics on masques and royal spectacles, tend to write more about the "effect" of such spectacles upon received notions of power and display.[39] The result is a static sense of masque as argument or deception but not necessarily masque as a temporally produced argument worked out in a set of performed strategies.

By convention, masques were performed only once. *The Gypsies Metamorphosed*, however, was performed three times: first at Burley, Buckingham's country house; at Belvoir Castle, seat of the Earl of Rutland, Buckingham's father-in-law; and then at Windsor (Butler 1991). The exceptional longevity of *The Gypsies Metamorphosed* is as important to an understanding of the masque as those more customary facts: dates, historical occurrences, and geographical place. James' pleasure in the piece caused him to have it performed again – not printed again or painted from memory, but done, again. With a King famous for being impatient about a masque because "they don't dance," it is folly to try and understand the particular workings of this Jacobean form without speculating on the bodies in motion, the music played and sung, and the cadence of the words being spoken.

None of this animating force cancels the critical interventions made about *The Gypsies Metamorphosed*. These include speculations about: (a) Buckingham, either Jonson's intent to "warn" James about his favorite, or how the masque functions as a complicated corrected view of the tarnished Buckingham; (b) continental politics; or (c) the representation of "colonial logic" embedded in the transformation of a ragtag people into Englishmen.[40] What is fascinating about the masque form is precisely the "expandability" of verse and song inviting something akin to early modern reception of emblems via the contemporary critical methods. Yet the masque was theorized by its makers as a form in which dancing, singing, and theatrical presentation opened the mind by sensuous apprehending of truth and beauty – a process impossible without sensory impressions produced aurally and visually.[41] As Jonson always negotiated the space between the transcendent and the obligatorily entertaining, he supplies in his best masques visions of beauty interlaced with joyfully comic moments. I suspect then that James I loved the playing of *The Gypsies Metamorphosed* because in the midst of commenting upon philosophical, cultural, political, and monarchical intrigues, Jonson offered a cornucopia of playing pleasures.

In the midst of the ephemeral and showy pleasures of dancing, music, and poetry, the staging of masques allowed Inigo Jones a space in which to create a collector's gallery of images. Jones as masque 'curator' offered a tutorial in sixteenth-century Italian art and architecture to an audience increasingly made up of collectors.[42] So some members of the audience would have appraised the set and the design, the costumes and the dancing as connoisseurs; the motion of the masque involved them in a representation of the pleasures of collecting, but also reminded them of the responsibility of having, keeping, and showing.[43] In *The Gypsies Metamorphosed*, when the Third Gypsy takes the palm of Thomas Howard Earl of Arundel, he grasps the palm of a great collector and patron: "What a father you are, and Nurse of the arts" (l. 615). Since in seven of its ten meanings cited in the *OED* (*Oxford English Dictionary*) nurse is a noun for a woman, Jonson once again eludes the linguistic consistency scholars dress him in. What is a collector nurse who is both father and caretaker? Is she a feminine protector and nourisher sprung whole from Jove's head? What does this mean for the maker of art, the work itself offered in search of a patron?

The gypsy fortune-telling as parable of collecting and giving sets the static collecting into motion: "By cherishing which, a way you have found/How they, free to all, to one may be bound/And they again love their bounds; for to be/Obliged to you is the way to be free" (ll. 616–19). If "they" is understood as the things Arundel collects or supports by patronage then Jonson inserts a provocative suggestion that the "arts" cannot be owned – "free to all" – though like good masquers they can perform obedience, loving their bounds in obligation to a generous protector and nurse is "a way to be free." Since bound and free serve again to bring us to the crux of stillness and motion, Jonson's wee ditty "read" over the top of Arundel's hand (at the Windsor performance) reminds the great collector of the nature of things in motion to be in motion. The rhyme has a dance-like movement: here they are "free" and away, there they come toward you offering themselves to your generous bondage, and finally, in your love for them and their free offering of themselves to the bond, they are free again. The parable of bondage and freedom can pertain as well to patron and artists, to King and subject, and in Jonson's case, Patron King to subject Artist. And the phrase "free to all" reasserts the power in a subject's choice to submit to a loving obedience. For centuries critics have commented on Jonson's love of unity; nowhere is it clearer than when one stops to examine even a small, serviceable bit of the masque and finds in it an allegory for the next larger circle of allusions, and the next and the next.

The Gypsies Metamorphosed itself stages concentric circles of giving and receiving: flowing out toward the King, in toward the masquers, out again toward the audience.[44] The first act of offering flows out of the giving of fortunes: the anticipation of how the telling will continue after the fortune of the King, the trepidation of some of the masquers as they sit with hands uncovered (instructed to remove their gloves) waiting to be chosen, to be told upon. Jonson's poetry accelerates the pace of the masque: the rhythms bounce and change so that even the reader can feel the quickening of pulse at the quickening of meter, the play of rhyme, the hesitation before the next fortune, the potential release of the dancing in between.

In a discussion of theatre and performance about his stage adaptation of *The Odyssey* (University of Michigan in 1999), Derek Walcott quoted the actress Irene Pappas who suggested that the closest theatrical form to ancient Greek theatre was the American musical. According to Walcott, Pappas specifically cited the intermeshed dancing, speaking, and singing, which echoes ancient Greek tradition, and the *percussive* nature of the language, dance and speech in the musical form. In *The Gypsies Metamorphosed*, Jonson seems to foreshadow not Milton or Dryden so much as Cole Porter. The delight in the extended rhyme, the percussive nature of the stresses in lines, the wit manifested in the looping recurrence of certain sounds and words suggest participation between listener and maker in their appreciation for erudition and lyrical panache. The affective power of musicals comes in part, according to Richard Dyer in *Only*

Entertainment, from the abundance represented on stage, an abundance the audience experiences not only as a visual spectacle but also as a received sense of bounty (1992). No less mitigated by political pressures or demanding audiences than the masque, the musical came into being by its costumes, outrageous sets, and huge production numbers. As with the musical, so the masque appealed to the senses through a display of power, yes, but also the power of more than enough.

All the senses are engaged in the fortune-telling of *The Gypsies Metamorphosed* as Jonson extends time in long lines with an extra emphatic foot (pentameter plus one); taking the King's hand Buckingham plants a kiss and peers into the future: "I'll kiss it for luck's sake; you should by this line/Love a horse and a hound, but no part of a swine" (ll. 279–80). Again the kisser, the kissee, and the prediction have worldly referents. Buckingham may give the King's fortune, but he is dependent upon being the recipient of it as well. Everyone in the first performance in the Hall at Burley, Buckingham's country home, would know how much the teller and the King were "obliged" in loving bonds.[45] In the moments of performance as soon as the eye and ear are involved, the audience is instructed by the meter of the poetry, of the song and thereby comes to expect, in this case, the elongated rhythm to continue. The body of a listener might move to the beat of the meter – particularly the final extra foot when the emphasis on "line" and "swine" arrests the movement – while the ear invites the mind to try and guess the rhyming words at the end of each line. While the masquers perform for the audience, they also offer invitations for the audience to heighten their reception of the singing, of the dancing in so far as they appeal to the senses of the spectators in rhythmic movement and sound.

After the Captain "discovers" the identity of the King and the dance/song occurs, the Captain returns to the royal hand, but his audience is now more than the mock-private one created by the fortune-telling. As the man is a King, so his fortune applies as much to his realm as to himself. Buckingham takes James' hand and turns (as the language instructs him by the "any") to the audience, "Could any doubt that saw this hand/Or who you are, or what command" (ll. 316–17). The bounce in the tetrameter is less intimate than the leisurely opening lines of the King's fortune. When the Second Gypsy takes over to tell the fortune of the heir apparent, the meter is emphasized by quick imperative spondaic lines: "As my captain hath begun/With the sire, I take the son/Your hand, sir!" (ll. 357–9). Now the attention shifts to hearing a quicker beat, and the play of give and take is made clear; the Prince must offer his hand to a Gypsy, though the last line of the first stanza gives back to the Prince his proper role, "Command, sir" (l. 362).

The pleasure of watching, of interpreting, of waiting – in the case of the masque audience who will find themselves the prey of gypsy soothsayers – cannot be separated from the poet's manipulation by rhyme and meter.

Meter and song sneak up on an unsuspecting audience member: like the much beloved sailor's hornpipe tunes which have the most inveterate landlubber swaying to the jaunty beat. In *The Gypsies Metamorphosed* the motion of back and forth is constant: the prancing over of a gypsy to the next fortunate victim; the alteration in rhyme; the suggestive praise (assessed by a knowing audience and rearranged if necessary into the real meaning) to the women at Burley; the ornery nudge that Jonson, who holds a pension, gives to the Lord Treasurer in the hopeful prediction that he will "put all that have pensions soon out of their pain."

When I used the words "'cornucopia' of playing pleasures" at the beginning of the section, I did so to suggest an overstuffed and ever-giving abundance. As with country dances that begin slow and speed up as a test of the dancer's prowess until the dance goes so fast it moves beyond the scope of the body controlling it, so with Jonson's acts of abundance, the 'anti-masque overdo.' An example is the signature accelerated rhyme of Patrico, the rogue priest of the gypsies. A virtuoso demonstration of the use of catalogue, itself a technique in oral composition which displays the speaker's capable memory, Patrico's catalogue of rhymes commences: "Sweet doxies and nells/My Roses and Nells/Scarce out of the shells/Your hands, nothing else/We ring you no knells/With our Ptolemy's bells/Though we come from the fells/But bring you good spells (ll. 803–10). The words ending in 'ells' would seem to run out before eight, but the rhyme scheme has a rising and falling lilt that goes on throughout the patter. The sound has the lilting of a pipe with a tumbling, fecund, seemingly inexhaustible rhyme, while the breath necessary to say/sing the lines also hints at virtuosity.[46]

Patrico's quick rhymes play to an audience Jonson introduces onto the masquing stage after the fortunes are told by the Courtier gypsies. The rude mechanicals metamorphosed, the clowns Cockerel, Clod, Townshend, and Puppy with their ladies Prudence, Frances, Meg, and Christian become a secondary audience more appropriate for the gypsies "other" trade, stealing. The discovery of the gypsies' theft of the poor trinkets is forestalled while a mini-masque within the masque of fortune-telling is repeated. Again the audience is treated to the pleasures of hearing and seeing fortunes being told, but soft gloved hands and loving prophecies are replaced by raucous jokes and tale telling: "You'll steal your selfe drunk, I find it here true/As you rob the pot, the pot will rob you" (ll. 842–3). These are the fortunes expected at an anti-masque.

Even in this set piece in which the country clowns are paraded before country squires, there is a heightened moment of reflection on the nature of generosity. Having taken precious trinkets from the common people's pockets, the gypsies return the much loved nothings. Using performance Jonson demonstrates the illusion of things kept, of things lost, of things returned. Any penitent sinner loves the story of the prodigal son, and any soul longing for loved things lost will love them restored. Patrico again in his signature rhythm conjures up the missing trinkets – these appear willy nilly sometimes with the right owner, sometimes not. The cynical can readily charge that the gypsies might easily give back such incidentals as nutmeg, pins, and ginger, but it is the largesse of the returning that makes for pleasure: "We scorn to take from ye/We had rather spend on ye/If any man wrong ye/The thief's among ye" (ll. 1011–14).[47]

The give and take in exchange need not be enacted in angelic selflessness. Dale Randall "argues Buckingham enjoyed the satiric thrust of the turning of him and his family into thieves" (quoted in McIntyre 1998: 69). The theatrical play that took place in an atmosphere of heightened self-consciousness mirrored the political world particularly acute in its own play of self referentiality. It would be folly for Buckingham to deny the King's largesse – when it actually materialized. Debts can be onerous and burdensome, but they are the stuff of seventeenth-century court life and Jonson, who relied on James, could spoof Buckingham, who relied on James, all in a theatrical gift given to James for his pleasure. Poets returned a patron's favor Barbour suggests: "by writing poems [and masques] the poet pays his enormous debt . . . the payment points up the inchoate status of literary property in 1616 . . . Like shares in a joint-stock company, Jonson poems earn new life" for his patron "as the poet's reputation grows. They constitute Jonson's currency" (1998: 509).

The fame of poetry that might increase the patron's 'stock' has a performed component: James might receive an immediate satisfaction by seeing the results of his patronage played out before him and then have that satisfaction extended in the publication of the masque poetry. The "currency" of Jonson's published poems circulated as well in less august circles. One of the songs from *The Gypsies Metamorphosed*, the Ballad of Cocklorel, gained Jonson fame and money in the sale of broadsides for many years after the performance. In the Ballad of Cocklorel, Jonson builds on the collusion between audience and players by offering at the height of the anti-masque an imaginative description of a social taboo. Turning the beauty of symmetry and equivalencies toward a satirical equivalence between a cave and an anus, the song tells a creation myth with its own big bang theory. Jonson creates a catalogue of bodies served to the Devil with a kind of giddy relish. He trusses and bakes those who are food for the Devil with the implements of rhyme and meter: "an overgrown justice of peace/With a clerk like a gizzard trussed under each arm,/And warrants for sippets laid in his own grease/Set over a chafing dish to be kept warm" (ll. 1110–13). The theatrical fascination with cannibalism has a long history: the theatre provides a setting where one can try out the idea of eating people without having to actually lift a fork and taste.

As Middleton manipulates the audience into imagining the forbidden by the intricate sexual language in his plays, so Jonson invites his listener to incriminate him or herself. Innuendo and description only come into full imaginative being if the listener/spectator lets the words form images in his/her mind. The "two roasted sheriffs" who "foxed and furred" "both living and dead" with "their chains like sausages hung about 'em" display themselves on trenchers in the mind (ll. 1090–93). Perhaps the spectator remembers a Dutch still life painting, mentally replacing the decorated boar with a fur-covered sheriff, though this would not be the curatorial focus Inigo Jones might have preferred.

The small village served up to the Devil is finally washed down with a "full draught of Darby" (l. 1119). The vast unimaginable yet provokingly imagined capacity of the Devil gives way to such a "breech with the wind/the hole too standing open the while/That the scent of the vapor before and behind/Hath fouly perfumed most of the Isle" (ll. 1126–29). Lest this out of context stanza (sung only in the Windsor version) seem to suggest a shocking lascivious interest in open orifices (as there of course is), Jonson uses the device to rail against the stench of tobacco, one of James' particular dislikes against which the King wrote "A Counterblaste to Tobacco" in 1604. But again it is the excessive, clearly Rabelaisian joy, of invoking bottoms and their audible productions that implicates the audience in their own particular awareness. The devouring hole of the Devil's mouth and the invention of the cave called the "Devil's Arse" are an anti-masque, anti-cornucopia where legions of officious officers are stuffed in a hole and blasts of stone-shifting air are let out.

After the smutty texture of anti-masque, the courtiers undergo lustration in transformation. The glove on the hand no doubt replaced at the moment of transformation marks a moment so small textually, so important visually, "the gypsies changed." But the veil obscuring the meaning of the masque to all but those who can understand, usually reinforced at this point in its transformation to the beautiful, never really covers *The Gypsies Metamorphosed*. Instead of the pure, powerful still truths replacing the wandering, thieving, lying gypsies, the end of the masque attends rather literally to the process figuratively suggested in the finale by most masquing performances.

Patrico, in need of a way to exit in character, suggests he give a blessing, as is his Friar Tuck-like job. What is blessed, wonderfully enough, are the very senses called upon to receive during the performance: "bless the sovereign and his senses" (l. 1326). "Order" is supplied not by dance and harmony but by the recitation of the senses in order of importance; Patrico begins with "seeing." The liminal world between gypsy and courtier is not yet closed; the blessing comes in the form of prophetic protection. The rhymes begin with "From . . . " and catalogue all that Patrico hopes the King's eyes may never have to suffer. The rhythm of the songs echoes the rhythm of Puck's spell over Titania's and the lovers' senses in *A Midsummer Night's Dream*: "From a strolling tinker's sheet/Or a pair of carrier's feet" (ll. 1353–4). Through an invocation of the imagination Patrico removes any disturbances from James' future as the song takes up seeing, hearing, smelling (particularly important after Cocklorel's ballad), tasting, and touching.

This moment in between anti-masque and transformation may be acounted, according to the spatial directions, liminal: the actor playing Patrico must cross the threshold between 'one world,' that of the anti-masque, and pass into the other, the Court – "I only now/Must study how/To come off with grace/With my Patrico's place . . ." (ll. 1298–301). At the end of the blessing, Jackman "ascending up" begins the most traditional of masquing songs and in the reverse of the descending tale of the Devil's Arse, the ascending songs taken up by the Captain and the gypsies "soar." It is a mistake, I think, to use the language of stage realism to understand what happens to an audience when the exaltation/exultation of song, harmony, and dance follow merriment and low playing. Satisfying endings are not always determined upon the basis of logic or truth in the sense of the transformed being perceived as totally new. Instead there is, potentially, the sheer weight of the audience's release into crescendo, the need to end, the desire for harmony, all of which together can make the ending one of culmination. Such a desire participates in the temporal nature of performance; complicated responses to what has been represented are not negated by the satisfaction of an ending. Like both the masque and play, time elapses for an audience's response as well, and in this time a spectator can remember, reassess, and even dismiss a work once enjoyed. In *The Gypsies Metamorphosed* the final transformation must needs be swift and at a high pitch to sweep away some of the anti-masque, and yet the audience has been readied for reception since the beginning. The motion of forward and back, giving and taking, expectation, fulfillment and surprise all make way for release. The end of giving is the end of performance.

2 Predominantly still

John Milton and the sacred persuasions of performance

THE ARGUMENT

Though John Milton does not generally make an appearance in books about performance, it is time we considered Milton's little acknowledged desire to write for the theatre. Even if that desire was thwarted by the political conditions governing the theatre of the time, it was a desire that influenced much of Milton's writing. *A Maske* is the only text Milton wrote and had performed. In it Milton creates a remarkable figure, the Lady, whose very power comes from a combination of stillness and motion. By staging her most persuasive addresses from a static, seated position, Milton manipulates not only the audience's perspective, focusing it on a third throne in the masquing hall, but also the audience's expectations by combining a still female body and an active female voice. Like Jonson, Milton works in a form already established as one displaying the aesthetic power of stillness and motion. But unlike Jonson, Milton uses the form to present theatrically the show of Christian struggle and triumph by comparing false illusion in the person of Comus to powerful representation in the person of the Lady. In Milton's dramatic writing, his characters often seem to take on actions even their author had not planned for the script. The Lady, while cleansing theatricality of its more sordid feminine history of inducing self-delusion, finds herself implicated physically by her engaged conversing with the villain Comus. Her mixed associations, the fixedness of print and printed rhetoric, the sensuous persuasion of corporeal performance and its consequences, combine to form a parable. It is for the spectator to draw from this parable the example of right actions and humble surrender.

In a theatrically innovative and pivotal scene in John Milton's *A Maske* the two seats of state, traditionally placed on a raised dais facing the stage, confront a third chair placed at the vanishing point of a single-point perspective, the apex of an imagined triangle.[1] When a masque was performed in great halls, the audience usually sat on the three sides of the room, a living wall enclosing the space for the meeting place of actors and watchers. In the empty space on the floor characters could descend to make presentations to those being honored, the watching royalty. (Charles I and Henrietta in courtly masques of the 1630s, at Ludlow their symbolic equivalent, the Earl of Bridgewater and his wife.) While this staging encouraged an audience's interpretation of the masque as a transaction primarily between the mobile players on the stage and the aristocratic hosts, the chair added by Milton in the center of the stage subtly shifts the customary view of the audience.[2] A Lady occupies the on-stage chair around which revolves the energetic, arguing anti-masque hero Comus. In *A Maske* Milton theatrically adjusts the audience's attention toward another throne, a throne where the authority is not simply the State in the body of an aristocratic daughter, Lady Alice Egerton, but the authority of the poet whose words become the "dancing vision" in place of spectacular action.

In the creation of this character for performance, the Lady, Milton figures an extraordinary collaboration of the aesthetic of stillness and motion present in the traditional form of the masque, adjusted by the urgent theatricality Milton employs in the later versions of *A Maske* that appeared in print. Where Jonson invented moments of playing pleasure in his masques and infused them with lessons about artistic power, collecting and bequeathing, Milton took up the masque form like Jonson as an opportunity for his poetry to be staged, but unlike Jonson he turned the playing into a drama whose center was a character of intellectual and *inspired* power. All of Milton's innovations, the seated form of the Lady, the dominant poetics of her voice, the ultimate surrender of her not to the expected intervention made by other aristocrats but to heavenly aid, depend upon Milton's deliberate representations of motion and performed stillness. Though my discussion echoes critical suppositions about Puritan masques, I am arguing for an understanding of Milton's creation of a *theatrical* form which might borrow the address to the senses in apprehension while restoring the self to the self in revelatory comprehension. [3]

Sacred drama and sacred text

The chair that holds the Lady at the center of our perspective is the theatrical property of the villain Comus. From her place the Lady commands authority in willful and dramatic language prior to her – potentially willful – silence. No icon this Lady, nor theatrical spectacle, rather a corrective to an audience's charmed awe with her reasoned arguments in favor of chastity, delivered firmly from the midst of the "sensual sty" of Comus' spectacular palace. The visual arrangement of the stationary chair allowed disruptive ideas to filter through Milton's lines of *A Maske* forcefully and persuasively, despite the mixed political company attending this Sunday entertainment at Ludlow Castle.[4] The language the Lady uses in interaction, while full of early Miltonic certainty, still emanates from the person of a recognizable member of the family. Milton gestures toward the tradition of the masque in order to remind the audience of the original form, that they might mark adjustment, adjustment made sometimes by way of gender as well as status.

The act of producing a poetic work for performance which espouses a religious ideology entangles an author in the public sphere where his or her potential fame as the author contrasts with the purpose of the work as persuasive theological argument. Milton in his own fervor adapted the sacred nature of ritual embedded in performance, since only through personal transformation, influenced by instructive performed poetics, could a community become a believing nation. In the art form of *A Maske*, Milton's louder poetic purpose could be muted by intermixing the reassuring, traditional presence of Henry Lawes, the court musician and Egerton, family music teacher, who intervened in the direction and design of the performance and played/sang Thyrsis (Diekhoff 1968: 4). Lawes' musical prowess and experience, as well as the ritual nature of the masque, almost liturgical with the code of masque-antimasque-resolution and reuniting dance, veiled Milton's transgressing purpose. The masque audience expected a display of the Egerton children, a rendering of the Welsh countryside and its inhabitants, some praise for wise rulers, and crisis resolution marked by the final dance. This the anonymous author gave while cleaning masquing house.[5]

Produced in several forms, *A Maske* in its public circulation evidences the confusion when script, performance, and print culture intersected in the 1630s and 1640s. For a short time after the performance, Lawes served as the young poet's amanuensis until the "oft copying out" of the poem tired the elder's "pen" (Milton 1973).[6] Circulation becomes a vital form of movement for the written and the printed, the breath as it were for the body of the text just as the performance in its steady procession through time breathes life into the play. Milton's adjustments and additions to the Bridgewater Manuscript serve as commentary not only on the maturing poet's experiences between 1634 and 1645, but on his idea of theatre, of what performance could and could not do and of what print could and could not convey.[7] The evidence of Milton's revisions suggests, as I shall argue, that he found the lack of visual drama available to print more vexing than the threat of spectacular seduction in performance.[8] In trying to convey the power and visionary nature of Christian struggle, Milton employs hyperbolic language and extended descriptions in the later printed version of the masque. Simultaneously in his writing of pamphlets in the 1640s and his printed revisions of *A Maske*, Milton attempts to compensate for the potential flatness of print by using metaphors of physical bodies, anatomical allegories to populate a dramatic stage and scene for the reader (see Chapter 3).

As a commissioned foray into the world of masquing, Milton's *A Maske* responded to the overwhelming presence of Jonson, recognized as the early master of courtly entertainments. Neither a writer of public plays nor an ex-actor (though he may have taken part in academic dramas), Milton chose to respond to the theatrical nature of the masque not simply by subordinating it to print, but by correcting it within the very display and immediacy performance allowed. Staging interactions between characters which challenged riot and opulent falsity, Milton displayed Christian example in action. And Christian example in action demanded an adroit mix of the still – the contemplative, the patient, the faithful – and the moving – the fire of zeal, the persuasive power of God's love, the "show" of conversion. Over and over again the young Milton writes in praise of "sacred drama," the sensuous experience of revelation which works as "the majestick Image of a high and stately Tragedy." "The call of wisdom and vertu may be heard every where," Milton writes, "not only in pulpits, but after another persuasive method, at set and solemn Paneguries, in Theatres, porches, or what other place, or way may win most upon the people to receive at once both recreation and instruction" (Second Book, *Reason of Church Government*).

Woody theatres and moving mounds

> Of Eden, where delicious Paradise . . .
> As with a rural mound, the champain head
> Of a steep wilderness, whose hairy sides
> With thicket overgrown, grotesque and wild
> Access denied . . . as the ranks ascend
> Shade above shade, a woody theatre
> of stateliest view . . .
> *Paradise Lost*, IV. 132–42

On that stage in Ludlow Castle, twenty-eight years before women performed in English theatres, the voice of a young girl addressed the audience playing the part of a central character. Accustomed perhaps to the sight of women, royal women, dancing in the spectacle of court masques, the audience would quickly identify the unusual nature of this lady's oral centrality, her extended speeches, her private, philosophical musings. Lady Alice sang and danced her first masque role two years before in Townshend's *Tempe Restored* which, according to John Creaser citing Orgel and Strong for verification, "was the first occasion on which any woman singer appeared on the English stage" (1984: 117).

Unlike the customary speaking women in masques who were professional masquers with little reputation to lose, a daughter of the Egertons might find such visible public speaking placed her in dubious company (Gossett 1988: 118–20).[9] Whorish ancestors, however, were to be banished from this stage by the chaste words and demeanor of a fifteen-year-old girl.[10] Speak the Lady does; but her threatening difference, Lady Alice's young female body, stays, for much of the masque, still. By freezing her into a speaking statue, Milton communicated a visual steadiness which might calm any fears of impropriety while he invited the select audience to view the process of her self-revelation, her education by trial, in fervent poetry.

As in *Epicoene* where the revelation of the silent woman becomes a mini-drama of the hidden master and the staged device, the form of the Lady seated (ll. 629–921) and the form of the work comment on one another.[11] A member of that sex commonly regarded as endangered in public and dependent on masculine protection speaks vigorously through a form typified by performed display and dependence upon lordly patrons. By controlling the most essential sign of performance, the vital body, Milton lowers the authorial risk contained in live drama. Requiring the "ear" of his audience to discern the Lady's speech, Milton thus subjugates sight, that is, the influence of Comus' spectacular palace, to hearing, a faculty gradually becoming theorized as a conduit for the intellect rather than a part of the system of senses perceiving. While the spectator should experience a revelation via intellectual understanding, he or she does so by way of performance. As is made clear in his theatrically conceived epic *Paradise Lost*, Milton will not settle for addressing only a spectator's comprehension, but the performed experiment of *A Maske* suggests he is working out *how* to stimulate apprehension in order to spark revelation and change without losing the spectator in a mist of the senses. He will move back and forth between forms of printed ephemera and poetic epic seeking to draw from each their strengths and mold a new form, a kind of holy, artistic amalgam.

The Lady's rhetoric in performance triumphs from a seat of feminine dependence and vulnerability, coincidentally the paradox at work in a true Christian life. Weak and defenseless virtue, such as the Lady's, must wait for heavenly aid to free it, suffering what looks like unbearable inactivity. The masque attendee who expects classic references and the action-packed maneuvering of Olympus' gods must adjust to the newer religion informing the drama in which the Lady's stillness actually mirrors Christ's own final struggle. Like her divine Lord, the Lady will fulfill her theatrical role by being thoroughly undramatic, by not acting upon Comus' forceful temptations.

The audience faces a theatrical choice similar to the Lady's, and in fact a dramatic choice which slyly echoes those of the popular romances created in the early modern five-act plays. While Milton has a theatrical axe to grind, his plot plays across the misrecognition always present in love play on the stage and the time-honored philosophical question posed to the theatrical spectators by Shakespeare and Calderon among others: how do you know what you see is what you think you see? (This is particularly tricky in the context of spirituality since faith must be based on things unseen.) Milton has designed clues for the audience to discern by equating the Lady and Comus with different forms of theatricality in the earlier scenes of *A Maske*. Comus is predominantly body, pure performance as signaled by his band of "unletter'd" (unprinted, unpublished, as well as illiterate) "hinds" (l. 174). His company having drunk of Circe's cup suffer the most extreme Protean change, a permanent change in nature, detumescent, having "lost their upright shape" (l. 59). Appealing to instincts activated at the site of their downward fall, the crew "undone by fond intemperate thirst" embody permanent falsehood, eternal masquers "their human countenance . . . changed . . . All other parts remaining as they were" (ll. 70–9).[12]

Echoing contemporary antitheatrical tracts, the poet decries this altering of "the express resemblance of the Gods," the face, into mere bestial disfigurement. The fears resemble those that inform Protestant fury over papist pretense. Among the multiple associations Circe offers Milton, David Norbrook writes, is her place in "Protestant iconography with the Whore of Babylon" (1984b: 105). In the effort to make chaste the theatrical, Milton can also clean up the slovenly false theatre of Roman Catholicism while salvaging the enlivening drama of the Christian life for Protestant believers. Milton adds an important qualification to purely sensual theatricality: the true horror of such bawdy, bodily excess comes from the victim's involuntary participation. No choosing spectators these revelers, but duped drinkers of Circe's dangerous cup.

The language of *A Maske* causes some confusion about who suffers the tragedy of such a curse. Rather than Bosch-like howling humans writhing inside horrid masks, the duped crew are "so perfect in their misery/[that they]Not once perceive their foul disfigurement/But boast themselves more comely than before/And all their friends and native home forget,/To roll with pleasure in a sensual sty"(ll. 80–4). Such unconsciousness leaves a spectator to the pain of recognition, mourning the rioter's loss alone since the bewitched themselves revel in blissful forgetfulness, a luxurious and "perfect" misery.

The dupable dancers in the performance were probably the slightly lettered hinds of the Earl's surrounding counties; Milton encourages the arrogance of the educated audience toward the lower classes taken by spectacle and illusion. He is not above a bit of Jonsonian derision for the common theatrical performers and their audiences, though he also works within the pressure of the genre. The folk dances, performed in the empty space where the players join the spectators, surely signal class superiority, but I suspect they also provided real masquing pleasures, pleasures created from the ordered disorder of anti-masque dancing. Milton, however, distinguishes between performance, riot, loss of voluntary choice, and persuasive display. His linking of gender to performance and print does not equate, as one might expect, the former with mostly effeminate nonsense and the latter with manly deliberation.

Yet when the opportunity arrives for establishing Comus' doubtful theatricality, Milton reverts to old antitheatrical type and blames Comus' trouble on the foreign, exotic intoxication, "orient liquor," of a woman's, indeed his mother's, cup. Circe's world of debauchery feeds on a power different than the satyr's permanently erect phallus, rather "rigor now has gone to bed" (l. 107). Night, a friend to Comus' crew, undoes the rigor needed for analytical thinking and right understanding since "tis only daylight that makes sin" (l. 127). More importantly for Milton's purposes, night makes revelation impossible. Comus' revelers participate in cyclical celebrations, dancing not in the sudden heat of passion but in the quotidian round, produced from the "dragon womb" of "dark Cotytto" (ll. 131, 129).[13] Conjured out of the repetitive cycles performance itself mimics, this "female" place erases the singular specific and masculine daylight of Apollo making "a blot of all the air" and allowing sin to flourish, not specific therefore not discernible. Here is motion as chaos and abundance as an invitation to carelessness.

Jonson and many antitheatricalists ridiculed the theatre audiences by associating them with the effeminate; Milton, however, contrasts bad effeminacy, bawdy theatricality, with his chaste feminine theatre. In some ways Milton and Aphra Behn (1640?–89) share an advantage: both are outsiders manipulating the forms of theatrical presentation popular in their day, a proselytizing "Protestant" in a genre of display and a woman in a theatre only recently allowing actresses let alone female authors. Even in her earliest plays, Behn has a remarkable sense of the power of motion as a corrective pattern on the stage (see Chapter 4) and Milton shows a powerfully persuasive determination to make theatrical power his in the service of his meaning.

The Lady, manly, godly reason in a female speaking body, creates an image of a 'good effeminacy,' one, Milton implies, even a man might imitate. In "Men in Women's Clothing," an article on antitheatrical tracts that express a terror of the effeminate, Laura Levine argues that Stubbes, Gosson, *et al.* fear most that "the spectator will automatically replicate what is on stage" (1986: 124). "Theater . . . being both effeminate and effeminizing . . . implies that things that are like women are likely to turn into women" (131). Milton manipulates that fear offering the powerful corrective that the very susceptibility, supposedly natural to the female spirit, allows for inspiration and spiritual power.[14] Adding women to Shakespeare's dyad of lovers and madmen, Milton suggests that lovers of God too find their way by seething apprehension even if the end of the moral tale does not find couples leaving the wood to wed but rather the spiritually triumphant Lady leaving a palace as enchanting as a wood to move toward divine grace.

Lest the "he for God only, she for God in him" poet sound as if he is championing the female, the vision of bad theatricality remains turgidly familiar. Cotytto's night womb provides the dark, the body and the female. Yet, Milton implies, these necessary black depths under the surface light allow the possibility of reflection, in the same manner as a mirror must have a blackened layer beneath the silvered glass. Milton employs the theatrical power where a mirror, a mime, an actor each represent back to the audience some version of the self, one's gestures, or other recognizable, embodied characteristics. If men watch the 'feminine' of performance and begin to perform the 'feminine,' they must find in the theatrical mirror a female version of themselves (a notion of femininity much more multiple and malleable because each spectator would see a different reflection). Rather than shunning these dangers, Milton solicits his audience's traditional associations with theatre, rearranging the terms of reflection, effeminacy, and spectacle.

To create an aesthetic of motion in stillness, Milton has at hand these associations which cannot be separated from the cultural value placed on the steady, unswerving male and the moving, unstable female. Having found his own 'feminine' reflection as Lady/employer of rhetoric often preferable and useful, Milton encourages both male and female spectators to attend to the Lady.[15] Depending upon just such influence, he presents this anti-masque of misguided riot and theatricality in order to correct it with chaste drama. A prophet must after all represent the motion of change not as unstable but as liberating. The word "conversion" contains the shift in position necessary for salvation, and the theatrical poet must show the movement as mysteriously measured and intoxicating as the choreography of meaningfully emblematic dancing in a masque.

Wandering onto stage after the anti-masque of Night (and her delusion inducing revels), the Lady represents a very different idea of femininity and choice of masque presentation. Undisguised, the dignity of her entry marked by her solitude, she speaks in preparation for her dramatic trial in the wilderness. The Lady stresses her author's emphasis on the ear, "her best guide now," instructing her audience to turn with her away from the trusting of mere vision and spectacle toward hearing in order to understand (l. 171).

In the Bridgewater Manuscript, the script most likely to have been performed at Ludlow Castle, the Lady's first appearance presents her vulnerable and resolved. Alone without manly protection she hears "riot and ill-manag'd merriment" and names Comus' performing crew in absentia as "unletter'd." Her demeanor composed, she "should be loath/to meet the rudeness, and swill'd insolence/of such late wassailers"; yet she chooses to move toward the noise (ll. 188–9). The Lady fears that Night, "envious," has "stolen" her brothers from her. Already established as the cover for Comus' carousing, illegible Night's performance threatens in another incarnation of "bad theatricality," stealing away from the spectators their distinguishing selves, as she might rob the Lady of her manly protectors (l. 194).

In the later printed edition, Milton develops the specific dignity of the Lady's spiritual journey, even further extending the (printed) spectacle of a woman's philosophical/theological musing.[16] Alone in this "desert wilderness," the Lady suffers "fantasies" "of calling shapes and beck'ning shadows dire" that "syllable men's names" (ll. 205–9). The "tumult" "rife and perfect" in her "listening" (active) "ear" produces questions, dislodges certainty of mind and purpose (ll. 202–3). A later Miltonic protagonist will undergo a like temptation with a sensuous Devil before he can "Publish his Godlike Office now mature": "O what a multitude of thoughts at once/Awak'n'd in me swarm, while I consider/What from within I feel myself, and hear/What from without comes often to my ears" (*Paradise Regained*, I. 196–9). Neither Jesus in *Paradise Regained* nor the Lady can control what "comes to their ears," but the poetic display of the struggle and triumph edifies the listening/watching audience. By associating her trial with Christ's, Milton creates in the Lady an atypical vision of public woman, shielded from the shame of commonness by her obedience and unique chastity.

This Lady of theatre cannot then be likened to Cotytto, to Circe, to the women whose reputations have more to do with Magdalene than with Christ. She enters her performance armed with divine precedent. In print, the Lady's speeches lengthen as she recreates for the readers what just took place and alerts them to how thoroughly alone she now stands (ll. 210–25).[17] Opening her mind to that of the reader, where her thoughts "may startle well, but not astound the virtuous mind," she orchestrates the revelation that her presence, her situation, her resolve should provide (ll. 210–11). A figure who stands remarkably alone would communicate her predicament through the spectator's various senses as they watched her stranded on a stage designed to look like a deep wood familiar to the Welsh audiences. In Milton's revisions for publication he supplies scenery, gesturing, and pointing out what in performance appears before the audience, describing how "Night," with her "dark lantern" closes "up the Stars," leaving the "misled and lonely Traveller" without heavenly guides. (The process of lowering the lighting by encasing the candles in a lantern would have an apprehensive effect on the audience: your senses would receive the dimming and ominous darkening well before you might articulate to yourself what is happening. (See Demaray 1968: 97–122.) Milton elaborates in the printed version of *A Maske* as if the Lady's physical presence at Ludlow Castle portrayed her struggle, but her physical absence from the text demands twice the number of images and descriptions.

Adapting the masque form of *A Maske* from the exterior show of chastity to a printed masque of the mind, Milton has the Lady announce to her readers the visions of spiritual sustenance appearing to her in her wasteland trial. "Chastity," she addresses the virtue as another character entering in masquing costume, "I see ye visibly" (ll. 214–15). John Demaray identifies Milton's early use of masquing techniques in his poetry with figures like "meek-ey'd Peace" "crown'd with Olive green" in "On the Morning of Christ's Nativity" (ll. 45–6; Demaray 1968). Welcoming her protectors with poetic flourish, the Lady directs an internal masque as if watching entrances onto a stage. "Pure-ey'd Faith, white-handed Hope and thou unblemish't form of Chastity" parade in front of her and ease her frightened mind (ll. 213–15).

The Lady's expanded soliloquy in print could indicate Milton's regard for his reader, her intellectual address demonstrating a collaborative measure much like Jonson's soliciting of his readers. Yet, Milton employs *more* language, *more* poetry, *more* argument to make print function forcefully as mystical revelation, a revelation accomplished by theatrical embellishments. And the intimacy he seeks with his readers cannot result only in mutual understanding but must point the reader toward his or her own responsibilities of action and choice.[18]

To reinforce the struggle of the Lady's trial, Milton increases the Lady's isolation in the printed version. At Ludlow Castle, the Egertons might have found the brother's neglectfulness offensive: in revision the Lady plainly states what she did not say in the Bridgewater Manuscript: "they left me" (l. 188). Abandoned to the night, the Lady of the text's thirty supplemental lines discussed above (ll. 210–40 in the 1637 and 1645 versions) preempt the brothers' philosophical discussion of her imagined struggles. Milton subordinates the brothers, whose long interlude exchanging ideas about their sister's chastity occurs only after the audience becomes acquainted with the Lady's predicament.

Shaping fancies into moving certainties

Having aurally tested herself in the isolation of contemplation and struggle, the Lady sings a supplication. Print and performance strain against one another with the record of the song. In both printed version and masque performance the Lady 'sings,' but only in one medium can she be 'heard.' The dollop of italicized print on the page setting of a song often represented the most elongated, elaborate, and memorable parts of masque performances. The temptation to glaze over songs as formulaic little ditties represents a reader's furthest separation from the world of sound necessary for a complete understanding of the masque.

In the performance the audience would be expecting a song: cued by the musicians, the potential motion of the Lady's body toward the front of the stage, the slight hesitation usually signaling a change from speaking to singing or the opening measures which freeze the singer in a prepatory position. Early readers or listeners to the manuscript version might conceivably know the song, in which case the reception of the words would be matched in the memory with the tune of the air. As sweet singer alone on stage, Lady Alice's social status finally accents her role; she employs her no doubt well-trained voice to equate her brothers with Echo's Narcissus. About to be caught in a "webbed parley" of her own, the Lady banters in her song with "the Sweet Queen of Parley" (l. 241). The Lady, already an unusually voluble female figure for the 1630s, sings a song playing on Echo, the female voice who through perpetual motion sacrifices invention of ideas for elegiac repetition. Echo, she who, Anne Carson reminds us, Sophocles names "the girl with no door on her mouth," is the subject of a song by a girl whose mouth is filled throughout this performance with language marked by rhetorical control and stylized improvisation (1995: 132). The song gives up one irony after another as the Lady provides Echo with visions of her brothers as self-deluded, self-absorbed 'narcissi.'[19]

The Lady's song conjures a witness whose presence during the Lady's semi-private struggle can only be "seen" as voyeuristic. The "side" left all "unguarded" by her brothers has been witnessed by Comus who, his first words imply, 'looks in' on her. Like the Elder at Susanna's toilet, or the rudeness of the male face in the window of Trutat's "The Reclining Bacchante," Comus peers in on a supposed private scene (see Berger 1972 for a discussion of the iconography of the male voyeur). Comus directs his powerful presence to the audience as he reinforces his position as a performer and enchanter of the senses.

In the initial exchange between Comus, representative of debased theatricality, and the Lady, budding representative of holy theatre, Comus discerns from the Lady's mien her unfeigned power. At first he confusedly interprets his response to the Lady's song, thinking she wields the famed power of Circe and her sirens whose seduction in "sweet madness" allows "sense" to be "robed of it self" (ll. 260–1). Yet Comus' language distinguishes Circe's persuasion – that erases choice with "potent herbs and baleful drugs" and entraps the "prisoner soul" – from the effect of the Lady's speech – that creates "sacred and home-felt delight" and "sober certainty" (ll. 262–3). The Lady's womanly, theatrical power bewitches in an entirely new way, restoring the 'self' rather than stealing it away. Comus' desire to make her his Queen by speaking to her confirms the Lady's stature.

Comus, like an old actor reciting outmoded lines, 'hails' the Lady with overblown praise. She cannot be bothered with old formality or traditional pastoral play-acting. "Nay Shepherd," the Lady says, waving away his praise which uselessly falls on 'unattending ears' (ll. 271–2). In this new theatrical form of display, the Lady's singing is for use, not the customary self display of talent, "not any boast of skill" but out of "extreme shift" (l. 273). Milton takes advantage of an ancient byproduct of masque performance; the instructive show of the Lady's dismissal of Comus' praise allows the audience to have 'attending ears'; not unlike court testimony spoken and then "struck from the record," the listeners hear the flattering words even as they admire the refuting modesty of the girl.

At this point the bawdy, body Comus might just have hauled off and hoisted the Lady onto his shoulder to make off with her. After all, Catherine Belsey writes, "Comus is about rape" (1988: 46).[20] Neither Belsey in the continuation of her essay, nor Milton in *A Maske* is quite so simplistic (and Milton's aristocratic audience would not have taken kindly to a hoisted daughter). Rather we *expect* Comus to be about rape; an expectation that Milton invites and exploits by presenting the Lady's vulnerability. Though the Lady remains in physical peril while subject to Comus' presence, her self-contained powers of speech and reason place her physical vulnerability in a subordinate position to the protected chastity of her mind. Rather than hoist her and silence her, Comus switches methods, choosing to imitate classical dramatic dialogue in an insinuating form of stichomythia to interrogate the Lady.[21]

On stage, performed interrogation and response function subtly, depending not only on what is said, but what it is said in response to, how quickly what is said is adjusted in the answer and posed back as a different question. Questions offered without calculation about an answer, formed without assuming the response, stage a measure of respect given from the addresser to addressee. It is astonishing how rarely women on stage entertain questions other than those already answered by other characters or strategically placed to confirm an earlier exchange in the play between men. When Comus begins to ask the Lady his questions in iambic pentameter, however, she becomes in turn responsible for her iambic response.

Well before Milton advanced a conjugal theory of "apt and cheerful conversation" in *The Doctrine and Discipline of Divorce*, he created characters whose dialogue set in print revealed their natures through a fixed representation of oral interchange. Such representations of dialogue between two characters in printed books of learning, tracts, and pamphlets of the late sixteenth and seventeenth century in England, I would suggest, 'picture' the process of learning by oral methods in printed form. Indeed the staged dialogue for didactic purposes shifts the awareness of the instructed from the singular reception and comprehension of an idea to an idea put in motion across an exchange, an exchange that interrupts statements to become query and answer. An invitation to apprehension by the senses, the 'witness' of staged exchange shifts perception between two figures and allows ideas to be developed through the tone of voice (many of the school texts are read aloud) and the process of the interaction as it changes pitch, perhaps moving from heated debate to resolution.[22]

Comus' questions are not wholly innocent; he encourages the Lady's forlornness while reeling her in on the promise of his knowledge about her brothers. "Were they of manly prime, or youthful bloom," Comus inquires, and we can almost see him twirling his false mustache while giving a sinister laugh (l. 289). Waxing homoerotic, Comus employs dramatic language to recreate the "faery vision" before the Lady's and the audience's eyes, bringing to descriptive life her brothers' activities under "a green mantling vine" (ll. 298, 294). Imaginary spectacle wins the Lady's trust. At first aptly discerning in their "unattending" response to Comus, the Lady's ears, undone by the desire to see and believe Comus' vision of her brothers, fail to 'hear through' Comus' language to his disguise.

Comus, now in possession of his treasure, directs her, assuring her their destination rises "from this shrubby point" (l. 306). This moment in performance, depending on Comus' gesturing hand, might have been very funny. Even the Lady seems to take the lively hint when she admits she could not find such a point, unless she had "well-practis'd" feet, considerably more seasoned than those feet she earlier named "unacquainted" (l. 310). The Lady consciously considers and accepts Comus' linguistic overture, "Shepherd I take thy word," arguing with herself that courtesy, though "named" at Court, is more often found in "lowly sheds" (ll. 322–4).[23] By taking the Shepherd's "word," the Lady makes a choice for experience, necessarily a choice involving temporal risk since if she simply said "no," the time of experience would end. Instead she chooses to venture farther, not only spatially, farther into the castle, but temporally, furthering through her response the time of the masque. If she is to be mistaken in this wayward trust, it will not be out of impetuous, unthinking action. She names her purpose to her audience, her willingness to choose a test of her virtue, asking "blest providence" to "square" her "triall" to her "proportioned strength" (ll. 329–30).

Shrubby points and kind shepherds can only be mistaken for landmarks and guides if the Lady is relying on her second best guide, her eyes. This seemingly disastrous change of guides, from reasoning ear to deluded eye, allows for the challenge between the merely illusionist theatre of Comus and the awakening, powerful, and chaste theatre of the Lady. She must forsake her mind and discernment, even if only momentarily, falling for the false promises of spectacle. Here one might make the argument that Milton, like many of his contemporaries, is beginning to separate the senses in their organic way of knowing from one another. By the mid-1630s, the writing on knowledge, sensation, and cognition begins to shift, and, as Elizabeth Eisenstein conjectures, one reason for the shift toward comprehension as an intellectual act less dependent upon the senses for understanding may well be due to the increased use of print (1980).

Continuing to mix the sensuously persuasive with the holy and didactic, however, Milton escorts his audience to the center of his careful theatrical construction, not an Anti-masque corrected (as might be expected in a Jonsonian masque) so much as a Morality Masque. A Morality Masque warns of its own dangers by displaying them vividly before the spectator; and performance of such dangers offers to the spectator an alternate response to the physical, visual seduction of the 'merely' theatrical.[24]

"Speak to me and be my Queen"

So we are returned to the pivotal scene in the masque: the Lady seated, Comus discovered, two models of dramatic representation encountering one another. Though the Lady's stillness might invite an interpretation of her unmoving body representing the stable power of print correcting the mobile and false theatrical body, her author is rarely content with either/or in his representations of oppositions (or his oppositions drawn vividly are rarely content to remain either/or). Milton, he who refused to shun the nickname given him by his schoolmates, the 'Lady of Christ Church', seeks instead to turn the doubled gender into a way of speaking. He creates for the Lady a 'crossaddress,' infusing her with a presence both visually and intellectually powerful. Her active, responsive mind fixed in an earthly immobile body shows the struggle natural to a Christian life when choice leads to debate and temptation. Theatrically displaying the Lady moved and persuasive and yet still and resolved in an active chastity, Milton mirrors in performance what he often tries to create in print out of allegories of stressed physicality: embodied language, words so vital they seem to have breath.

While ready to use the spectacular, mobile images and physical description to his own advantage, Milton still insists that words determine action, not action words. In this way he creates a temple of "logolatry" as Michael O'Connell terms the Puritan linguistic version of the Catholic spectacle of "idolatry" (O'Connell 1985: 287). Though such a temple can be a theatre, Milton creates this theatre of words in the form of an anti-spectacular woman. By mixing traditional equations of gender, rational speaking man in the body of vulnerable young woman, by mixing media, print's authority/authenticity with performance's immediacy and (potentially didactic) display, Milton rescues theatricality from its own excesses and print from its own limitations.

Milton demands that his audience witness the Lady's words without elucidation by motion or action. The power should be in the sound of the Lady's pronouncement, possibly emphasized by her rhetorical gestures, and the content of the poet's philosophy. Most dramatic action in *A Maske* is reported, harking back to the stateliness of Greek tragedy; sensational monologue or dialogue – language not actions – create tension in the absence of a performed narrative plot. Neither the Greeks nor Milton disavow the power and presence of performance by an emphasis on language; rather the person of the hero, the echo of the Chorus, the tension of tragic interaction transfix the watching audience in ideas inseparable from the experience of the story. That the Lady's predicament ensues from her being transfixed by Comus' large, visual power does not detract from her author's use of her immobility. Having risked a trial, entered into a compromising relation, the Lady must now call upon her reason, the only means available to her since she cannot take action, thus demonstrating through her voice her resolve to proceed through her ordeal.

The intensity of the poetic bantering between the Lady and Comus heats the middle of the cool masque of Chastity. Comus and the Lady do not distract themselves by the conventional flattery of the patrons, a distraction inviting the customary shift in audience attention between raised stage and the raised dais containing the seats of state (Diekhoff 1968: 6). Such division of the audience's attention, like Comus' earlier outmoded flattery, belongs to a debased masque form Milton intends to correct by fixing the audience's attention on the seriousness of heady debate, the enactment of intimate, erotic, philosophical interchange. While audiences were accustomed to look to those seated on thrones for pronouncements and for reactions, the pull of Milton's intense language made for the literary equivalent of single point perspective. His counter strategy demanded that an audience see/hear the focal point of *A Maske*, not the watching royalty but the speaking Lady.

Milton like Jonson must move between the power of controlling the focus of the viewer without completely subduing the action into lifelessness. There is then something of the collectible in the Lady's still position, a stillness that is to remind the reader/spectator of the kept chastity of her body. Since in the crudest of ways fathers kept their daughter's virginity as a treasure to be traded for money and alliance, the display of the Lady as a pawn in a patriarchal economy poses a problem for Milton. This is one reason her voice is so important, it must disrupt the familiar figure of the seated beauty as portrait displaying family wealth and potential heirs. Instead, Milton must make her a powerful presence whose power points toward the unseen power, an unseen power not limited by the economy of bride exchange.

As he requires chastity to "sall[y] forth" in *Areopagitica*, so Milton conflates the theatrical action of dialogue with a private term of intimate interchange. Converse, "the action of living or having one's being in a place or among persons," implies daily-ness, repetition and spontaneity, qualities at odds with the masquing stage (*Oxford English Dictionary*). No definitive performance, no singular demonstration attended with the "oohs" and "aahs" of admiration and surprise mark a conversation. Jonas Barish identifies Milton's creation of a similar paradox in Book Five of *Paradise Lost* where the proof of Adam and Eve's unfeigned piety, the "validity of the prayer," rests in "the changefulness which for others embodies the most reprehensible feature *of* theatricality" (1981: 96). If "spontaneous worship, in the Miltonic Eden, resembles a kind of perpetual motion, an endless sequence of unique happenings," then conversation, both between God and his creations and Comus and the Lady, represents a pious theatricality in which the participants reveal themselves to one another (in the case of the masque to an audience as well). Conjoining two seemingly opposed attributes, steadfastness and changeability (stillness and motion), Milton plucks from theatricality its most vital component, motion, but moves the Lady's intellect and reason across the stage as a dramatic substitute for her body.

It is worth remembering that Milton's prophetic purpose models itself upon an oral tradition of prophecy. And that oral tradition depends, like gift exchange, upon motion. Without a performance the orally composed, the aurally received cannot exist. While Moses returned with tablets on which were written the Ten Commandments, his messages and revelations were delivered in speech to the receptive and non-receptive alike. Milton must create a role that incorporates the newer technology of print into the prophetic mode, and the prophetic mode is not a mode of reason and argument, but of persuasive address to the senses which will not seek to instigate logical concurrence but cause conversion and belief.

Milton's desire to cause words in their abstract divine essence to govern bodies in their daily physical existence, however, creates a language replete with earthy insinuations. The act of engaged speaking (and the creation of engaged speakers that audiences hear and see) would awaken the body along with the mind into converse or conversation "in the biblical sense." "Criminal conversation" was a seventeenth-century term for sexual intimacy and intercourse, a term used in legal courts to obtain a separation or divorce (Stone 1977: 38). The Lady and Comus seem fully aware of the dangers of heavy speaking; he hopes to speak to her and she will be his "Queen," while the Lady worries that if she unlocks one set of lips in this "unhallow'd air," the other will soon follow (l. 757).

Milton prepares his audience at the Masque to understand and distinguish between "apt and cheerful conversation" and deceiving, sensually motivated ploys. Asides no longer necessary, disguise sundered, the much remarked upon wand of Comus, though not waved, remains prominent. Chaste and unchaste theatre unmask through theatrical conversing revealing simultaneously to each other and the audience the philosophy responsible for their natures. Unlocking her lips glues the Lady to her seat. By speaking at all, and by choosing to acknowledge Comus' words, the Lady commits herself to some sort of converse. Rejecting the mandate of 'stay silent and virtuous or speak and be compromised' customary for seventeenth-century women, the Lady chooses to speak with persuasive vigor. Comus may not "touch the freedom" of her mind in seducing her body, yet his desire to "speak to her" in order to make her "his Queen" releases a mode of discourse usually unavailable to female characters who are not already queens (l. 663). Without the Lady's struggle and choice in the face of Comus' intentions, the heightened language of the scene would be unnecessary, erased by the brothers' easy rescue and return of a young, predominantly silent, girl.

Her (in)actions, her vibrant speech makes clear, cannot be mistaken for a natural passivity or a patient waiting for brotherly intervention. This inactivity is her choice, more her choice perhaps than even her author realizes. Although Milton creates a plot in which he holds the Lady still, her inability to move would seem to happen more as a consequence of her susceptibility, finally, to the power of spectacle. In all the recorded versions of Comus, including those with stage directions, Comus' *conditional* threat, "If I but wave this wand/Your nerves are all chain'd up in Alabaster" (ll. 659–60), is never followed by the necessary action given in stage directions or spoken by the characters, 'Comus waves his wand.'

Thus on stage and in print the Lady assumes her stillness voluntarily or by an internal and not an external enchantment. Using the stage directions as guides, one must assume that whether the Lady knows it or not her most powerful speeches come from being susceptible. Yet the Lady's confused engagement with the seductive Comus is crucial to the plot of a masque mirroring the drama of divine humility, the theatrical imitation of Christ's behavior. The Lady's willingness to test herself by entertaining Comus' enticements produces the *display* of chaste choice, of 'knowing' virtue.[25]

Theory and practice collide in the person of the Lady who in her trial prevails, while her body cannot erase the evidence left after a test of virtue. Acting in this universe exacts a price. The beauty of the Lady's combined motion in her passionate words – accompanied perhaps by proud and attentive gestures and the motion of her head – hints at the *unseen* parts of her body figured continuously in the early modern period as dangerously mobile and wanton when unchecked. At the end of *A Maske* the Lady, having embodied chastity articulately and persuasively, will be glued to her seat by a seemingly uncontrollable and disconcerting secretion. The evidence of motion, of being moved, paradoxically immobilizes the Lady via a secretion we are led to assume is out of her control. Mesmerized momentarily by the seduction of Comus' theatrical presence – an appeal to apprehension which would leave the spectator in the bleak land of "blear illusion" – the Lady misses the import of the conditional, the "if" in his threat.

Thus the wand offers an opportunity for the Lady to temporarily "immanacle" herself. Before she can triumph in Milton's terms, the Lady must see all around her, the visions of theatrical spectacle, the lure of physical intoxication, and then she must prefer spiritual intoxication. Her author writes in the hopes that chaste theatre and poetry can make the mind tipsy while leaving the body only temporarily implicated, and in the end fortified against empty persuasion.

Comus too must participate in Milton's theatre of choice; not swinish enough simply to take the Lady, he engages in conversational seduction in the hopes that she will drink the liquor willingly. Having likened himself to Apollo, no sun-clad power of Chastity but rather a ravisher of women, and her to "root bound" Daphne, Comus takes the advantage of mobility to address the Lady's aspect: "Why are you vext, Lady? why do you frown?" (l. 666). At first, the Lady might simply be seduced by Comus' spectacular self and palace, but too soon she is lost in her answers to him, in conversation, seduced by Comus' desire to attend to her words. He looks at her, he listens to her – in performance he would move around her – wooing her by returning, amended, her own words.

Though the audience can hear wiliness in Comus' language and spectators might see his plotting mirrored in his stalking body moving about the chair, the Lady, whose training in Reformation asceticism confronts the ornateness of Comus' Catholic spectacle, is in the process of learning to discern seductive show from sincere truth.[26] Comus' temptations are fully of the "taste and see" variety. He encourages the Lady to "look," trying to secure his visual power over the oral/aural Lady: "see here be all the pleasures/that fancy can beget on youthfull thoughts . . . And first behold this cordial julep here/that flames and dances in his crystal bounds" (ll. 667–73). The tempting mirror, the dancing flame of Comus' cup offering spiritual self forgetting and temporal immediacy must be seen by the eyes and tasted by the body. All these lures flicker and move catching the eye by reflection and sudden glimmers of unexpected light. Yet Milton does not simply dismiss the visual as the untrustworthy sense to be overcome by the ear; the Lady with whom the watching audience can identify doesn't stop looking, she doesn't shield her eyes, instead she incorporates her ear and eye to create a fuller discernment.[27]

As a poet Milton cannot afford to abandon the senses of his reader through which the reader perceives and knows. But his use of the frozen body of the Lady, like Jonson's deployment of delay, acts as a momentary artifice of separation. Her stillness is for effect, as if she were blindfolded and thus dependent upon a sharpened sense of hearing and smell. So in this scene because she is seated, the Lady sharpens her 'free' senses in an unfettered, mobile reception that infuses her speech and her responses.

When Milton embellishes the Bridgewater Manuscript in the 1637 and 1645 versions of *A Maske*, he again helps the reader *to see*, as the spectator would, the young Lady Alice fending off her tempting rival. Letting the reader know his victim has "dainty limbs," suitable according to Comus for "gentle usage and soft delicacy," Comus shows the reader how the Lady scorns him in converse, holding on to her "harsh" ways like "an ill borrower," refusing to drink from his always extended cup mortal "refreshment" (ll. 680–8).

Continuing his reinterpretation of gender and genre, Milton presents the Lady in a Miltonic variant of the Pygmalion/Galatea story. At first mobile and alive, the Lady becomes stone in order to speak vigorously. Whereas Shakespeare's statue in *The Winter's Tale* seems to breath with "veins" that do "verily bear blood," thus giving evidence of artistic power mimicking the motion of life, Milton's temporary statue (the Lady) proves the strength of his art by her seeming disregard for movement of the body equipped as she is with "freedom of the mind" (*The Winter's Tale*, V. iii. 64–5). Even at such a disadvantage, a disadvantage not unlike anonymity or femininity, the Lady will triumph over false illusion by showing self-possession, not as a statue for another's possession but as a self-contained, attentive perceiver of her theatrical dilemma.

Comus, more the theatrical performer than an awakened reader of Christian virtue, looks to the Lady's trapped position and assumes she lacks something, if not yet her seal of maidenhood. When he suggests she drink the cup as a restorative, his slip in perceiving her stillness as a lack shows the Lady the way to respond. She knows she has lost nothing of vital importance in this contest: her immobility of body only a secondary consideration, Comus cannot "restore the truth and honesty" he forfeited by his theatrical ploy of disguise (l. 691). The Lady knows she needs no "restoring"; she refuses to become the creation of such as who are not "good men": "good men give good things/And that which is not good, is not delicious to a well-govern'd and wise appetite" (ll. 703–5). Her choice is neither starvation nor 'banish'd appetite' – indeed she desires the "delicious" – but the enjoyment of good things from good men in good time.

Both parties in this conversation listen to what the other says. Noting his slip and her rebuff, Comus suavely redirects his powerful energies to the Lady's proclivity for the serious and answers her with philosophy, long and evocative lines of philosophical monologue. Not one of the Lady's "budge doctors of the Stoic Fur," Comus sings a hymn to Nature based on abundance enjoyed unto satiation (l. 707). By consuming, by enjoying, excess naturally prunes itself, Comus argues, wooing the Lady not with a vision of tousled passion and strewn bedclothes but with order grown from enjoyment rather than an abstinence which causes overproduction and chaos, the land "strangl'd" in "Nature's waste fertility" (ll. 706, 729). Comus' Nature produces valuables to be collected, "all worship ore and precious gems," from her "own loins" (ll. 718–19).

The Lady's mortal coil, Nature, Paradise, must all be saved from themselves, not despoiled by unreasoned growth or untimely moisture. Cotytto's womb in the dark false theatre of night and Nature's rich productive loins belong to the generous world of abundant cyclical life. Neither offers the legible security of narrative climax; each process repeats itself, undoes itself, remakes itself, wastes itself, replenishes itself. Comus partakes of this world in his masculine character of traditionally "feminine" pursuits. And the Lady critiques his 'use it or lose it' refrain in her feminine voice of 'masculine' reason.[28]

Recognizing that her surrender to an argumentative exchange compromises her even if Comus' arguments themselves can be rebuffed, the frozen Lady worries she has "unlockt" her lips too eagerly. Virtue has none the less clearly listened to her captor, perceiving his intent to seduce more than her body, "the incorporal rind," in overcoming her "judgement," a more permanent violation, by "obtruding false rules prankt in reason's garb" (ll. 758–9). The Lady fears she sits undone: since she does speak to Comus, is she now his Queen?

Though not yet the "apt and cheerful" talk envisioned offstage in marriages by the domestic reformer of the 1640s, this conversation takes place between comparably powerful if opposed voices. When the engagement necessary for private conversation breaks down, the Lady turns the dramatic tension away from herself and Comus, addressing the silent public witness to this conversation. Breaking the spell of converse, the Lady colludes with her auditors by referring to Comus as "*this* Juggler," leaving him a mere street performer and "Impostor," feigned creature of debased theatre.

On the masquing stage Comus misses the Lady's subtle cue/clue, her use of the disconnected pronoun, "this Juggler" instead of "you Juggler." He does recognize, though, that the "talk" has changed, become "mere moral babble" rather than an argumentative exchange of philosophies (l. 807). In the 1645 printed masque Comus hears the Lady – put out but aware she has dismissed him from her intellectual bed – and matches the Lady's third-person maneuver, calling her "She" who "fables not" (l. 800). In the Lady's vehement printed finale, an aria consisting of twenty-one lines beginning with her extremely rhetorical "Shall I go on?," the Lady dismisses any previous conversational intimacy: "Thou hast not Ear nor Soul to Apprehend/The sublime notion and high mystery/That must be uttered to unfold the sage/And serious doctrine of Virginity" (ll. 784–7). So there. The rupture onstage would have been immediately apparent to a watching audience as the Lady turned her head away from Comus and toward them signaling the beginning of her disenchantment. For the reader of the poem in print, however, this rupture must be made plain in an extended argument where the textual Lady clearly turns from her tempter in the unmistakable language of rebuke.

Virtue and chaste theatre redefine themselves by disowning the spectacular seductions of Comus; we as audience have witnessed the conversation, the tempting dialogue, the decision to abstain. Drama affords Milton representation of that which often lies secret, enacted in private moral struggles unacknowledged. What better form for a Puritan to represent a good work whose self-proclamation would tarnish its power, but whose dramatization enriches all who see or read it? For the audience Milton creates a spectacular argument for chaste virtue, for the reader, an invitation to picture the struggle through the power of the poetry and *see* with the mind.

A sacred theatrical then, this Lady, this dramatic piece. Her triumph shining through her words despite Comus' sensual palace and despite the aristocratic setting where the "sensual sty" and the courtiers were not necessarily strangers. Set in stone she performs her rectifying service for her author, then proves troublesome in the last act. The entrance of her brothers visually confirms the intellectual *fait accompli*, the divorcing act of 'dis-conversing.' The choice of the audience as a more suitable object for address by the Lady signals an end to the possibility of her succumbing to a private tryst with Comus. With the end of the trial comes divine intervention. Comus resorts to force upon perceiving her linguistic separation from him, and promptly the brothers enter, break his glass and begin the unraveling of the enchanted scene.[29]

The Lady, through with Comus, can only return to the society she wandered away from, though she will return changed. Richard Halpern rightly warns that "the virtuous resistance of the Lady may become revolt if it is not relinquished at the proper moment" (1986: 94). So why doesn't the Lady stand up?[30] The entrancing spectacle gone, she does not relinquish her chair, nor use her voice. She allows her brothers to assume that she is frozen, unable to explain. How odd that dramatic divorce like marriage at the end of comedy seems to render women silent too; without the challenges of Comus, the Lady submits to the ministrations of all around her, not speaking the reason she so persuasively displayed a few lines before. She must become all 'show,' miming her acceptance of Sabrina's releasing moisture and joining her parents after treacherous separation. Her listening partner has vanished, his glass broken, his wand intact.

Throughout these scenes of reason's triumph, something is wrong in the material world. What keeps the Lady confined, Sabrina tells us, is "gums of gluttinous heat" on the "marble venom'd seat" which only the touch of "palms moist and cold" can unloosen (ll. 916–18). Critics who have dared to analyze the sticky substance have predictably assumed Comus' wand to be the premature culprit.[31] Yet Comus' seed would, any experienced disporter knows, tend toward runniness; female moisture by way of excitement or fertility remains "gluttinous." Sabrina's cure, like a cold douche, washes away the evidence and freshens the maiden.

This explicit reminder of the physical consequences of sensuous perception demands a denouement initiated by Sabrina who anoints the hands, the lips and the genitals of the Lady. A new goddess of a new kind of theatre, Sabrina answers her summons from under the "translucent" water, a summons put to her ear – "Listen and save" (ll. 861, 866). With Sabrina, the Lady makes a better choice of female patron than when she solicits Echo earlier in the masque who "livst unseen," unknown and whose voice only mimics the speaker's plea. Sabrina, however, emerges in an image of clear representation, as a harbinger of discernment, of apt listening and, consequently, redemption (l. 230).[32] When she rises Sabrina announces her watery, uncontainable nature, a goddess of fluidity not stability, borne across the earth on "printless feet" (l. 897). The correcting motion of clear water, not agitated and muddy, undoes the unnatural stillness suffered by the Lady.[33]

Indeed Sabrina enacts a printless feat when she anoints this new chaste theatre with drops on the areas most in danger and most moved by Comus' temptations and his threats. First on the Lady's breast and then in an old, oral ritual of the thrice-made gesture: "thrice upon thy finger's tip/thrice upon thy rubied lip" (ll. 914–15).[34] Finally, like re-vision and re-marriage, the Lady is allowed the opportunity to be "tried" again. Freed by Sabrina's cleansing power into an 'intact chastity,' the Lady practices a chasteness in her trial which readies her to be 'revirgined/revised' by the "chaste palm" of the goddess. The ritual necessary for such feats can be reported in print, but the musical incantation of the performed charm – words by Milton, music composed by Lawes – loses some of its mythical power in the reading.

While Richard Helgerson's aphoristic description of Milton as free "from the old aristocratic shyness about print but invested with the numinous presence of the old performance culture," has a persuasive beauty to it, the actual practice Milton is left with is easier for the critic to encapsulate than for the writer to make (1987: 20). In Milton's creation of theatrical print the evidence of the passions upon the body, a printed simulacrum of those unpredictable bodies in performance, disrupts the coherence of his imagined scenes. In her intellectual dismissal of a seductive proposition, the Lady has triumphed, but her chair holds evidence of struggle and of the possibility of pleasure. When Sabrina descends, the Lady rises, presumably educated herself to trust her ear over her eye, to 'listen and be saved,' rather than to 'look and be lost.'

In "'Gums of Gluttinous Heat' and the Streams of Consciousness: the Theology of Milton's *Maske*," Deborah Shuger argues that for Milton the fact that the Lady does not consent makes her captivity "morally trivial and without repercussion" (1997: 6). Yet Shuger's intriguing argument about wet dreams, confession, the show of internal struggle and the self in Protestant theology lacks any recognition or interpretation of the masque as a performed form. Though the "consent" the Lady shows may not be wholly conscious, she is duped by the show of the wand to assume herself chained to her seat. The gums then may be more aptly understood as the "birdlime" (a term Shuger glosses from seventeenth-century usage) of one's own erotic weaknesses, but the show of the performance still makes this scene complicated by stage practicalities and the demands of resolution at the end of a masque. If "it costs Sabrina very little effort to free" the Lady, is it not possible it is because the Lady prepared the way by turning from Comus? More importantly, neither the poem nor the masque of *A Maske* "divests the body's unwilling captivity of any moral significance" (7). Instead the show of the struggle – the pure but immobile Lady rebuking the impurity of will-less motion and the description of the physical traces of desire and temptation – are in service of the audience and of performance. Shuger emphasizing the influence of Augustine and Catholic humanism on her consideration of *A Maske* assures us she does not mean to suggest that Milton was a "closet papist" (7) But I do mean to suggest that his project was something like that of a closet dramatist.

Closet dramatist not so much in the sense of a Samuel Daniel but in the sense of a Protestant dramatist: one whose intent to show purity through the trial of the inward senses demands not only vivid poetry but also an innovative show of the necessarily non-dramatic. In this regard Shuger's interventions are helpful when she posits the loss of "confession" after the Reformation as an intensifying of "the felt disjunction between one's public identity – the person who speaks that others may see him – and the unspeakably complex and strange inner creature known only to oneself" (15). On the one hand, the memory of what one has done or imagined, good and bad, "constitute the self" according to Aquinas. On the other, Calvin suggests that the "sins committed in a day" are so numerous that the memory – Aquinas' self – "gets confused" (10, 15). By show of inward struggle and by denouement of grace, the "dea ex machina" of Sabrina offering release to the passive body of the Lady, Milton teaches his audience about a self in formation. Seeing or reading *A Maske* the audience must keep in their memory a recognition of virtuous piety brought about through reception by the senses; yet, this recognition cannot be applicable only to the individual body of the "Lady" and her specific trial, but must be an example for the potentially virtuous acts of the communal body of the faithful.

Until Milton's revisions of the 1645 *Maske*, this memory is created predominantly by seeing and hearing. The tension of the still and the moving already delineated in the body of the Lady and in the pressures upon the printed poem is echoed in the tension Shuger sees as a residue from Classical and Renaissance sources. If motion as it shows itself in the body almost always constitutes impurity, according to many of the ancient and early modern theologists, then the inward version of this struggle, impure thoughts moving across the mind and agitating the soul, becomes an experience to be shown as Shuger quotes Philip Sidney from "the secretest cabinet of our souls" (1997: 17). Such a construction of the need to display confusion and resolution makes the self a kind of collector's corner to be inventoried and pondered. Rhetorically Comus and the Lady, from their different traditions of theatre, use the stage to walk the audience through demonstrations of wonders. In Comus' world his desire is to enchant, ensnare, and even potentially add the spectator to the collection; in the Lady's, hers is to review, remind, and refresh the spectator who must then leave the display not attached to the physical and particular Lady herself but to the life of grace she struggles to lead. In fact, to return to the perspective Milton manipulates when he seats the Lady on the throne in front of the seats of state, perhaps the vanishing point, one can say only with the lightest of analogical touches, is becoming the trajectory of the self poised and disclosed, revealed and relinquished, subsumed into the body faithful at the moment of resolution.

3 Theatrically pressed
Pamphletheatre and the performance of a nation

THE ARGUMENT

This chapter examines the years generally considered a "gap" in performance history between 'Renaissance' and 'Restoration' theatre. Though the established theatres were for the most part closed from 1642 to 1660, performances of pamphlets, of playlets and other forms of ephemeral print took place in public theatricals or a pamphletheatre. Because of the crisis of production and the pressure put upon print to replace or to reinvent what had been the domain of the public theatrical, the works of the period and their reception give evidence of the continuing collaboration of textual creation and performance. Through the examination of stillness and motion in the public, popular sphere of pamphlet writing, performance, and reception, I argue against the false separation made by limiting the history of seventeenth-century performance and theatre to the periods before and after the Interregnum. The subject is vast: the chapter does not offer a survey, but rather points to ways to consider the pamphlet exchange of the Interregnum in terms of performance 'companies' of dissenters and public reception of pamphlet writing, as well as offering specific examples of works created for the pamphletheatre by John Milton and Richard Overton.

One morning in 1997 New Yorkers woke, collected their 'paper of record' and noticed to their horror, if they had a moral attachment to the form the news arrives in, that *The New York Times* had gone 'color.' For the citizens who chose the *Times* primarily for its 'serious' and 'comprehensive' news reporting, the gaudy color pictures slapped onto the front page of each section betrayed sober reporting for flashy, advertising tactics. Color signaled a difference in intent for the paper. While the columns and columns of newsprint flowed down the paper in an orderly fashion, there to be read and then discarded (or recycled), the dressing up of the paper seemed to render the news itself a visual object . . . more importantly . . . an object that could be comprehended visually, not solely by reading.

The editors of *The New York Times* were responding to a technological change in the public reception of news, one that had begun years before but now seemed too pervasive to resist. The popular and garish *USA Today*, recognizable because of its bright blue box on the front page that resembles a print version of a television screen, reassured its readers with its abbreviated columns of text that they could scan the entire article, rarely having to turn a page. This emphasis on appearance and brevity responded to the much reported, often by *The Times* itself, revolution in "visual culture," "young people" learning the world by sight, by icons, by pictures on a television or computer screen.

The pamphletheatre and reading aloud

> Reading is not uniquely an abstract operation of the intellect: it brings the body into play, it is inscribed in a space and a relationship with oneself or with others . . . reading aloud [has a] dual function of communicating the written word to those who are unable to decipher it themselves but also cementing the interlocking forms of sociability. A history of reading must not limit itself to the genealogy of our own contemporary manner of reading, in silence and using only our eyes; it must also (and perhaps above all) take on the task of retracing forgotten gestures and habits that have not existed for some time.
>
> (Chartier 1994: 8–9)

In moments of historical transition when the production and reception of forms of communication shift, the older forms do not immediately (nor inevitably) sketch a graceful bow on their way off the stage. Often people resist such innovations holding still harder to the familiar; and even those who study a way to create in the new mode find themselves borrowing the strengths of the old, reinventing and adapting to the change in dissemination and reception. When the Parliament banned public theatrical performance during the Interregnum in England in September 1642, writers and audiences were forced to adopt alternative forms for public presentation and reception about contemporary events. Material once used for plays at public theatres was imported into forms such as the droll, the 'motion,' and the pamphlet playlet. The exchange between pamphlet writers and readers, the production and reception of the pamphlet, became a form of public theatrical that was at its most intense during the period when theatres were closed.

Established methods (habits) of reception exist as well in the scholarly world. In literature and drama studies the Interregnum, formerly known as the time when there was no theatre in England, tends to be lost between the Renaissance and the "long Eighteenth century" (1660–1800). Even "early modern" as an encompassing term has not always encouraged consideration of the seventeenth century as a whole. With few exceptions, the years 1630–60 are left to historians or those working specifically on the political literature of the period.[1] Yet the writers and actors, directors and playwrights who took up the drama after the Restoration had not been in exile in France; in England time did not stand still between the playing of city comedies in the 1630s until the reopening of the theatres. Rather the experience of daily life in the Interregnum with the publicly performed debates between, say, Royalists and Ranters, between those eager to have a King restored and those eager to imagine a government without a monarch, left its mark on both the writers for and the players in the theatre of the Restoration. As Nigel Smith suggests, the years of the pamphletheatre do not constitute "a gap in the history of English drama so much as a subject in itself, an instance of the survival of one form temporarily inside the skin of another" (1994: 92). Susan Wiseman also queries the critical fondness for the idea of the "gap," but I want to suggest not that we take this period as a subject in itself – filling the gap – but as inseparable from the culture of theatre in seventeenth-century England.[2] The tactics of persuasion and presentation employed in the pamphletheatre, borrowed from the theatre and adapted for the press, would influence the making of the drama for the rest of the century.

As it is impossible, I argue, to understand theatre history without considering how performances were played and received by the audience, so it is impossible to understand the transformation of a culture in its production and reception of print without exploring the varieties of the reading. Like the practice of collecting, the practice of reading involves activities that partake of an interchange of stillness and motion. Reception of a performance as of a text heard aloud has a dynamic quality; the reader/spectator can be moved and can return the motion to the players or performer of the text.[3] In considering Jonson's and Milton's work I suggested the receiving spectator as part of the dynamic of the aesthetic power of stillness and motion; though the structures where reception occurs have changed with the closing of the theatres in the Interregnum, the receiving spectator becomes the receiving listener still participating in the dynamic of stillness and motion made manifest in public with the 'production' of pamphlets.

Roger Chartier in *The Order of Books* builds upon the essential if static beginnings of the scholarly examination of print culture by introducing a migratory term into what had been represented as a stable relationship of reader to object, the book.

> Readers and hearers . . . are never confronted with abstract or ideal texts detached from all materiality; they manipulate or perceive objects and forms whose structures and modalities govern their reading (or their hearing) . . . a text, stable in its letter, is invested with a new

meaning and status when the mechanisms that make it available to interpretation change.

(1994: 3)

Chartier cites Michel de Certeau who presents the reader as a traveler, even a 'poacher,' moving across the landscape created by the writer (1). This approach shifts our attention away from monolithic ideas of the 'book' and 'print,' demonstrating that the manner of reading and hearing influences how a writer manipulates a text in order to address the audience. "In the sixteenth and seventeenth centuries the reading style implicit in a text, literary or not, was still often an oralization of the text and the 'reader' was an implicit auditor of a read discourse. The work, which was addressed to the ear as much to the eye, plays with forms and procedures that subject writing to demands more appropriate to oral 'performance'" (1994: 9).

Because "oral exchange remained the primary mode of receiving and transmitting cultural capital" and yet the seventeenth century was a period "in which significant advances were made in popular literacy and the new technology of print," pamphlets provide one in a "dynamic series of interactions between spoken and written forms of communication and record" in the seventeenth century (Fox 2000: 12, 11). Further, the public reception of the pamphlet texts opened public spaces in which the literate and the illiterate were able to listen, much as the theatres had done before 1642. In *Winter Fruit: English Drama 1642–1660* Dale Randall argues that "it is tempting but too simple to say that closing of the English theatres triggered the appearance of many mid-century pamphlets that bore the formal trappings of plays" (1995: 51). But it is not so much the cause and effect of theatres closed and/or pamphlets fashioned after plays that is intriguing, but the substantial growth of pamphlet writing (whether amplificatory or dialectical) occurring in these years. What I take to be an intensification of the public theatrical space came about through a mix of pamphlets produced and read aloud in squares and in taverns. Added to this public 'noise' of pamphlet debate was the circulation of the first newspaper printed in 1641 (while there are forerunners, a 'steady' press had its beginnings in the Interregnum (Sherman 1996)).

Since the production of pamphlets increased from twenty in 1640 to nearly one thousand in the following year, the public space of debate had to expand, multiplying the possibilities of performance in proportion to the larger number of pamphlets written to address and to dispute (Randall 1995: 52).[4] That so many writers chose to dramatize the debates in play form meant at the most fundamental level that the reading aloud of pamphlets necessitated changes in voice and in attitude as the reader moved from the language of one character to another. The readers would no doubt import acting techniques they themselves had learned or had witnessed into the oralization of the text.[5]

The public space of reception for pamphlets was, like the public theatre, a space of exchange between pamphlet reader and audience.

> Popular writing had existed in England since the sixteenth century, yet the literature of the civil wars was new in that pamphleteers fused the technique of preexisting low genres with openly political argument and brought political debates from behind the closed doors of parliamentary chambers into the noisy, dusty, crowded streets.
>
> (Achinstein 1994: 11)

Sharon Achinstein in *Milton and the Revolutionary Reader* argues that Milton's work must be understood in the context of the English Revolution which she calls "a revolution in reading" (3). Without the critical interventions of Chartier and other scholars, this sentence can too quickly become textual since the customarily flattening vision of a revolution in reading would have individuals hard at work in solitary study and response.[6] However, if "readers viewed a drama of political exchange in public," then readers are not sedentary bodies isolated in their imagining of the new nation, but multiple and immediate in their necessarily communal responses. These bodies, these "readers" might indeed be able to cipher a bit, write not at all, but they could "read" in public, hearing pamphlets, debating them with other "readers": "pamphlets and ballads were often consumed in public, shared, or passed around from one person to another" (Achinstein 1994: 12). The encounters between ideas presented in various forms and those listening to the presentation involved the kind of sensuous reception discussed in the first two chapters of this book. The body of the reader/auditor as well as the sound of the writer/reader often met in an exchange of performances.

In his article "Popular Verses in the Early Seventeenth Century," Adam Fox cites invaluable evidence about the performance of song and ballad gained from what we might think of as the 'anti-archive' of the Public Records Office. We are indebted to the complainers in the early modern period: antitheatrical tracts from the early seventeenth century offer descriptions of early modern theatre practice that might otherwise have been lost while the evidence given by those who testified against the slanderous or scurrilous ballads and songs and poems of the mid-seventeenth century enable us to 'hear' what was being avowed, rejected or parodied in this oral and printed exchange. These ballads and songs exist at the intersection of print, script, and performance.[7]

One must imagine this 'theatrical' space and its performers and auditors. The markets and squares of London and outlying towns where pamphlets could be heard continued to serve, as they had in the medieval tradition, as "ritual thresholds." Jean-Christophe Agnew suggests that such spaces inspired "the same spontaneous group identity that anthropologists have elsewhere linked to such liminal settings as pilgrimages" (1986: 32). With this analogy we might equate the 'journey' of a society toward political reform to a pilgrimage with stops along the way where the proselytizers preach, the listeners can be convinced and converted, and thereby the numbers of the faithful swell as they make their way. Pilgrimages invoke a world of ritual and theatricality set amongst the daily converse: arresting for a moment the quotidian action in the square in order to open it up for the theatrical production from which could result a community of those watching/hearing the theatrical performance.

Both the act of pilgrimage and wider dissemination of print culture form two components of the 'imagined community' of nation according to the theories of Benedict Anderson (1991). For Anderson the imagined bonds at the inception of a nation and the shared temporality created by newspapers begin in the nineteenth century. Yet early modern scholars have borrowed from the work not only of Anderson but also of Hans-Jürgen Habermas to theorize what they see as earlier instances of both the imagined bonds forming a national identity and of the creation of "public space."[8] Many citizens in England in the Interregnum joined the "pilgrimage" of an imagined journey toward a government designed and implemented by the people. The sites that gave life to this imagining were public spaces in which the production and reception of pamphlets circulated ideas, rebuttals, and revisions. While the choice to buy a pamphlet and read it alone or among friends required a decision and an action, in a public space someone might be walking along without thought of reform or rebellion and be caught by the voice of a pamphlet reader, he or she might stray toward the group ready to receive or dissent or, having had his or her fill, wander away.

Of course public squares and other meeting places had functioned before the Interregnum as places for listening to proclamations, ballads, and other public notices and they would continue to do so after the Restoration. However, the sheer volume of pamphlet production between 1642 and 1660, and the people's responses to the political crises in England and Ireland, insured the public spaces were full of the charged language of political debate. This theatrical language became, in Nigel Smith's term, "a transposed language of a disembodied and suppressed stage, of speeches and actions without the actors to give the characters living form" (1994: 74). Yet giving voice to the characters was a way of giving them form. The changed public space called for changed public performances, and a shift in the interpretation of those performing. The shared idea of a nation as both an audience for national ideas and as performers of those ideas was driven by the printed publication expanding in this period. In a discussion of "dialogue pamphlets," pamphlets which stage a discussion between characters, Susan Wiseman writes: "the pamphlet dialogue (sometimes the pamphlet playlet) in the market of news and its possible performance contexts suggests that it offered an invitation – issued from a variety of political perspectives – to rethink public roles." The "dialogic and rhetorical nature" of the pamphlets, which I argue derives not only from theatrical dialogue but also from the pedagogical sources like Comenius, "located even the private, individuated, purchaser and reader as participating in public events" (1998: 20).

While there was a "migration of dramatic resources to the arena of the pamphlet," more traditional forms of drama did not disappear entirely during the Interregnum. Recently scholars have been in the process of correcting the received notion that in the years 1642–60 there was no theatre. Revivals of traditional plays were often clandestinely performed as both rebellion and reminder, while plays "were printed and widely read" (and widely read meant widely heard) with some plays "explicitly acknowledge[ing] the importance of the pamphlet" (Smith 1994: 73). Actors often became preachers, switching one oratorical style for another, and companies transferred to Holland and France where they continued to play (70–92). Even the news came in the form of drama, performed for a society F.J. Levy suggests was "accustomed to treating the theatre and the world of politics as somehow interchangeable" (2000: 263). This "interchangeable-ness" of theatre and politics did not constitute a jaded dismissal of all politics as 'mere' theatre, rather it amplified an understanding of the demands on the public 'man' of performing his part well and being judged by his audience if he did not do so (see section 'The actor and the pamphlet' below).

Print produced, played, and perishable

Before moving to instances of theatrical delivery and performative writing in the pamphletheatre, however, let me rehearse some of the ways in which the pamphletheatre shares aspects of the collaboration of the moving and the still discussed in previous chapters. Pamphlets were produced in print, as were plays; though 'ephemera' these texts circulated as potential parts of collections, idiosyncratic as the collection of ephemera might seem.[9] The language used to suggest value for the production, circulation, and preservation of pamphlets invoked categories of gender as it had in the earlier pamphlet exchange which occurred at the turn of the sixteenth century. In *The Marketplace of Print*, Alexandra Halasz employs theories of commodity exchange to interpret the selling of print in the public sphere in the 1590s and early 1600s. She suggests that "male-identified notions of ownership and stock in cultural signs establish the 'necessity' and value of the purchase, while the female-identified notion of ephemeral pleasure insures continued purchases" (1997: 173). The 'feminine' seduction of play/pleasure/passing set against the 'masculine' virtue of owning (keeping still) suggests that something only becomes real – takes on value – when one owns it. Not simply when it is in print, but when that print is in one's possession. Yet this particular moment of ownership, or of a capturing of the ephemeral, cannot last. Collectors who think of their objects as feminine – beautiful things acquired and displayed – depend upon the renewing effect of circulation and a spectator's acknowledgment.

Halasz reminds us that by the end of the sixteenth century "the legal monopoly on printing was a *de facto* monopoly on textual property . . . a peculiar form of property because it consists not in owning something, but in having control over a particular text" (1997: 24). In Halasz's terms the property of print that one owned only came into being by its circulation – as in gift exchange. Oddly the material object of print was not the "object" owned, rather it was the control of the object in motion. Much work has been done on economic circulation or the cycle of consumption in early modern England; what I am concerned with here is a world of display and performance in social settings that seems to oil and keep 'new' the precious object. While the ephemeral pleasures guarantee "continued purchases," the collector must find ways to display his/her collection so that the precious objects become 'new' again in the eye of the beholder. Hoarding provides only the most private of pleasures. (Remember Morose's concern that Epicoene not seem dumb or artless at Court). The danger for any object, ephemeral or not, comes in the loss of energy when the pamphlet is not read or the play is not performed or the object is not admired. With pamphlets, their dissemination, not only in print but in public spaces being read aloud, oils the machinery threatening to grow stiff from disuse.

The circulating energy of the pamphlets was also due to the style of writing pamphlet authors employed. A number of writers left evidence of their efforts to dramatize the rhetoric in pamphlets that the language might 'stand in' for the absent dialogue in the mouths of players. The heightened language portrayed mock situations of speech and of listening, of debate among characters in front of an implied, listening audience. The nature of reading in this period abetted the intent of the writer to create a staged relation between writer (speaker, character) and reader (audience). With styles as diverse as those of John Milton and Richard Overton, pamphlet writers did more than simply enumerate the reasons for readers/auditors to embrace their positions. Instead they often placed the auditors imaginatively in the performance of the nation the pamphlet strove to represent.[10] In Overton's case the metaphor of the theatrical included the recognition of the political life as public performance, of public servants who must be "substantiall and reall *Actors* for *freedome* and *liberty*" (Overton in Boaz 1997). As Sharon Achinstein attests, "writers about the theatre before and after the Interregnum were influenced by the period, not simply in terms of ideology, but in terms of form and performative power" (1994: 12).

In very different registers and to very different purposes the texts of the pamphletheatre pushed print toward theatrical effects: from the corporeality of Milton's metaphors or the moving tableaux of the nation Milton rhetorically staged in *Areopagitica*, to the oratorical writing style of the Ranters. The Ranters had a style Byron Nelson characterizes as:

"associational, violent, threatening, repetitive, conversational, seductive, solipsistic, illogical and playful . . . theatrical and artificial in their use of dialogue and role-playing, riddling and prankish wit, and jesting personae" (1992: 61). The principal 'actor/playwright' of the Ranters, Abiezer Coppe in his *The Second Fiery Flying Roll* combines "a playful farrago of voices . . . the miserly 'harlot' who disapproves of beggars, the St Paul-like convert who is smitten with guilt . . . the sensitive soul . . . the king-like figure who pays homage to the beggar" (69). Byron Nelson surveys Coppe's writing to elucidate a Wittgensteinian "language game" played by the Ranter, games that "have clear, immediate social use, are governed by rules . . . shift emphasis from the meaning of words to their use" (67).

I would further suggest that those very games Wittgenstein took to be "playful gestures" that are without a capacity to "capture the real nature of things" have a corollary in the performance of pamphlets in the seventeenth century. The language games, acted out in print, instigate gesture and play in the text and compel the reader/auditor to be transformed into an interpreting spectator. The 'stakes' of the game of religious persuasion and national imagination in the Interregnum seem less those of simply changing the auditor that he or she might know and believe, than those of an exchange intended to incorporate the auditor as player, with a national and religious role to perform.[11]

If "it can be argued that Wittgenstein's declining belief in the representational value of language is akin to the Ranters evolving awareness that language can neither bring in nor accurately describe the divine," then this 'language for use' employed in the manner of performance seeks to initiate actions rather than invite belief.[12] In this way the listener/actor could already be understood to be a part of the company of others, incorporated into decisions which were represented as communal rather than hierarchical. If in the copious production of pamphlet literature we begin to see something of Wittgenstein's despairing sense of the failure of representational value, this tendency becomes even more marked in the drama/comedy of the coming Restoration. In the plays we see an early cynicism, often imputed to Wycherley and Etheredge, born of the disjunction between saying and meaning.[13]

The active audience participation in early modern theatre facilitated the reception of pamphlets and later plays which required a simultaneous understanding of what was being said and whether it could be understood to represent a breech in meaning or not. These 'self-conscious' spectators might more easily adapt to the 'pretend' of theatre from both the vantage of inside the fiction and out. Even in a culture like that of the United States remarkable for its own habit of self reference, it is difficult to explain how self-consciousness creates a pact of awareness between performer and player in which both take their part in the making of the performance. Scholars have often accounted for this give and take by picturing the rowdy crowd of the public theatre as so loud, so raucous, so indifferent to the stage presentation that the 'free for all' could be dismissed and the plays studied as texts. In Adam Fox's depiction of the production and reception of ballads and songs we see the potential response of an audience to plays and to pamphletheatricals:

> [T]exts could be invented within a community in response to a live and current issue, could be read out in specific situations, and might evoke a number of measurable responses ranging from hysteria to hilarity . . . fluid and dynamic composition[s] . . . which slipped in and out of oral and written forms, coming from people and speaking back to them, both reflecting common opinion and helping to shape it. The impression given here is of an interaction between text and readers or hearers of a kind which is not often retrievable at this social level. There is a sense of that dialogue between author and audience which is facilitated by reading.
>
> (1996: 127)

In a sense Fox's considered and imaginative rendering of the exchange of texts among hearer, speaker, and reader, falls aptly at the midpoint of this book. The motion of give and take in his description, the "slipping . . . coming from . . . speaking back . . . reflecting . . . shaping," charts the course of the still and the moving in the public reception and the fabrication of public performance of print. Though one can see all sorts of signs of the beginning of the separation between the receiving senses and the reasoning mind, not the least of which is the Wittgensteinian distrust of language and its power to represent meaning, the world of 'write and read,' 'speak and hear' is an entangled one. This dynamic world is neither set in its (stereotypically) enlightenment ways, nor amorphous in its (stereotypically) unfixed early modern embodiments. Here again we find ourselves in the midst of the seventeenth-century transition (described in the Prologue) that teaches us, I argue, about the shifting modes of the production of performance. As we have come to expect, the modes of production represent values given by the society to the power/danger of the making still and the press/loss of the moving.

The motion of the "dialogue between author and audience" in pamphlet reception came in part from the perishable nature of a pamphlet. The ephemerality of pamphlet literature acknowledged by writer and reader/auditor alike exempted the pamphlet from the status of "timeless" literature, a fixed position of art. Pamphlets could be produced by printers "quickly and cheaply" and readers "consumed such works with a fury exceeded only by the fury of the press to replace old pamphlets with new ones" (Achinstein 1994: 10). The material production of pamphlets made for a printed form that was marked by the urgency of the *un*collectable. Because the production of pamphlets was fast, objects not designed to last, this form of print announced itself as a conveyer of ideas in process. Like newsprint, the form was expected to perish, to be tossed away, to be responded to quickly. The hunger for call and response brings to mind the world of five-act plays where a different play could be performed every night, a capacity for production unthinkable in late twentieth-century theatre. In the sixteenth century the performed world of pamphlets had even included a traveling 'stage' since the Elizabethan Marprelates in the 1580s traveled with "collapsible presses" (11).[14]

Thus these "pamphlet wars," as James Holtsun's edited collection styles them, demanded "timely" responses and swift rebuttals (1992). Unlike larger folio texts, the pamphlet could be pocketed. Like plays, pamphlets appeared in quarto form; "usually pamphlets were eight to sixteen pages long, long enough to argue a single point and to support it with marginalia full of references to other pamphlets and literary works" (Achinstein 1994: 10). Though akin to speech in that the pamphlets were expected to disappear, not to be saved, the trappings of print – sections divided by numbers, marginalia providing an immediate amplification or clarification down the side of the page – gave the pamphlets order and a measure of fixity.[15] When performed the printed pamphlet functioned socially to represent the community to itself, as both Milton and Richard Overton were well aware. "The texts destined by their author and (more often) by their publisher to the most popular public often contained formulas or themes that came directly from the culture of the tale and oral recitation (Chartier 1994: 20).

The "company" of reform players

After the closing of the theatres, performers of plays moved indoors to private shows: re-formed masques played at Cromwellian Court, short drolls or scenes from plays were performed in private theatres.[16] Public play performances sometimes materialized with bands of actors performing sudden shows which could be suddenly dispersed. Only at the plucky, if a bit tacky, Red Bull Theatre was the ban on public performance persistently tested by illegal shows. In public spaces the exchange of pamphlets and their public recitations created a form so clearly tied to performance that Byron Nelson calls the intervention a "creative" act of "guerrilla theatre" (1992: 71). Groups of auditors listened to tracts often written by the very playwrights and players so summarily put out of business. Margot Heinemann, writing about popular drama and the Levellers, suggests that while "suppression of the public playhouses crushed the old drama out of existence, the printing press in the 1640s worked with a freedom and a range unknown before" (1978: 73).[17]

When historians of early seventeenth-century English theatre examine the conditions of playing, they consider the texts of the plays, the structure of the theatres, the writers for the stage, the acting companies, and the composition of the audience. In the world of pamphletheatricals one sees signs of each of these components; for example, it would be fascinating to study the short-lived nay much debated "Ranters" as if their political activities were those of a radical acting company with its principal players and sites of performance.[18] Or to survey the work of the Diggers or the Levellers or indeed the Royalists, from whom we have the largest body of play texts.[19] Byron Nelson suggests the fine "performance skills" of the Ranters contributed to the "vividness" of their "street theatre," a vividness reported not only in their own writing, but also in the attacks from the "bitter anti-Ranter tracts" (1992: 60). For information about performance in public spaces in the Interregnum, the performance scholar, like the theatre historian, studies trace texts. For theatre, one uses plays, poems about playgoing, records of attendance, actors' memoirs, theatre companies' financial records, antitheatrical tracts; for pamphlets, one uses pamphlets, reports from trials, diaries, and records of individuals, representation of the performed moments on the pamphlet stage pictured, heroically or satirically, by other pamphleteers.[20]

In this interpretation, for example, the Ranters might be considered a company whose strength is in the performance of comedies. Nelson suggests the Ranters had a strange affinity with the despised Archbishop Laud in that they too could be said to be fostering a revival of the tradition of "popular mirth and festive outlook" (1992: 64). The spectacle of hyperbolic play remains in the outraged reports of Ranter overacting: anti-Ranter tracts complain of "Abiezer Coppe preaching naked, then throwing apples or nutshells as he is being interrogated by a parliamentary committee . . . [of] the Ranter shoemaker who believed 'good meat and drinke, tobacco and merry company to be Gods' . . . [of] Dr Paget's maid stripping 'her self naked' to join a roistering band of Ranters as 'they improve their liberty'" (60).

The Ranters as a 'company' were notorious for a religious practice cum ritual dating back to women's festivals in Greece, cursing. According to Anne Carson, the performance of cursing, "aischrologia" means "'saying ugly things' . . . certain women's festivals included an interval in which women shouted abusive remarks or obscenities or dirty jokes at one another" (1995: 132). The ephemeral in the practice of cursing reinforces a certain effeminate association with wandering and the lack of force in words which are tossed out: that is, both wasted and forcefully spoken. The Ranters' blasphemous form of play gave their detractors theatrical ammunition for their tracts in which the anti-Ranter pamphleteers "exaggerated images of the Ranters by casting them as sensational characters" (Gucer 2000: 78). The sensational characters anti-Ranters tracts created were not unfamiliar to any who had seen the early importation of *Commedia dell'Arte* from Italy to England and other improvised forms of comedy where characters reveled in ritual cursing. However, the *Commedia* players and the women in Greece tended to hurl the insults back and forth between comedians rather than speak them out as a general form of cursing employed by the Ranters.

The authorities who worried over the multitude of printed pamphlets let loose upon the public often styled their worry with language about the fear of the uncontrollable. The Ranter performances of cursing fueled the fear of the copious – read incomprehensible – the potentially blasphemous. That the accusations made against the Ranters found voice in condemning those orgiastic maids and shoemakers mentioned above should come as no surprise since the habit of condemning the feminine, wanton, and uncontrollable in performance, made more heinous by the incomprehensible and blasphemous, always comes to rest in the equation of such looseness to female sexual promiscuity. Much of what was uncontrollable was improvised, a form of performance easiest to employ in times of political upheaval because it is suddenly made and as suddenly dispersed with no evidence except the report of witnesses. Throughout the century the streets could be the site of performances, but particularly during the Interregnum the forms of performance undertaken depended upon an "improvisatory dimension" which allowed for social commentary and could incorporate and transform interventions from spectators (Randall 1995: 156).

The stage manager and the sacred in pamphletheatre

In *A Maske* Milton obviously wrote a text to be performed, seeking to represent the 'drama' of Christian life dynamically. Such texts are marked with printed conventions: the placing of the character's names at the beginning of their speech with a period to indicate speaking, the dialogue exchanged between the two, the implied and printed stage directions. But scholars tend to forget that *Paradise Lost* was initially conceived as a five-act play (see Demaray 1980 for Milton's outline of the epic in five acts). In between the writing of these two (dramatic) works Milton vigorously participated in the pamphletheatre: *Of Education* (1644), *The Reason of Church Government* (1642), *An Apology Against a Pamphlet called "A Modest Confutation of the Animadversionis upon the Remonstrant against Smectynmuus"* (1642), *The Doctrine and Discipline of Divorce* (1643), *Areopagitica, A Speech* (1644), *Tenure of Kings and Magistrates* (1648), to name only those published before the death of Charles I.

Many scholars, particularly Sharon Achinstein, have explored Milton's career as a pamphlet writer, analyzing his work in light of history, of religious debate, of literary influence, and of biographical context (Norbrook 1984; Smith 1990; Helgerson 1987; Hirst 1995; Achinstein 1994). The pamphlets are full of examples of Milton's quirky, sudden, and illustrative analogies, and the prose rewards study many times over. Though unable to write for a public theatre first closed and then reopened in celebration of a monarch he opposed, Milton created a prose theatrical enough to earn scorn from his critics as if they could see in his work a performance under way. One critic went so far as to accuse John Milton of being a "scurrilous mime":

> Reader, If thou hast any generall or particular concernment in the affairs of these times, or but naturall curiosity, thou art acquainted with the late and hot bickerings between the Prelates and Smectynmuans: To make up the breaches of whole solemn scenes, (it were too ominous to say Tragicall) there is thrust forth upon the Stage, as also to take the ears of the lesse intelligent, a scurrilous MIME, a personated and (as he himself thinks) a grim, lowring, bitter fool.
>
> *A Modest Confutation* 1642)

Following this smug antitheatrical aside – it would be difficult to read "to take the ears of the less intelligent" and not think of William Prynne who had lost his ears to Archbishop Laud – the angry respondent to Milton's 1641 pamphlet in support of the "Smectynmuans" continues his diatribe, condemning the pamphleteer poet for, among other overstimulating pursuits, being a frequenter of playhouses. This confuter of Milton's pamphlet uses the most common verb used in the first half of the century for an actor's craft to describe Milton's printed acting, "personate."

The urgent form of textual animation Milton employs must go beyond the relating of stories to the showing of actors moving in a pantomime of political and domestic choice. The two sources Heinemann suggests animate the Leveller style of pamphlet writing are both sources Milton plumbs as well: "One of the main influences on Leveller style was of course the Bible . . . the most effective writers were also inspired by the other great source of instruction and culture open to ordinary Londoners, the theatres and the published texts of their plays" (1978: 69). Though no ordinary Londoner, Milton writes of his desire to press his work into a model of the "sacred drama" of the Bible.[21]

Had Milton found a suitable stage for his work, he might have re-formed the mystery play into a poetic pageant to rival secular drama. In the Trinity Manuscript, Milton left sketches of potential dramas containing remarkable detail and intriguing plot descriptions. For example, under the title *Baptistes* Milton writes, "beginning from the morning of Herods birth day" and goes on through the plot and scenes, some full of Cecil B. DeMille like possibility: "Herod had well bedew'd himself with wine . . . the Chorus consists of Lots Shepherds com[e i]nto the citty [*sic*] about some affairs . . . with musick and song to the temple of Venus" (Trinity: 37). Most artists immediately understood the aesthetic, erotic, dramatic appeal of the Salome, John the Baptist, Herod story, witness Fra Lippo Lippi's exquisite fresco cycle in Prato. But Milton's dramatic imagination ranged widely, developing the scaffolding for many plays including "Adam unparadiz'd,"

"Sodom Burning," "Asa or Aethiopes," with the preparatory outlines running to twenty or more scenes.

A reformer with a penchant for the theatrical, Milton understood the stage's potential for showing history and representing a nation forming and re-forming. In his "Scotch stories or rather British of the north parts" he proposes a Macbeth play, beginning with Macbeth's arrival at "Mackduffe." The problem of beginning the story after the killing of Duncan might be solved by the "appearing of his ghost" – upping the Shakespearean ante by having two ghosts in the show (Trinity: 41). In another project left unscripted that displays Milton's dramatic preference for beginning at the beginning, Milton sketches out twenty-one scenes for the drama, "British Troy." There is something of *Titus Andronicus* in the details; almost every scene description contains the words "slaine by." The earlier rulers of Britain do not come off well, they are "in thire cups," killed for "ravishing" another's "wife," and they make bad choices which reverberate through the history of the nation: "Egfride . . . slaine in battel against the Picts having before wasted Ireland and made warre for no reason on men that ever lov'd the English . . ." (35). One cannot help but hear the telling of history as a narrative of love gone wrong, though those in Ireland might differ with Milton's notion that they had "ever lov'd the English."

Milton so vividly incorporated his dramatic plans into the writing of his pamphlets that, according to his contemporary James Howell, Milton deserved to be "hissed at rather than confuted"; he deserved an antitheatrical dismissal from the 'pamphlet stage' rather than a printed, reasoned rebuttal (Masson 1881, v. 3: 62).[22] The arguments in several of Milton's pamphlets take moving and complex life from an imagined world – one theatrically perceived and physical – of free men in a utopian land of virtuous trial and communal rejoicing. When the ardent performer was driven from the pamphlet stage by too passionate responses to his tracts, it was in part because he gave his arguments embodied life and what they "bodied forth" was socially unmanageable.

License like performance is a risky thing. If apocalypse demanded a certain poetic drama in *Paradise Lost*, championing individual choice in the Interregnum world of religious debate required Milton to render dramatic the wrongs of mismarriage – *The Doctrine and Discipline of Divorce* – and censorship – *Areopagitica* – (to name only two subjects he addressed). While rendering dramatic the wrongs of a bad marriage and censorship, Milton simultaneously renders dramatic the calm, goodly, reasoned outcome when the barriers to divorce and censorship were removed. In his dramatic pamphlets Milton chooses different forms than Richard Overton and other writers who create pamphlet 'plays.' He creates printed oratory and dramatic soliloquies (as he will in *Samson Agonistes*, the bitter elder to his more idealistic Interregnum pieces), as sites of dramatized pedagogy where the voice of the lecturer persists through the representation of different scenes. For Milton such dramatic representations of ideas cannot simply be expressed in reasonable argument – offered for comprehension – they must be clothed in recognizable, moving shapes in order to present an apprehensible pageant of the English nation.[23]

The shapes Milton creates in his writing do not all take the form of idealized heroes and heroines. The pressure brought to bear upon the writing seems to produce involuted, grotesque creatures born of Milton's tortured conjunctions. Consider the odd marriage at the opening of the revised second edition of the *Doctrine and Discipline of Divorce*.[24] "She" who has duped the irate, because wrongheaded, readers of Milton's first edition is that all too popular teacher Custom. "Silently received for the best instructor," Custom enters with her "sudden book of implicit knowledge for him that will, to take and swallow down at pleasure" (222–3).[25] Like those readers who must be called from the "ale-houses" in the pamphlets of the late sixteenth century examined by Alexandra Halasz, Milton's readers swill in common, but they swill metaphorically, ingesting unwholesome Custom (Halasz 1997). "Reading" here as in *Areopagitica* is a taking in which does not stop at the head; the words and ideas must pass imaginatively through an intellectual digestive tract. From such tasting and reading grotesque faces "puff up" with "pretended learning," swell with a "visage of counterfeit knowledge and literature" (1985: 223).

If drunkenness, or even a more seemly tipsiness can be seen upon the face of the drinker, then, in Milton's analogy, the effects of 'reading wrongly' can be discerned in the body of the confused. Clearly reading here is not a bookish solitude since the language of Custom is not only the falsely printed, but also the falsely preached and the falsely performed and read aloud. Milton gives his poisoned Lady in a mini-marriage, an anti-masque of wrong conjoining between Custom, the "mere" face without substance, and Error, a "blind and Serpentine body without a head" (223). Accepting "what he wants," Error supplies "what her incompleatness went seeking" (223). Presenting these two abstractions as dismembered bodies allows Milton to 'show' his audience the physical disabilities Custom's and Error's influence wreaks upon them. Joined together by lack, incompleteness, and wanting, Custom and Error in Milton's incarnation sicken the reader's/hearer's body. An audience can more readily perceive the visceral reality of physical illness than the abstract reporting of a moral malaise.[26] In considering a later form of print that was often received and shared in public – the nineteenth-century novel published serially – D.A. Miller explores the genre of 'sensational' novel. His reminder that a sensational novel is written to produce sensations in the body of the reader aids us in recognizing how Milton's pamphlets are similar in that they might be called "sensational tracts," written in order to "shock and instruct" (Miller 1989, see "Cage aux folles: sensation and gender in Wilkie Collins' *The Woman in White*").

For Milton and many of his contemporaries the malleable form of the female, as idea and as character, proves a recognizable and useful shape, a representation not only suited to intellectual male trade, but also to the form of oral, theatrical presentation. The listening/reading audience has before them not simply ideas, or ideas given visceral shape, but pronouns attached to ideas. It is rarely possible for any audience not to imagine "she" (in whatever form the idea of "she" takes for them) when they hear the word "she." In a world where many pamphlets instructed readers in the right behavior of men and women, Milton's abstraction called Custom comes very clearly clothed in the abstraction called female. Thus Milton's wedding of that serpentine Error, he of the long, phallic body with the literally wrong headed Custom mixes the sexes into an ill body politic. It is like Milton, however, not to assign "she" only to the villains in his piece. Truth comes in the shape of "she" as well.[27]

In *Areopagitica*, Milton stages "a speech" in the service of his vision of a reading nation. A form of performance employed to persuade in sound, oratory influences as it disappears into the air, not available for later analysis unless the listener has a perfectly retentive memory. In printed incarnation, according to Nigel Smith in his essay on *Areopagitica*, oratory becomes an "emulsifying agent . . . binding together different concerns which are so many fragments of truth" (1990: 103). By now the interdependence of the still with the moving should be immediately apparent in the amalgam of the sound that dissipates even as the speaker's voice creates a bond among the listeners who become a united audience sharing a common experience.

Milton populates his pamphlet with objects – books – and emblems – Truth and Virtue – whose vulnerable 'bodies' barely escape death at the hands of 'tonsured imprimaturs' and maenadic religious philosophers.[28] The objects, however, are not piled up for collected use; instead the danger, according to Milton, who is still young, is that the objects will be inert enough to be censored, or that censors will not be flexible enough to give the books their freedom.[29] At times the pamphlet seems to produce an antic cartoon for the listening and reading public where things otherwise invisible are illustrated to show the reader/hearer corporeal consequences that he or she may understand intellectual freedom.

If for Milton the object of the book becomes corporeal, ideas soon join his anthropomorphized crew. Truth, as one of Milton's main characters, outdoes Proteus, that patron saint of actors, admired and feared for his swift changes in nature. Like the books he suggests risk being strangled in their cradle by censoring hands, Milton figures Truth as endangered at birth, orphaned by the Parliament's order, the order itself a "Stepdame to Truth . . . disenabl[ing]" the righteous of "what is known already" (1985: 543). Having only just appeared, Truth swiftly changes in the next paragraph, becoming fluid; she is now uncontainable, "a streaming fountain" of "perpetual progression" (543). There is a certain intellectual freedom Milton grants the feminine, as if he has seen the price of a rigid, unchanging spirit traditionally associated with the masculine. Later in his work, one can sense a weariness which turns into a resigned acknowledgment of the need to control actions and interpretations. As is historically true, with this tendency toward such conservative control comes the reification of the position of women in the hierarchical balance of power.

However, in *Areopagitica*, according to its then still transgressing author, the Parliament do not understand Truth's liquid nature; in trying to contain her, they find her slipping away from them as water through a licenser's fingers. Water stagnated by the blockage "sick'n[s] into a muddy pool of conformity and tradition" (543). "Our richest Marchandize," this fluid Truth must circulate in order to increase abundance (548). The necessary character on this stage of license, law, government, and individual morality, Truth appears as Milton robes and disrobes her dramatically. Elaborately 'setting his stage' for his most risky argument, Milton makes ready through Truth's appearances his rebuttal to that always already formulated question in any censoring/ruling body's mind – "how will we control the 'dissemination' of truth?"

The paradox of stasis and movement exists in the political arena, for example in the controlled access to unruly ideas, perceived as dangerous in their copious, unchecked freedom. Only by calculated dissemination can hierarchical bodies balance the free movement of circulation. Since Milton intends his Truth to champion motion, to be revealed only when unbound, she cannot appear in the scene as a reified statue, clothed in glory, rather she must shift and change so that her author might argue for the freedom of mind unchecked by restraining law. Truth as an entity is not meant for the shelves of a single collector.

The progression of the story of Truth in *Areopagitica* reads like Milton's sacred drama sketches. The muddle and confusion, like the chaos of a third act in a five-act play, offers liquid Truth taking shape again, reborn as a mythic character who "came once into the world with her divine Master, and was a perfect shape" (549).[30] This new lineage, an original lineage usurping the upstart Parliament's claim to Truth as exclusively its own, quickly vanishes into tragedy when "hew'd," her "lovely form [is] scattered to the four winds" (549). Thus the "sad friends" of Truth must search for her parts "limb by limb." While one limb does not the whole Truth make, to censor the search risks losing the retrieval of an essential member.

The audience witnesses in Milton's pamphlet the search for Truth undertaken by those who, while seeking for different limbs, all strive to re-member the body. Milton's mixed vision of method and intuition renders the search for Truth as a kind of occult Ramism, as in *Paradise Lost* where Raphael and Adam's act of Reason in joining and dis-joining engages them in a mimetic work of creation. Milton's searchers seek for what they "know not" by what they "know, still closing up truth to truth as we find it (for all the body is homogeneal [*sic*] and proportional)." A process that brings, if not the full form of Truth herself, the satisfaction of a harmony more blessed because it is not "the forc't and outward union of cool, and neutrall, [*sic*] and inwardly divided minds" (551). The physical characteristics of the virgin puzzled over together may produce a right rendering of Truth; the act of puzzling over the mysteries of an abstraction metaphorically represented as female produces masculine harmony.

As the final act of Milton's argument comes toward a close, with an author's prerogative he sees Truth whole, re-members her now "strong, next to the Almighty," needing "no policies, nor stratagems, nor licensings to make her victorious" (562–3). To all appearances unrestrainable, even next to the Almighty, Truth returns four pages later, in her original role, the shape changer. "Give her but room," directs the stage manager of the pamphlet, "and do not bind her while she sleeps, for then she speaks not true as the old Proteus did" (563). Ironically in a pamphlet giving books the status with corporeal beings, Milton argues that things (and by extension people) lie when they are *bound*, a condition of printed publication. If kept too close, out of circulation, ideas and their authors become the hated "feigned" thing of empty theatrical show. Milton displays an alternative unbound drama in a bound form of print that might evoke Truth as she moves, changing shape, appearing and re-forming.

From the free flowing river, to the dismembered daughter and virgin, to the amorphous unifier of sects, Truth consolidates her properties into Milton's most daring characterization of her. Staged as if in a performance where fantastical things are in motion, Truth, Milton surprisingly suggests, "may have more shapes than one" (563). In a particularly delicious rendering of her role, Truth, Milton writes, may be on one side or the other "without being unlike herself" (563). Toleration thus finds a champion in the multiple Truth since one can say "here is truth" only to find her "there" as well, and not unlike herself.

By figuring Truth in all these scenes as she changes costume and suffers dismemberment, Milton presses the frozen "nay forc't and outward union" of printed argument to represent a realm of temporal change. To figure multiplicity, a dangerous sign of lack of coherence for many Christians, risks a lack of control. Milton, having embodied the visual character of Truth as multiple, defies his audience to dismiss his argument for the freedom of the press as 'not truth.' In Milton's printed theatricals, he can continue the abstract fantasy of control in a way bodily performance might undo, yet he leaves the unpredictability as part of the argument of the work. "The tract is inconclusive" Nigel Smith writes "because of the need to show how truth is to be gathered" (1990: 118). Inconclusive tracts one might argue are open ended, unfixed yet fixed, even inconclusiveness does not change form from reading to reading.

Though Smith hints at an important part of Milton's strategy in the pamphlet, the tract is not so much inconclusive as it is written to encourage repeated readings. In fact, *Areopagitica* is altogether conclusive in that Milton proposes a method of reading that allows for multiplicity, thus his text must needs be re-read. One might even suggest Milton creates an ethic of re-reading: by suggesting the multiplicity of Truth he implies the search cannot ever end, there can be no triumphant closing of the text in the satisfaction of having 'got it.' According to Truth's own multiple nature, it might be truth, or an essential limb thereof, and thus deserves recognition while its stage, the pamphlet, deserves attention and attendance. It is left for reader/listener to participate and indeed to judge, invited to listen again and again to a performed speech "staged," as Milton writes, as if delivered to the Star Chamber, oratory pictured in the court of political and social law.

The actor and the pamphlet

If, as Derek Hirst argues, "the drama of justice was perhaps the most visible feature of the Public life of London in the first half of 1649," the *show* of law has always been good material for dramatic performance (1995: 247). Historically, courts of law, national and local, have provided playwrights since Aristophanes with material easily adapted for the stage. In ritual, drama was judged by the gods; in daily life, justice meted out by the demigods of authority. The 'stuff' of trial, evidence, testimony, argument, prosecution, and sentencing performed aloud and in public was paraded in front of the audience like a set of carts on which the different stages of the mystery cycle appeared. The purpose of the trial was not only to discover but to show the truth, a reordering of the world by aligning the stories told to the judgments made about those stories. In the several crises occurring in England during the years of 1642–60, court trials were frequent, much debated, with the most unsettling trial having the new wielders of authority sentence to death God's representative upon earth, the King. Reinforcing earthly justice, the Bible supplied important models in trials of wisdom (Solomon) and revelations of political cowardice (Pilate); the potential for public theatrical performance of trials was immediately exploited by the makers of the pamphletheatre.

As Margot Heinemann suggests, few writing during the Interregnum were better pamphlet dramatists than Richard Overton (1978). To be a great pamphlet dramatist meant not only that Overton used characterization, action and tension to dramatize his vivid sense of justice and injustice in the English political world, but also that he was an extraordinary political theorist and his dramatic pamphlets enhanced the audience's desire to participate in his representation of the free nation. "Readers were to act not only as spectators of the debates, but were to become a kind of jury in deciding matters" (Achinstein 1994: 103). Overton staged for his readers mock trials where the "debate" became a drama among allegorical figures dressed in robes corresponding to political affiliations. In *The Arraignement of Persecution* (1645), Overton sets out his pamphlet in play form with the members of the "Court of Assizes" arranged on the page like Dramatis Personae. They include Justices Reason and Conformity, "Mr Unity-of-the-Kingdom", "Mr Blood-of-Princes" as members of the "Grand Inquest," and, in the "Jury of Life and Death," "Mr Liberty-of-Subject" and "Mr Light-of-Nature". It would take no careful listener to hear the division of good and bad according to the final list of persons under "Sir Symon Synod" who make up his jury and include "Mr Council-of-Trent" and "Mr Pontifical Revenue" not to mention the rather more otherworldy and boldly included "Mr Antichrist."

In this playlet, which "is believed to have served as a model for Bunyan," the scene very definitely opens (Heinemann 1978: 83). There are speeches, stage directions for the calling of the several characters 'into' the Court – an ingenious way to use the text to create an inside and outside for the listener/reader since the pamphlet has spatial pauses between lines and actions:

> JUDGE: Well then, let Sir Symon be called into the Court.
> CLARK: Call Sir Symon Synod.
> CRIER: Sir Symon Synod, come into the Court.

When after this brief set of calibrated actions the Judge 'turns' to Sir Symon, we cannot help but have temporally supplied the calling, the door opening, Sir Symon entering. It is far different textually and imaginatively than the narrative collapsing of time and motion, 'The Judge had Sir Symon called for, and he entered the Court.'

The most superfluous member of a textual cast it would seem would be the Crier. Yet, if the drama is to play out immediately for the spectator – if Mr Persecution must be tried afresh each time the pamphlet is read aloud or read silently – then the Crier by name and profession performs the important oral function of rendering the command of the Judge and the entrance of the character as necessarily aural rituals. This oral summons provokes the action of characters onto the stage – public square or courtroom.[31] Since all these characters are, furthermore, walking allegories, the crying of their names is the telling of their natures. Where a description might be furnished (as Milton so often does) in prose, Overton uses the names and then their speeches and actions to establish their physical sight and sound. If the *Arraignement* was ever performed in a tavern, in a meeting house, on the street, one can imagine how the readers would play with the voices of their characters.[32] False accents were an essential part of comedy on the stage; a hokey Spanish accent would no doubt be suitable for "Mr Spanish-Inquisition." Since "Mr Desolate-Germany," member of the Grand Inquest, serves as an emblem of a potential future for England – "let them looke upon the Germane Desolations, depopulation, warre, famine and Pestilence occasioned by Papal supremacy over our consciences" – his accent while recognizably

German might not be played for mocking laughs but rather sober realizations.[33]

Overton's playlet with its "large cast of persecutors and tolerationists, judges and jurymen" according to Heinemann suggests the "*mass* involvement at the peak of the Leveller movement" (1978: 83). The fundamental shift in representation, as seen in Milton's work, followed from a shift in the writer's expectation of the audience. If the seventeenth-century theatre expected a knowing and engaged, frequently contentious, response from its audience, the pamphlet writers addressed their readers as potential fellow makers of a 'new world order.' Where Spenser used allegory for its narrative and aesthetic persuasion – offering a tantalizing invitation to the reader to decipher the 'real' meaning – his allegories, though politically complex, still fitted the pieces of the puzzle into a political hierarchy. For Overton, however, his actor/allegory characters played themselves out before the reader in modes of toleration not reinforced by the Parliament or the religious authorities. The reader was to judge, to discern a puzzle, to be instructed but also to constitute him or herself as an *actor* in the public world of the new nation.

Though there are still some questions about Richard Overton's biography, it can be fairly said that he was involved in the two great mediums of public production of his time: the stage and the press. He acted in a Latin comedy, was known to be connected to the "Cambridge dramatic circles" and by 1640 was a printer/pamphleteer (Heinemann 1978). While certainly not the only figure who went from acting to pamphleteering, Overton deliberately drew on his theatrical experience to write playlets, to create vivid and theatrical moments in his prose pamphlets, and to construct a theory of the public role of representation. In writing from prison Overton gives direction for the right acting of the true Parliamentarian (*An Appeale* 1647): "Such as are the representers of Free-men, must be the substantial and reall *Actors* for *freedome* and *liberty*, for such as is the represented, such and no other must the figure of representation be".[34]

There is a paradox in public life which can be subsumed in the religious doctrine of monarchy where the King's earthly body might indeed be a bit too earthly but his divine body remains above the fray. In theorizing a more secular world, a practical believer in liberty understands the mature responsibility of representation. While late twentieth-century US politicians and journalists speak of "the appearance of wrongdoing" to suggest the disconcerting gap between ethics and show, what Overton's "figure of representation" suggests, I argue, is an actor's understanding of the demands of a role. Consider how he continues: "such as is the proportion, countenance, favour of the man, such and so must be the picture of the man, or else it cannot be the picture of that man, but of some other, or of something else, as the picture of a grim, meager, frowning face is, not the picture of an amiable, friendly smiling countenance" (Wolfe 169).

If we set Overton's directions about outward appearance against Thomas Heywood's *Apology for Actors* 1612, the instructions to the "actors for freedom and liberty" resemble the instructions to the actors for the stage: an actor should "keepe a decorum in his countenance, neither to frowne when he should smile, not to make unseemely disguised faces in the delivery of his words . . . but to qualifie every thing according to the nature of the person personated." The "person personated" translated to the public stage becomes a figure of representation. My purpose here is not to accuse Overton of making "all the world a Leveller stage," but to get at something extremely important in the theatrical persuasion used by Overton and Milton and others of other persuasions. While one must interrogate constantly the right interpreting of outward show and the deduction of false dissembling, all communal action has within it the demands of careful representation and responsible public acting. To be a woman or man deserving of equal freedom, one cannot act the Tyrant. What is yours by natural right can be forfeited by grabbing centerstage and in doing so infringing upon the rights of those on stage with you.

Overton knows what it means, he suggests, for a leader to feel one thing and need to act another. In the acting manuals of the time, as Joseph Roach astutely argues, counterfeiting demands what is at times a disconcerting commitment to engendering the feelings of the character one is about to play (1985, particularly the Introduction). When these Parliamentarians, the "figures of representation" who stand in for the "*Free-men,*" enter the public space of political decision making, they must inhabit the character of freedom vividly enough to make their constituents know they are acting the part they have been chosen to act. If a character begins to mutate into the face of a tyrant ("grim, meager, frowning"), then the people who depend upon the representation have a right to remove the unsatisfactory performers and substitute those who can play their roles well.

As the 1640s progressed, more and more pamphlets articulated a fear of being ruled by endlessly swaying "Opinion." What Overton seems to be arguing here is that the dedication to the service of representing free-men has an experiential, visual component on which the discerning member of the audience can rely. Opinion is a particularly windy character whose corporeality cannot be attested; but examining countenances (as they are displayed in front of you or reported to you in pamphlet re-animations such as the Putney Debates) gives the spectator a way of discerning dissembling by reading the performance as more than the words said. By now any good reader of mine has thought of a thousand examples of the good actor who fools "all of the people, all of the time," but it is Overton's purpose to teach his fellow free-men both the skills of vivid representation of freedom and the skills to discern it. If it is an idealistic vision, he is in good company.[35]

Such idealism did not negate the distrust in the "representational value" of language, its ability to immediately communicate ideas and ideologies without doubt or nuance. In the years of the pamphletheatre performances, writers creatively, performatively responded to the actions of their leaders when those leaders amended and sometimes betrayed the vision of the nation represented in the pamphlets. When the theatres reopened, they reopened in the context of eighteen years of public theatricals. Though many in the audience may not have been familiar with the repertoire of city comedies on the boards in the 1630s, they were familiar with their role as receiving and participating spectators, interpreting social, national and, increasingly, domestic representations from the vantage of experienced pamphlet playgoers.

4 Decidedly moving

Aphra Behn and the staging of paradoxical pleasures

From the instructions embodied in her prefaces to the creation of her five-act plays, Aphra Behn designs a theatrical world negotiated through motion. Behn's articulation of her purpose solicits the reading and theatre audiences to understand the compact they actively make with her, as with her characters and the actors on the stage. In her plays, Behn builds framed theatrical moments and in turn breaks the frame in order to provide the audience with a set-up of fixity and the correcting (sometimes simply inevitable) influence of motion. Though each chapter in this book examines the use of gender in creating terms of value, in Behn's work the examination extends to the female characters invented by a female writer for female players. To be reminded of this historical fact is not to encourage an exercise in essentialist nostalgia, but rather to recognize the lucid examination of gender offstage and on by a very ironic maker of plots and theatrical schemes. In the theatrical world Behn stages the exchange of bodies, of money, and of wit reflecting the social world where there exists an increased anxiety and excitement about trade of all kinds. Through her plots and her characterizations, Behn makes comment again and again upon the world of the still, the withheld, the lasting, and the world of the moving, the offered, the ephemeral.

Prefatory addresses to the reader

"Good, Sweet, Honey, Sugar-candied reader," begins Aphra Behn, tongue firmly in printed cheek as she addresses the reading public regarding her play *The Dutch Lover* (I, 221). Jonson's equivocating in his desire for readers/appreciators, Milton's fervent, impassioned address to his 'fit audience though few' meet their rhetorical match in Behn's overblown direct assault on the 'favor' of her literate public. With a startling ease of address she mocks the female supplicant role, laying it on thick to entertain her audience and, without pedantry, further her argument. With Behn in the 1670s we move well beyond the years of the public back and forth of the pamphletheatre. The discourse between audience and writer begins to take on signs more familiar to twentieth-century readers, that of the relation of author to private reader with book in hand. The copia of ephemeral print in the Interregnum, worrying to those who saw the pamphlet display as a sign of disorder, was disciplined to some extent in the decade after the Restoration.[1] As late as 1679, however, Behn claims the printed production of *The Dutch Lover*, both her Epistle and the printed text of her play, have the status of active, ephemeral, shared print – it is an "idle Pamphlet" (I, 221). "I must have a word or two with you," Behn tells us in her Epistle using the mock privacy of print to "single" out her reader (I, 221). Behn's egalitarian tone to her audience, an invitation with didactic purpose to be sure but still an invitation, allows more than one response, suggesting exchange, or conversation.

Teasing her audience, she regards them as self-conscious readers responsible for the contract between reader and author:

> if you will misspend your Time, pray lay the fault upon yourself; for I have dealt pretty fairly in the matter, told you in the Title Page what you are to expect within . . . having inscrib'd Comedy on the beginning of my Book, you may guess pretty near what peny-worths you are like to have.
>
> (I, 221)

Encouraging the reader to pay specific attention to the printed apparatus – Title Page – she assumes the buyer of this "peny-worths" can choose with freedom the "Book" they are presumably holding even as she instructs. Once in possession of the "comedy," the reader may not, after some furtive enjoyment, disown his/her participation in the buying of the book. For her part the author deals fairly with the audience, neither falsifying the character of the work, nor hanging "a sign of the immortality of the soul, of the mystery of godliness, or of Ecclesiastical Policie" to mask the entertainment (I, 221). The potential for explanation in person by the author, once hinted at in the early work of Jonson, has in Behn's time begun to change: she places more weight upon the textual apparatus of the book itself than on her own voice in it. Behn acknowledges her control ends at the edges of her text in print, and the reader must take up the work with attention to the bargain between writer and reader who will not necessarily encounter one another, except perhaps at the playhouse.

Behn employs a mode of demurring familiar to readers of "ladylike" rhetorical openings. Declaring large words are beyond her, Behn frets she will "misspell" the names of the great subjects. In the flowery "honey-baby" opening, Behn constructs the expected feminine appeal so as to comment from it and on it. Once erected, she strategically demolishes it by crossing over the (demure) line into irony. Partaking in the pleasures of print, the tactics of rhetorical construction, Behn does not disappear; she becomes more visible, unleashing her ironic wit in a swift attack upon masculine institutions.

The work of an author who employs motion demands a critical language which can account for that motion and its effects; I hope by the arguments in this book to focus our critical attention on the use of motion and stillness on the seventeenth-century stage, and it is to Behn I owe the initial endeavor. The forcedness of Jonson's push me-pull you placating and haranguing even when mixed with wistful desire, and the deliberate addition of corporeality by the use of physical analogy in Milton's prose are in contrast to Behn, a poet and writer whose métier seems to be motion. Even in *Oroonoko*, the work she is best known for, Behn's narrative voice teaches by animated story, the tales often represented as being told in the moment, re-imagined by those who lived them. Her meditation on "natural learning" in the novel, one she continues in her plays *The Young King* and *The Dutch Lover*, stages itself to the readerly imagination in much the same way her preface demonstrates that admirable artistic work must move the spectator to change by the sensuous evidence portrayed through showing (see p. 110).

In her preface to *The Dutch Lover*, Behn claims ignorance of words she ought to know because she fancies such airy syllables "strongly ought to mean just nothing," probably originating in the mouths of "so many ignorant, unhappy souls" spending "ten, twelve, twenty years in the university (who yet poor wretches think they are doing something all the while)" (I, 221). Behn extends her condolences, employing sympathy, that female specialty, to tweak the scholarly noses. Mocking the academic genre of preface, Behn raises a skeptical eyebrow at those who prove "in Folio" an idea speciously dignified only by bloated exposition in print. Because dubious pedantry appears hopelessly textbound, Behn cannot understand why printed plays – made of more modest ambitions – should not share the shelf "among the middle if not the better sort of books" (I, 221). Note that while Jonson imaginatively ordered future shelves for his books in his creation of authorial persona, in the 1670s, according to Behn, those shelves exist for more than just a scholarly audience.

The material object of the book, and decisions about where to store it, allows Behn to make manifest the nature of the ephemeral address in which she is engaged and to pose the question of whether to conserve "idle pamphlets" upon permanent shelves, render them a part of preserved knowledge. A preface to a play submits itself to the reader's time, generally before he or she reads the play, perhaps after he or she has seen it on the stage. A single reading suffices; Behn supplies information that might be read once, unlike the story in the drama which may be enjoyed again and again. Behn's Preface makes an argument to the moment which fades after the reader has gleaned the necesssary information. While in the Interregnum there had occurred a "migration of dramatic resources to the arena of the pamphlet," in Behn's work we see a reverse migration as she employs a strategy from pamphlet writing, pointing out the ephemerality of her "idle pamphlet," in her mixed media of preface and play (Smith 1994: 70).

Other residues of the public performance space alive in the pamphletheatre can be traced in the Preface when Behn compares the aims of a playwright and of a preacher. Equating the orality in performance to vocal performance in the street, Behn looks to the failed reforms of "frequent preaching." At least the plays are honest in that "no Play was ever writ with that design" (I, 223). "Intended for the exercising of men's passions not their understandings," plays are "the best divertisement that wise men have . . . Comedie was never meant, either for a converting or conforming Ordinance" (I, 223). While Behn clearly articulates her artistic intent, to "exercise men's passions not their understandings," in the spirit of mock humility she underestimates how she employs entertainment in the service of influencing an audience's reception of meaning.

In fact, her prefatory writing and her plays demonstrate that theatrical means of representation are for Behn the *most reliable* way of changing understanding. Behn posits an art whose "value" remains in the experience, the exercising of the passion. To seek to address the passion rather than the understanding does not mean to jettison instruction or persuasion. Rather Behn implies throughout her work that rhetorical, linguistic, logical persuasion often produces only fleeting changes; like Bacon Behn suggests that which is impressed by the senses remains more permanently inscribed on the memory. It might not surprise us then that one method Behn uses to bring about such changes are scenes that work like masques or emblems. In *The Theatre of Aphra Behn* Derek Hughes seeks to "clarify Behn's status as an intellectual" by examining how she "expressed her ideas through the stage" (2001: 11). This is a welcome intervention in Behn's studies and in theatre studies since so many critics are not accustomed to seeing intellectual ideas manifested in staging, in the design of the play, in the use of "all the resources of meaning offered by the theatre" (11).

When Behn sets out to use all the resources of meaning offered by the theatre, she does so I propose from the vantage of the senses. Behn's method of addressing the senses harkens back to the performed world described in the Prologue: one of sensual instruction based on apprehension. Yet she seems to mix contemporary ideas of categorization, that of passion and understanding for example, with a borrowing of method and story from Shakespeare and other playwrights of the early seventeenth century. With these borrowed and invented tools, she crafts performance as a means of instruction toward change. And that means is rarely one of conversational persuasion or mean spirited tricks. In many of her plays – *The Forced Marriage, The Amorous Prince* – the errant find themselves attending a 'show,' a theatrical miniature created to transform the wrongdoer; the transformation is represented by Behn as having been brought about by experiencing a gradual change as the drama unfolds. Writing about Behn's adroit use of the stage Dawn Lewcock argues that her use of visual effects "affect the perception of the audience," changing their "conception and comprehension of her plots and/or her underlying themes" (1996: 66–7).

Evidence of Behn's instructive manipulation of stillness and motion on the stage appears in one of her first plays, *The Forced Marriage*. In seventeenth-century theatre practice the custom was to open the curtain at the beginning of the play and to leave it open through the acts. In *The Forced Marriage* the curtain, Behn writes in her stage direction, must be down at the beginning of Act II, and when it is raised, the audience sees a tableau of a marriage ceremony in which the wrong couple is being married. Like a figure in a Titian painting turned toward the viewer as if to draw attention to the static nature of the scene in which he or she is a part, the bride, Erminia, looks back toward the viewers and Philander, the man she should be marrying. Sword half-drawn, Philander looks upon Erminia with desperation while other characters gaze on the appropriate or inappropriate object of their desire and the curtain falls. Completely silent and thoroughly displaced in the common pattern of comedy, the moment of the wedding remains in the audience's mind, a visual memory as Behn separates the mismatched pair and unites the true lovers in a continuing series of show and learn, show and change. The 'pedagogy of motion' Behn employs in these scenes proceeds temporally; the spectator is corrected through a series of tableaux or scenes that replay for him or her the history of the problem, rehearse possible consequences if it continues, and then display solutions. Because the ideas unfold slowly before the character, he or she experiences a temporal learning. The character displays a growing awareness, apprehending through mind and senses what the right action will be in light of the instructive tableau set before not only the character but also the audience.

Nine years later in her preface to *The Dutch Lover* Behn, having described her theatrical philosophy in terms of instructive showing, shifts the scene for her reader to the performance of the play itself. Behn brings the reader with her on opening night where she witnessed a fop, "a thing, Reader . . . a Smelt" who "opening that which serves it for a mouth" informs all round him to "expect a woful Play, God damn him, for it was a woman's" (I, 224). Were she to dignify such foppish stupidity with an answer, she might "take a little pains to make him know how much he errs" (I, 224). Now the reader feels the force of her purpose. Seeming to defer a discussion of the disadvantage women suffer in education, "waiving the examination why women having equal education with men, were not as capable of knowledge," Behn still makes sure the query is set in print (I, 224). Reminding the drama-going, drama-reading public "that Plays have no great room for that which is men's great advantage over women, that is Learning," she cites her model Shakespeare who "was not guilty of much more" learning "than often falls to women's share" and who pleases audiences more than the classic Jonson (I, 224).[2]

Dismissing proleptically those eighteenth-century critics who would later read Shakespeare as literary dramatist, Behn gives him his due by the only evidence admissible, a recounting of a performance. "I have seen a man the most severe of Johnson's [*sic*] Sect, sit with his Hat removed less than a hair's breadth from one sullen posture for almost three hours at *The Alchymist* [*sic*]; who at that excellent Play of *Harry the Fourth* (which yet I hope is far enough from Farce) hath very hardly kept his Doublet whole" (I, 224). A lover of theatrical performance will always fall for the burst doublet over the appreciative nod. Since none of her contemporaries excepting the Laureate Dryden, according to Behn, "write at such a formidable rate" as Shakespeare, a "woman may well hope to reach their greatest heights" (I, 224). Further, the burst doublet proves the power of moving stagecraft to elicit a mimetic motion in the breast of the spectator, and, as she proves, Behn is a playwright who knows how to use her opportunity for 'temporal tutoring.'

Having claimed her place and her inheritance – she may admire the author Jonson but she emulates the oral, performing Shakespeare – she announces herself a theatre professional who does not entirely love performance. Like other playwrights, she suffers the memory of the performance of the play as one of vulnerability: "Know then that this Play was hugely injur'd in the Acting . . . My Dutch Lover spoke but little of what I intended for him, but supplied it with a great deal of idle stuff, which I was wholly unacquainted with until I heard it first from him" (I, 224–5). Though Behn's work celebrates movement, and its capacity to stir the passions, as a professional playwright she wants no cavalier dismissal of her text.

Behn cites pragmatic reasons for the unpredictability of performance, namely that she had given the actor the part because she "knew him so acceptable to most o'th'lighter Periwigs about the Town" (I, 225).[3] Like screenwriters whose dialogue dies in the mouths of Hollywood's hot properties, Behn, whose report here indicates she had much to do with the actual choice of cast and early productions of the plays even if she could be surprised on opening night, found herself subject to the company's clowns and heroes/heroines, the favored actors and actresses of the day.

Behn's impatience with this particular performance distinguishes between the play injured "in the acting," as it was on opening night, and the play injured *by* acting. Writing in many genres, Behn hoped for literary fame for all that she put into print – her poetry and her short fiction as well as the later printed versions of her plays – but she conceived of her plays as works to be performed. "Mrs. Behn's plays are often full of detailed stage directions and very specific instructions on scene changes" notes Edward Langhans in his work on Restoration promptbooks (1981: 56).[4] Such attention signals her creation of plays to be played. Behn knew the theatre for which she wrote her plays; when she carefully creates scene, act and line with those "specific instructions," she can imagine where on the stage the players might be, how they might move, and when the scene changes.[5]

The critical tenet in literary studies in the late twentieth century that "there is no author," derived from Foucault's essay "The death of the author," depends upon the invisibility (by death or absence) of the author. The author as playwright, however, can experience a more immediate form of death during a performance of a play. For no matter how fictive the construct Aphra Behn is to us who read her, when she attended a performance of her own play, the audience's reaction and her presence in the theatre undid the protective veil of blind print, showed the Lady writer *at* her work. As the earlier chapters suggest, the conjunction of print, aurality, orality, and performance in this century opened fault lines where the media could mix. The sound of Behn's voice at rehearsal as she read the text of her newest play, the presence of the woman writer giving an interpretation of the work for the actors would influence the makers, women and men, of the play she had written. These moments of play reading, rehearsals, performance, offer a conjunction where the still and the moving intersect and sometimes clash. An actor might want to use his or her talent for improvisation to embellish a character while the author, having written the character specifically for the improvisers, remembers the written words of the text even as she hears other words spoken as the play is performed (Milhous and Hume 1985; Holland 1991).[6]

Behn brings evidence of her management into print; the Preface has the rhythm of an evening at the theatre. Imagining the owner of the quarto holding the work in his/her hand, she directs the reader's attention first to the title page, then to her personal exposition in the Preface, then to the play, by way of referring to the reader's possible experience as spectator in the Duke's Dorset Garden Theatre. Finally, she sums up her introductory remarks with the finale of the printed work, the Epilogue: "Lastly my Epilogue," an epilogue unsatisfactory to her because written by a lesser wit but still an epilogue "to make out your penyworth, you have it here." The printed contract, my writing for your penyworth, fulfilled, she says "Adieu," leaving the reader to his or her own private reading of the text (I, 225).

Moving pictures; or, The Lady's Not For Keeping

From Behn's active prefatory texts we begin to understand how she intended her plays to work, but it is only by trying to 'produce' Behn's scenes as performance that I can demonstrate the opportunity performance allows Behn. She sets forth the pleasures of motion, of giving and exchanging *within* the economy of performed time. As a critical practice in each of these chapters I seek to 'animate' the work by reminding the reader when and where and how actions might have taken place on stage, animating the possibility of vocal nuance and gestural subversion to recollect the aesthetic, elemental effects of moving art forms on the receiving body/mind. The give and take of Behn's particular work in the theatre can only be interpreted through an understanding of staging, of motion, of moments carefully choreographed and collected together to be dispersed again. Working in a performed medium, Behn can illustrate the cultural patterns of exchange in human relations as well as the less practical, non-quantifiable 'productions' of emotion or experience which gain vitality from circulation and which stagnate when a character attempts to collect them. As is Behn's way, she parodies the mercantile aspect of sexual as well as dramatic relations while making interesting visual and aural commentary by propelling women into ambulatory commodities who trade and who trade themselves.

What follows is an examination of the staged moments Behn creates to present her characters and the audience with an interchange of fixity and motion. Behn portrays the consequences for those who obtain power by hoarding, withdrawing, creating scarcity and those who spend and move. The consequences are enacted for the characters and the community represented on stage as well as the community offstage, who recognize themselves in the representation. (We cannot be reminded enough that in seventeenth-century theatre practice an audience was not roped off from the stage by darkness or the fiction of realism but invited to participate in lively exchange with the players, playwright, and settings.) Even her characters well versed in their own participation in the emerging market economy of the seventeenth century can choose to engage in the pleasures of the freely given, to circulate and trade without guarantee of an equal, or indeed any, return.[7] Behn's frequent description of her main characters as "inconstant" renders them a kind of moving emblem of the world in motion. However, instead of the inconstant moving until it is reincorporated into the norm of the constant, the inconstant is often in a potential position to teach by example an ethic of the freely given.

In the literary economy of writing for the stage and for print, Behn participates as an author and owner of her work (though she would not have been paid at first for the written object of the play but rather for the longevity – the third night proceeds – of the performance). While clearly Behn is savvy about the circulation of her texts for money, she often writes into her plots a quasi-utopian or, in the case of *Oronooko* according to Laura Rosenthal, a "nostalgic" sense of longing for forms of exchange not tied to money. Behn's ideal exchanges result in the creation of communal bonds (1996: 142). Jessica Munns sees in Behn's prefaces a struggle for control that Munns articulates in the language of debt: "is the reader who has paid for the text in control, or the writer controlling the reader: who is in whose debt?" (1993: 54). Yet Rosenthal's description of Behn's evocation of gift economy in *Oronooko* seems to come closer to Behn's representation of a gift economy – no doubt in the case of her rendering of African life drawn from a "primitivist mythology" – that "binds communities and creates noble friendships" (1996: 142).[8] In *Oronooko*, though the gift economy has "profound internal conflicts," nothing "becomes more pernicious in Behn's novel than when English commodification violates" the exchange of gifts (141). In Behn's plays she continues to intervene in the midst of a world engaged in economic exchange, for which she has a pragmatic respect, by correcting purely economic relations.

Directing the motion and energy embodied in performance, Behn exploits the possibilities of performed exchange, frequently mocking the characters who try to hoard and entrap. As poet, translator, short fiction writer and playwright, Behn recognizes the attraction of the performed work's immediacy *and* the satisfaction of the printed text's longevity. Her women characters on stage and in fiction celebrate the ephemeral power of oral performance and movement while planning for their own versions of permanent fame and stability. Yet Behn's work stages the digressive adventure of movement, the interruptions and reversals of fortune that accompany the attempt to secure one's love, one's work and one's livelihood, even at the price of being left with 'nothing to show for it' . . . but the show. In her work the price of an acquisitive love can be more exacting than the 'perishing,' in erotic terms a repeated 'dying,' which comes with playful inconstancy and movement. Commodities at liberty, collectors' items who control their own exhibition, Behn's women characters in motion endanger the stability of the socially constructed display case that is marriage.

Behn's emphasis on performance, motion, and mobility extends beyond her creation of character and set design into the very structure of her plays. Behn has an extraordinary visual sense of how the stage contrasts stillness to motion, how interruption can be hilarious or tragic, how a long complicated trick merits the time it takes to be played. Like other early Restoration playwrights, Behn often designed an entire act out of one scene; an uninterrupted swirling motion in which characters meet each other, flee from one another, overhear one another, and quarrel with one another. At the Dorset Garden Theatre, the company excelled in the mobile intrigue play, and Behn wrote complicated plots and subplots appropriate to their specialty.[9] Extending well beyond the proscenium into the pit, the Dorset Garden forestage worked to thrust the street before the audience. In the interior scenes, set back behind the onstage box seats, one might catch glimpses of where Behn had hidden men, women, and cuckolds underneath blankets, behind curtains or disguised as a chair one's mistress has sat upon and draped her robe over.[10]

Though one finds such instances of Behn's innovation in each of her plays, two spectacular scenes, one from *The Rover*, Part I, and the other from *The Feigned Courtesans*, display her orchestration of stasis and motion as instructional moments in performance. In *The Rover*, Part I, Behn reconfigures the traditional seventeenth-century equation between wandering wantonness (motion) and virtue (stillness). Taking place at carnival time in the Catholic country of Spain, the story follows the fortunes of Hellena, a young girl sprung from the convent, her sister Florinda, a traditional lover fixed upon an Englishman but pledged to an old Spaniard, and the courtesan Angellica Bianca whose enterprise of selective circulation is endangered by the presence of Willmore, "the Rover." Within the past twenty years this play has received a great deal of critical attention that analyzes Behn's relation to her courtesan, and by extension to the public display of trading, whether the trade be one's body or one's words or one's theatrical imagination.[11] For my purposes, however, I will limit my discussion to Behn's use of visual stasis and motion in one particular scene from the play.

As Act II opens the audience has already learned of the various complications obstructing the joining of Florinda to her love Belvile. We have also been tantalized by an exchange between Hellena and Willmore in masks. But like the more conventional female characters created by playwrights of the seventeenth and eighteenth century, Angellica Bianca does not enter until the second act.[12] The stage direction from Act II, scene i of *The Rover*, Part I, constructs a visual masterpiece haunting the recent rediscovery of Behn's work: "Enter two Bravoes, and hang up a great Picture of Angellica's [portraying her] against the Balcony, and two little ones at each side of the Door" (I, 30). Angellica Bianca as courtesan to be adored hangs atop the scene as a captive image sold for a fortune. Behn contrasts Angellica's stillness to the band of roving young women in the first scene of the play, women who don disguise and seek their own "fortunes" in love. Few feminist critics reading the play can pass by Behn's dramatic balcony without experiencing the shock of recognition in the arrangement of display, buyers, and woman "so wondrous fair" framed in three likenesses (Diamond 1989: 42–6). Insisting on the audience's understanding of a scene created by a directorial eye, Behn has two "bravoes," stage hands, arrange the set while the characters on stage and by extension the audience watch the making of an orchestrated spectacle. Angellica Bianca's self advertising, as created by Behn, displays the artistic representation of female beauty preserved and motionless in portraiture and the concomitant offering of that beauty for a price.

Behn's elaborate scene of adoration at the shrine of the tripled whore should have provoked the audience's visual associations with religious imagery. Though Behn borrows the basic set decoration from Thomas Killigrew's *Thomaso; or, the Wanderer* [the only "stolen object" as she writes in a Postscript to the play (I, 107)] , Killigrew hangs the picture of Angellica on a "Pillar" and three scenes on adds as an afterthought "there must be two little pictures posted upon the pillar" (1664: 335). Behn's deliberate set up, staged for the audience and designed around the balcony, allows her to use the side entrances where the actresses/actors come onto stage. Rather than draw the audience's attention to a single pillar as Killigrew does in his play, Behn's arrangement requires that the other characters look up in admiration while Angellica appears to 'hide' on the balcony where she is still seen by the audience.[13] Imagine the big picture of the "white Angel" with two smaller saints on either side, a secular 'altarpiece,' with secular indulgences for sale. Most of the action is taking place close to the pit on the right or left side of the forestage. Hung from the balcony over Angellica's door, the trinity of representation invites worshipers to conflate a woman's oldest Christian professions, whore and madonna.

Because this is a scene in a performed play and not a display in a gallery of paintings, Behn can set before her spectators the fixed, intractable *categories* of religion, display, beauty, trade, and women as they are jostled by the mobile action of theatrical illusion, provocation, and circulation. Performance in its kinetic ability to take the audience through time, progressing through the story without having to confine it all to a single visual reproduction, does not deny or negate these categories so much as reconstitute them. The arc of the performance produces for its participants the effects of time, change, and incremental recognition. In this scene Behn's design does not simply illustrate the common conflation of stage and courtesan's drawing room, but emphasizes the odd nature of monetary exchange for the intangible. What constitutes customer satisfaction in a whorehouse, a vestibule, a theatre? What vestiges of such satisfaction can one find upon the body of the spectator/participant? Behn simultaneously accentuates the still, familiar sight of a pseudo-altarpiece within a moment of theatrical illusion in which the courtesan carefully arranges her representations. Behn will, later in this scene, use the portability of the smaller paintings as a catalyst for actors whose mobility, whose penchant for circulation, cannot leave the static unmolested. At first, however, Angellica waits like a playhouse to be patronized, her 'proscenium' a framed portrait, very much like the proscenium frame that will gradually set the boundaries for the stage in the next century.

Unlike the private boudoir of women in *The Rover*, Part I, Act I, where Hellena and Florinda enter alone onstage and discuss male characters not yet seen by the audience, in Act II Angellica Bianca's public 'boudoir,' a courtesan's gallery, invites male discourse. Willmore and the English gentleman Belvile, Frederick, and Blunt (from the *country*), banter while the design of Angellica's house comes into being behind them. The lack of Angellica's flesh and blood presence allows certain performances from her would-be purchasers. Again the playwright plays with the still stand-in for the courtesan – the portraits – and the moving bluster of the men. But she uses the moment to show how the homosocial contract requires the idea of a woman without the corporeal messiness of her moving and talking self. In Behn's day and now, a woman walking by a group of men in a public place at the moment when the air begins to fill with ogling and commentary knows that if she stops to confront the men, rather than walking by, their 'scene' will have to be emended or abandoned. A woman's visibility followed by her absence, or at least her receding, creates the space, the 'stage' for summary and critique – women provide spectacles to be discussed, collected, and traded: "how about that one?" (see Chapter 1 for Jonson's treatment of the unveiling of the silent woman in *Epicoene*). Evaluating the rare, rating the comparative value of the goods requires a stillness, in this case provided by absence, where a moving presence might jolt the scales of appraisal. It is the collector's expertise that is as much on display as the wonder of his newest 'piece.'

Angellica makes a pragmatic business out of woman as spectacle. Though she seems to hang untouchable above the boorish scene, she encourages (by her willingness to be objectified) the masculine commentary about woman as merchandise.[14] She creates and exploits a marketplace based on scarcity – the male buyer wins the prized position of authority from which to report on the unsurpassed Angellica. Behn creates the vibrant tension by demonstrating the transaction between 'rare' woman and her would-be collectors, figuring it on the stage, and then reinterpreting the possibilities when mobile characters disrupt a scene whose initial action depended upon the stillness of absence and assessing.

In such rich contexts Behn sets her cavaliers in motion on stage under the sign of beauty. Belvile dismisses the "fair Sign" advertising an "Inn where a Man may lodge" if he is a "Fool with his money" (I, 30). Blunt, more representative of hypocritical British colonialists, mocks the overt display as "Impudence" practiced in this "Country" so unlike his own (though he will soon be out of pocket, not because he paid for a whore, but because he did not recognize one when he saw her) (I, 30). Confusing his role as usual Blunt asserts: "we're no Chapmen for this Commodity." Indeed Angellica would never be silly enough to have Blunt for her peddler; his bluntness, his literal speech, would undo fame and circulate her name, her reputation into commonness (I, 30).[15] Besotted Willmore, ignoring his blustering companions, plays notes upon the true lover's strings, turning soft, bemoaning his poverty "when it hinders my Approach to Beauty, which Virtue ne'er could purchase" (I, 30). Willmore is, however, as much without virtue as funds.

The whole scene involves gazing on the Picture, turning from the Picture, reading the accompanying signs: theatrical gestures heightened and mocked by Behn. She portrays the spectacle of men seduced as Leontes by an artist's perfect – almost (but not quite) breathing – rendition of 'woman.' Taken in by the portraits, Willmore and Blunt begin to woo the representation, as Bassanio woos his casket in *The Merchant of Venice*. Portia, good heroine, follows Bassanio's raptures over her portrait by prompting the man back to reality when she verbally taps him on the shoulder: "You see me, Lord Bassanio, where I stand. Such as I am" (III. ii. 149–50). Portia suspects Bassanio may be disappointed in comparing the casket likeness, frozen beyond change or death, and the thing herself. In her comic world, Behn translates such virgin worry into Angellica's savvy business instincts. The man who will have Angellica will pay according to his first desire born out of a representation; cash-in-hand, Angellica regards his possible disappointment with flesh and blood as his own worry.[16]

The restrictions of a legendary courtesan's life provide a form of pleasure: "their Wonder feeds my Vanity, and he that wishes to buy, gives me more Pride, than he that gives me my Price can make me Pleasure" (I, 31). Angellica enjoys the ancient reward given women who forfeit active choice: the spectacle of men burning for her beauty pleases her more than the physical satiation of money or purchased sex. Adoration and fame immobilize the body; Angellica reports her satisfactions as wholly intellectual. When asked by Moretta, her servant, why she has not suffered the "disease" of women, being in love, Angellica turns Beatrice's sprightly dancing natal star from *Much Ado About Nothing* into "a kind, but sullen Star, under which I had the Happiness to be born" (I, 32). A merchant of the ever-emerging middle class, Angellica has had "no time for Love" (I, 32).

In the exquisite set up of this act, the framed gaze inevitably causes conflict in a world Behn represents, one based on an economy of artificial beauty, the display of said beauty, and its scarcity. If desire is inflamed by seeking the most beautiful object, the most famous example of a species, then the equation will always be the "one" sought by the many. Even the motion of trade and travel depend upon the conviction that the journey will end with either the witnessing of the finest collection or the bringing home of the rarest collector's item. The beauty must be artificial if it is human since all human beauty changes and can even be said to be different according to the time of day, the presentation of the beauty or the emotion on the face of the beloved. Performance acknowledges in its representations the longing for preserving the beauty of an object, of a lover, and of a moment and yet in its relentless life in time insists on the change that rebukes the fantasy of acquiring and keeping the living body.

Thus above the still representation on the balcony Behn reacquaints the audience with the living inspiration for the staged portraits, the courtesan herself, a fourth picture come to life. Angellica, taunting the men below her by allowing a quick glimpse of her face, instigates motion. Where her absence allowed the men to peruse the idea of her in conversational exchange, even her fleeting presence undoes the space of controlled appraisal. The dynamic of performance can only entertain a certain stasis for so long before succumbing to pressures of plot, of physical motion by the actors, and of a corrective push as time elapses. Each man, like a member of an anarchic dance company, begins his routine: one demanding a duel, another abandoning his betrothed for a taste of heaven, the third seeking to replace an uncle who last shared the courtesan's bed – in short, moral chaos.

Willmore undoes the trinity of pictures by snatching one and thus breaks up the fight while simultaneously releasing the unwilling voice of the frozen beauty. Angellica must respond to his unexpected initiative by stepping out of the silent position of the admired. Like those who inhabit the cheap seats in the theatre, Willmore jeopardizes the delicate visual arrangement with his boisterous and rude manners. Moretta fears prophetically that Willmore will "ruin us, we shall never see good days, till all these fighting poor Rogues are sent to the Gallies" or galleries, banished to the cheapest seats in the house (I, 35).[17] By his stealing of "a trifle," his dismantling of the symbolic altarpiece, Willmore wins admittance behind the proscenium into Angellica's chamber, and eventually into her arms. By stealing at all he upsets the staid market economy entrusted generally to an orderly process of seller and buyer uninterrupted by another class of trader, the thief.[18]

What Willmore enacts in the fiction of the play, the audience in the galleries often exercised in the liminal world between fiction and the everyday: the license to break the barrier between spectator and possessor, the frame of forestage and proscenium, a separation potentially dismantled by force or by noisy opposition during a performance. Though no doubt the playwright found this audience's disruptive force irritating, Behn, herself an outsider storming the male-sequestered proscenium, portrays the hapless Willmore lovingly, finding in his energy a welcome disruption to convention. Behn also portrays Willmore's energy as a force for a return of that which should be freely given – love – to the cycle of give and receive rather than the stilted exchange of beauty to the highest bidder. Willmore's flaws, his lugubriousness, and his ready rhetoric win the audience's amused heart as he woos everything in sight (and many things he cannot see for drunken blindness).[19]

If *The Rover*, Part I, simply and fondly adored and wanted "more of Will," without female characters who exhibited a "will" of their own, Behn's play would join the company of plays celebrating lovable rakes in the early Restoration.[20] But the play juxtaposes the active Willmore with the active Hellena. Behn magnifies the performed and printed role of a less accounted for dramatic dismantler, the rakish actress. Hellena dresses in her creator's perfect moniker for performers, she is "inconstant." Since the very livelihood of actors depends upon their protean transformations, Hellena embodies her *raison d'être*, performance. Her task reveals the collaboration of a performer's dependence upon the still and the changing: she must establish a consistent Hellena that the audience recognizes while engaging in the multiple permutations necessary to move from her character in Act I to her character in Act V.

Hellena's self invention involves disguise and veiling, a manipulation of the displayed, admired beauty. Where Angellica remains silent, courting attention by the wonder inducing stillness of her portrait, Hellena sets out on the street in costume wooing by the sound of her voice and the quickness of her intellect. Ever the actress in performance, Hellena schemes and intrigues and wins her Rover by matching wits at roving. The lovemaking of women and men to both women and men allows Behn to contrast the freedom of a life of inconstancy to the cruel fixity of a life in which one is unjustly mated; unpremeditated constancy, Behn implies, belongs more to property than people. To choose a lover is in some sense also to offer oneself. The exchange of gifts set in motion in performance allows for the repetition that renews because what is constant is the pressure of circulation, the flow of action and time offering characters and spectators new opportunities to congregate, interact, and withdraw. Stale vows taken once or marriages left to die in tedium work against the energetic state of loving bequeathed to some of Behn's female characters. As often in her work, choice distinguishes tedium from vitality, a voluptuous repetition born of cyclical satisfaction and longing, not the horrible repetition of forced marriage and its dispiriting constancy.

By placing Hellena's energy – a rare instance of true female energy upon the stage – in relation to Angellica's immobility and reduced choice, Behn unmakes the cultural vision of women reduced to statues to be adored. Mark Lussier suggests that Behn's use of the "language of money" allows her to "reveal mental and social relations as based within the male economy of desire, where women are objects of exchange" (1991: 380). While Lussier notes some essential truths about the economic world in which Behn is writing, the space of the stage can easily be lost when only construed in the linguistic analysis of economic theory. If, as Lussier suggests, Behn is writing for a stage preoccupied with the coming of banks, paper money, and obsessive exchange, she also, I argue, creates on the stage a space for bodies enacting give and take in the midst of a world ever more framed by the values of commercial exchange. While "economic discourse" might eclipse "other metaphorical language" in Behn's comedies, Behn sets that language against a language of gesture and theatrical action. Through her persuasion by performance Behn shows her audience how giving and receiving (particularly by women characters who transform themselves for a time through performance from objects of exchange into traders), being in motion across the time and space of performance, demonstrates the consequences of choosing to give and to let go despite loss, of one's heart's desire, or, for that matter, of profit (380).

I am not suggesting that Behn makes a sophisticated critique of emerging capitalism, but I am suggesting that we as critics have established language and precedent (Lussier frames his argument by using the work of Raymond Williams) to identify economic strategies while we have very little critical precedent or encouragement to recognize instances on stage of the freely given. Behn's performed world creates spaces for exchanges of intangibles – flirtatious language, pledges of love and friendship, play between audience and actors which can result in the give and take of reinterpretation – within a fundamentally intangible art form. Such creations need to be figured into the equation of response to emerging capitalism as well as into the equation of how performance works *as* a space of exchange in a space of exchange in a society engaged *in* exchange.

At the end of the play, Angellica finally "loses" Willmore whom she mistakenly regards as her property to acquire and keep by armed threat (Angellica enters the scene with a pistol). Responding to Antonio, a man of property, the "Viceroy's son," Angellica laments "yesterday/I'd not have sold my interest in his heart" (I, 98). That Angellica understands a kind of lover's usury in her passion for Willmore, the "interest" she has in him like a merchant's venture trusted to the speculation of trade, allows her to mistakenly think she might sell her amorous stock to another trader. A heart is the thing that must be freely given by the owner; in the circulation of gifts sometimes the cycle of exchange creates "increase" but such intangible extras cannot translate into the measurable world of profit (Hyde 1979). "Keeping," as Behn's knowing women remind the audience in *Sir Patient Fancy*, "becomes as ridiculous as Matrimony" (IV, 12). To be kept, or to be held, or to be enslaved, or to be married when the bond strangles is to be out of the motion of acting on choice and desire; it is to be interpreted as an item in the display case of the domestic/social world.

Acts in motion

Where Angellica's visual display and Hellena's taking to the street bring before the audience contrasting instances of stasis and mobility, in Act II of *The Feigned Courtesans; or, A Night's Intrigue* Behn assembles moving duets, trios, solos in choreographed ensembles of giving and taking. Lovers, ideas, books, and players all circulate through the one-scene act culminating in a zany's performance of a tale about motion, performance, and withholding. Behn's cast in the play includes the mis-betrothed Marcella, who is trying to escape from Octavio into the more suitable arms of her choice, Fillamour. Cornelia, Marcella's sister who engineers the courtesan disguises, provides for herself by roaming and finding and liking. Two subplots complicate *The Forced Marriage* scenario. Laura Lucretia, who crossdresses as a courtesan and as a man, is promised to Julio, brother of Marcella. Laura Lucretia is a "rogue" woman – not paired with another woman in the same predicament – whose circulation throughout the play often further disrupts and confuses the plot. She has set her heart on the unworthy Galliard, Fillamour's friend and Cornelia's partner in inconstancy and wit. Meanwhile a comic trio based on the *Commedia dell'Arte* – Petro, the wise and crafty Italian, Sir Signal Buffon, a young spark in Rome, and Tickletext, his not very effective governor – dance in and out of scenes parodying national stereotypes, demonstrating imperfect language acquisition and suffering from literal mindedness in a country – Italy – whose pleasures are represented as intensely theatrical.

As the act proceeds, each vignette equates performance, motion and play with giving and receiving. Set in "The Gardens of the Villa Medici," the first characters to enter represent the authorities who force marriages: Uncle Morosini – Behn's Italianate pun on Jonson's many humored Morose – "an old Count," and Octavio, whose name in the Dramatis Personae list is followed by "a young Count, contracted to Marcella, deformed, revengeful" (II, 309). Two pillars of patriarchal, familial control over daughters/nieces enter into the gardens, meet and speak, while the servant Crapine (in Morosini's household what's in a name has little to do with a rose) approaches with "no News" about the absent nieces (II, 326).

Crapine's entrance initiates the almost unceasing motion in the act; he crosses the stage while escorting Morosini and Octavio toward an exit. As the men leave, Marcella and Cornelia, in their first entrance, "drest like Curtezans," pass by (II, 327). Morosini and Octavio hesitate just long enough to establish for the audience that the former knows not his nieces nor the latter, his betrothed. Since the women move from the contained immobility of family to the free space of women moving in the street, their features become individually unrecognizable, simply common. In this case motion itself serves to disguise the two women. According to Behn's representations of the life of women, it does not seem too farfetched to understand the patronymic or married name as a label indicating how the female collected in the domestic space should be regarded, itemized, and shelved. Since the women are not properly "tagged," Morosini and Octavio assume them to be "Whores, Sir, and so 'tis ten to one are all the kind" (II, 327) – not unique and worth collecting, not the property of a specific man and worth restraining.

Paradoxically, because their 'commonness' frees them from the pressure of being on display as goods for the appraising eye, these two women gain a staged privacy, remaining on stage for a brief moment by themselves. Marcella, carrying a book – the transportable commodity *Ovid* – conducts herself as a constant woman, imagining nothing more daring from her time on the street than to glimpse her beloved Fillamour. Cornelia, however, takes to the courtesan dress with happy relish and snatches the book away imagining a "better use for famous *Ovid*," better presumably than reading it. In a truly refreshing response to all those who have read "famous *Ovid*" with increasing concern for the female body count, Cornelia asks: "And prithee what a pox have we to do with Trees,/Flowers, Fountains, or naked Statues?" (II, 327).[21]

Mocking print in one of its most classical embodiments, Cornelia regards the book not as an instrument of learning, nor a revered repository of ancient culture, but as a useful prop for her own scene. The women banter in a manner perfected by Behn in several of the comedies – a discussion of the nature of women and love carried out in a parody of Socratic method. Marcella, though sprightly enough, cautions the wilder Cornelia (originally created as was Hellena for the rakish Mrs Barry), allowing Cornelia to take the stage for her outrageous responses.[22] Like Hellena who must intermix stasis and motion, Cornelia 'takes' the stage for her scene, displaying her comic power in language and play before she surrenders centerstage to another player. Cornelia proves mobile and powerful through her ability to improvise words and scenes; as we will see . . . she has a plan for little Ovid.

"What a damnable wicked thing is a Virgin grown up to a Woman," starts Cornelia (II, 328). A virgin, carefully held out of circulation and exchange, lacks imagination, according to Cornelia. Imagination would unsettle the contract of a virginity offered to a suitor as a unique, non-circulating commodity which can be symbolically collected under the name of the husband. Marcella reminds Cornelia of her duty to her own: "A too forward Maid, Cornelia, hurts her own fame and that of all her Sex" (II, 328). Cornelia no doubt directly addressing the female members of the audience as Barry the actress, and as Cornelia the character, might have momentarily moved out of the fiction to convey Behn's own frustration with her Lady listeners: "my Sex shou'd excuse me, if to preserve their Fame they expected I should ruin my own Quiet" (II, 328). Marcella, all agreement, still worries about "the World." Cornelia, fed up, returns, "Hang the malicious World" (II, 328). Playing behind their vizors, again no doubt directing themselves to the matching ones in the audience, the women speak of Love and whoring as trades separated only by a little "Honor"; yet they do not replicate Octavio's maliciousness by considering the women engaged in the trades as indistinguishable from one another. The female character who chooses for herself moves out of the containment called virginity (whether in physical reality or simply in imagination), engages in acting, disguising herself, and joins in the erotic exchange as a partner to men who have an established place on the street.

As they are now, neither women of quality nor actual courtesans, Cornelia and Marcella risk "the leuder scandal" of being "honest jilts," maids who promise and then renege. According to Behn's dramatic economy false promises merit more shame – the word scandal is used only for jilts – than an honest monetary transaction for sex (II, 329). False promises stop the cycle of exchange, withering the give and take of intercourse into hoarding, deceit, and suspension. In delineating the choices facing the two women, Cornelia defines the performing professions and markets of exchange open to women not under a guardian's or a husband's financial protection. Without money, once the women's only detachable valuables are sold, only one "jewel" remains to be "parted with," a jewel that can be sold over and over again (II, 330). Their freedom of movement would cease were they to find themselves without funds since money lubricates all sorts of trade. Behn's characters make choices about giving and taking from positions defined by a market economy; the characters are pragmatically respectful of their need for money in order to circulate. But Cornelia sways Marcella by encouraging her to imagine a worse constriction than poverty. She describes the scene of the nieces' homecoming: "you to the embraces of the amiable Octavio, and I to St Teresa's, to whistle through a Grate like a Bird in a Cage . . . let's walk and gain new Conquests."[23]

A convent and a "deformed, vengeful" man's embrace represent the enclosures resisted by the outdoor, active, intriguing life of a courtesan. Structuring the play to contrast these opposites, Behn opens the act with Morosini and Octavio; the men's threatened return would banish Marcella and Cornelia from the stage, secluded and kept, held, like the book Cornelia carries, an item of private property. The women elude the men who could not recognize them when on the street, the men who would imprison them in the other opaque cage of female invisibility, virtue. Unlike Angellica's role in *The Rover*, Part I, where high-priced courtesan life encloses female energy as surely as the house of an old man, Cornelia's version of "gay" whoring comes closer to the "pickeroon" women Behn defined in her prologue to *The Forced Marriage*.[24]

Yet Cornelia moves in the demi-theatrical world of the *feigned* courtesan, not really participating in the practical market of a daily whoring life. Her lovers who sigh and sue for her hand do so because of her youth and her novelty in town. She enjoys the fame of the "new," a condition as untested as the virgins she mocks and a fame which might land her in the contract of still beauty Angellica inhabits. Although inconstancy like performance might still prove the preferred life to one of dull tedium in a married state or in a convent, Behn is never naïve about the price of female roaming. Disguise might work from time to time for women in seventeenth-century society, but civil and legal authorities write the ending to the stories performed on the city street. At best Behn's plays can serve to jolt by motion and energy what Judith Butler labeled the "sedentary" assumptions – those categories of collecting – of how women act, what they want, what would happen if they could run free (1990). And at best they do.

Arcing the motion round the stage to draw the third set of protagonists into this cycle, Behn moves the two women "down the Garden" (II, 330). Actors mimic a vital part of exchange when they concede the forestage to their fellows; all acts of giving and taking, of exchange and circulation, require a balance of timing when one is the recipient of attention, actively participating, and when one becomes a part of the collaborative community on stage. The next set of strollers in the garden, already discussed by the women, enter and see the feigned courtesans as they recede into the inner stage. Galliard, like a bored boy suddenly come to life, states the obvious, "Women!" The cry of an anxious lookout in a perpetual crow's nest, his exclamation of a 'sighting' induces immediate response. The women "drest" like courtesans are game "for our purpose too . . . let's follow 'em" (II, 330). Fillamour, who sounds like he has already attended a performance of *The Rover*, Part I, reminds Galliard of the lesser spoils gained by looking: "What shall we get by gazing but Disquiet?" (II, 330). If honest the women will cause sighs, if not honest – Fillamour suffers his scruples alone here – "they are not worth looking at" (II, 330).

The energy of the play hardly wavers with Fillamour's brief desire to stop and look, to arrest the plot; instead the action and exchange swirl more characters about, moving Julio, Fillamour, and Galliard toward the exit only to have them run into Marcella and Cornelia. Each encounter, each re-assessing of the exchange of love, of women and men, of feigned identity supplies the audience with an accruing sense of Behn's varieties of mobile possibility. The never ceasing mobility itself, I suggest, maintains an open conduit to the audience's senses communicating the 'argument' of the play, instructing the audience somatically about the limits of trying to fix into category, into property, into subjugation the body of a being made manifest by circulation, internal and external. While watching a stage on which several characters pause to play, move across the stage, greet each other or suddenly flee, the spectator might experience a moment of wanting to arrest the motion: perhaps from a particular fancy for one of the characters or a confusion about what was just said to whom and why. But a moving act like the one Behn creates tutors us in the inescapable demand of time: no hand can press the pause button, reverse and repeat, rather we must let that moment go or remain stuck in frustration and miss the next part of the moving action. At the stage doors, Laura, who has been enjoying the love of Galliard while he believed her to be the courtesan La Silvianetta, enters tripled in her disguises – first Laura, then courtesan, now a "Man" accompanied by her page Silvio and her attendant Antonio. Fillamour and Galliard, ever distractible, turn and follow Cornelia and Marcella "down the Scene," leaving Laura to look after them from the forestage and speak (II, 330).

Laura tells the audience the tale of her assumed identity while explaining the advantages of crossdressing: "This Habit, besides many Opportunities 'twill give me of getting into his acquaintance, secures me too from being known by any of my Relations in Rome" (II, 331). As she begins to move toward the exit, she is just in time to meet the (other) feigned courtesans trailing their gallants. Laura informs the audience of her intent; though she exits toward the backstage, she will enter another way "round the Garden and "mix my self amongst them" (II, 332). Behn instructs the audience and we know to expect Laura's return, meanwhile we give ourselves over now to the lovers, wit, and wooing, about to take place on the forestage between the prominent quartet come front and center from their previous stage position "down the Garden."

Cornelia controls the space of the forestage, creating the scene with the aid of her Ovid prop, very pointedly directed by Behn she walks "about reading" (II, 332). Cornelia's arrangement of her scene suggests she has seen some Flemish or Dutch paintings (such as Behn might have seen in Holland or England). Her author suggests Cornelia assumes that the "picture" of a woman reading is pleasing to the appraising eye and Rembrandt, ter Borch, and Vermeer agree with her. Behn endows Cornelia with a collector's acumen since Cornelia bases her scene upon the centuries of virgins depicted holy book in hand; a woman reading is a woman at devotion. In another revision of Shakespeare, Cornelia's articulated plotting of this scene reminds the viewer of Polonius' and Claudius' 'trap' of Ophelia walking about with a book in her hand as a bait to catch the conscience of a prince. Giving Ophelia volition and agency, Behn has Cornelia stage herself as collectible, a supposed catch suspended for Galliard's always already raised net.

Behn dispatches Marcella to retire to the inner stage where she can lean "against a tree" and leave her friend to her mobile tableau. Ovid will do as well as St Paul in convincing Galliard that Cornelia is "at [her] Evening's Devotion" (II, 333). The two begin an exchange of wit upon the close conjunction of Devotion and devotion in which Galliard, ever the boy, suggests that Cornelia not "ruin a young Man's good Intentions, unless they wou'd agree to send kind Looks and save me the expense of Prayer" (II, 333). While Cornelia teases back the scene shifts toward Fillamour, who should, while the two rovers engage, become more and more brazen about looking at Marcella. So sure he knows her to be his Marcella, he interrupts the banter center forestage, "offers to run to her," only to have "Gal.[liard] hold him" (II, 334). Performance can highlight the distance between what one thinks one 'knows,' and one's confusion in the protean visual world of what one sees. Centuries of drama turn on the trick of a lover not recognizing the scarcely disguised beloved, but perhaps the tension illustrates a fundamental experience of watching theatre – a spectator gains knowledge incrementally, or allows it to be reconfigured, through reinterpretations of the seen and the heard.

The 'true' lovers' plot interrupts the play lovers' banter, threatening to disrupt it. If Fillamour discovers Marcella, he will undo the 'feignedness' of the courtesans, and, by doing so, return two young women of quality home. A lover's fidelity might abruptly end the roaming, cutting through the need for disguise and intrigue. Luckily Galliard lacks the imagination to conceive of Marcella outside and unprotected. Fillamour, all action, keeps offering "to go" while his friend restrains him, "pulls" him, and finally subordinates himself – going off to the side with Cornelia – letting another couple take the center of attention. Fillamour comes forward to address Marcella in her guise of the courtesan Euphemia. For all his 'noble' love, Fillamour cannot distinguish his beloved under the guise of courtesan, cannot imagine her actively saving herself from her uncle's plot. He will have to learn to use his imagination to reinterpret what he sees, allowing for more wit and spirit in his idea of his beloved before the two can meet in a freely given exchange. Marcella becomes the scourge and minister to Fillamour's misapprehension; hoping Heaven will "punish him" later, she takes up a bit of the sacred task herself. Out of her disappointment Marcella finds a sudden natural talent for dissembling; she portrays the courtesan vigorously, lashing the ignorant lover with terms of the trade: "to Women of our Profession there's no Rhetorick like ready Money, nor Billet-deux like Bills of Exchange" (II, 335).

The choreography of moving actors and actresses circulating, commenting, or testing disguises ruptures as the well-managed vignettes break apart and almost every member of the cast appears on stage. Fillamour's misrecognition and Marcella's anger sunder the minuet of small groups center stage, forestage, exiting and entering. Marcella, the constant lover who participates in the portrayal of a feigned courtesan only to free herself from the wrong lover and eventually give herself to the right one, turns collector, preferring the hard exchange of money to the soft bantering intercourse of a lover's words. Like Angellica's face over her balcony, Marcella's words seem to loose a chaos born of competition and scarcity. Hers is an action which is the direct opposite of Willmore's stealing of the portrait from Angellica's balcony: his action frees the exchange from the trappings of property while Marcella acts to revoke her willing offer. She will not give herself to Fillamour, and thus the giving and receiving, the circulation on stage, dissipates into the raucous armed combat preceding plunder and the taking of spoils.

The pleasure, the entertainment of the chaotic scene is in part made by the sheer number of bodies on the stage. Richard Dyer in *Only Entertainment* sees in certain forms of entertainment – musicals, dance, films – the pleasures of energy and abundance at work in making the form "entertaining," an abundance communicated to the audience by multiple bodies in motion on the stage (1992; see Chapter 1 for a discussion of Dyer's work and Jonson's masque). While offering some sense of "escape" into a world where one might sense "things could be better," these forms do not "present models of utopian worlds," but rather allow the spectators to experience "what utopia would feel like" (18). The freely given can also effect in the spectator a sense of abundance, the opposite effect of calculation and measurement. Dyer hits upon an affective quality of bodies as perceived by the spectator – in Behn's case an abundance of them – moving energetically and wittily across the stage. There are eleven bodies entering and exiting the approximately thirty-foot long and twenty-five foot wide forestage during the fight scene that ensues from Fillamour and Marcella's misrecognition in Act II.[25] Because most modern theatregoers are likely to see plays with casts of two and four, one easily forgets how difficult a feat of staging it is to keep that many bodies in motion on the stage without losing sense of the scene and how exhilarating it can be to watch so many bodies in motion at once.

After the chaotic fight splits the orderly circulation of groups meeting, intriguing, flirting, plotting, and perambulating about the stage, Behn sets up the comic commentary in the scenic stage behind the forestage which ends the act. Sight gags born of panic, Sir Signal "climbs a tree," Tickletext "runs Head into a bush, and lies on his hands and knees" (clearly only buttocks are left to protrude toward the audience) while Petro fights with the Gallants (II, 336). The garden of earthly delights willy nilly becomes the garden of earthy comic sights; an anti-masque of display switching the picture of Cornelia at devotion with one cast from an entirely different genre of Flemish painting. The buffoons, the rude mechanicals, enact a subplot commentary on exchange through a tale told to idiots, signifying the exchange of nothing. After the customary scatological laughs about a snuff with the inescapably suggestive name of Cackamarda Orangate, Petro instructs the dupable Tickletext and Sir Signal about the proper way to "act a story" (II, 341).

Clever, free like his sisters in the trade, Petro is a consummate performer. In his feigned masculine whoring role of pimp, he is not hindered by considerations of quality, Petro embodies the preferences of action and performance when he tells Sir Signal that when acting the story, "no matter for words or sense, so the Body performs its part well" (II, 341). Petro rejects spoken logic, ironically spoofing farce while he creates it. The comic appellations for Tickletext and Buffon suggest a pair of objects, and Behn renders them much more immobile than other characters.[26] So much an object is Tickletext that he enters at the end of the play adorned with an inkhorn on his head and carrying a folio. His costume resembles that of the seventeenth-century French villager described by Natalie Zemon Davis who is made to wear paper and text as a sign of communal derision (see "Printing and the People" in Davis 1975). Behn's Tickletext visually spoofs the textual man.

Petro's satiric methods are pleasures in themselves as well as didactic tools instructing the men about words and slavish literal interpretation. When Petro suggests to Sir Signal that he "flourish," the printed direction records his obedience "[He flourishes]" (II, 339). Tickletext, playing mock audience, applauds him, "Most admirably performed" (II, 340). Signal wants Tickletext to join him in pretended fun, to "out-do me in the Art of presenting," an art joining giving to performing (II, 340). Playing the overly gracious host, but linguistically conflating free giving with warfare, Tickletext "retaliate[s] with this small gem," disposes of his diamond. Sir Signal, audience to his governor, in turn praises him: "Most rhetorically perform'd, as I hope to breathe, Tropes and Figures all over" (II, 340). Because the men inhabit a too literal world, they render things in motion heavy. A literal interpretation often results in frozen knowledge, the circulation of speech abruptly ending in the "thunk" of an idea falling to the ground. (Blunt's name in *The Rover*, Part I continues this connection since his name suggests his literalness and his fate is one of being duped into falling through a trapdoor.) While Sir Signal means to praise his fellow, his manner turns rhetorical *copia*, "Tropes and Figures," into unmanageable objects strewn carelessly about, seeming to clog the very entrances and exits of the stage.

Petro, ever the actor, gets remuneration from the two men by way of his own talented dissembling. The performer in exchange for the spectator's purchase of a place at the theatre 'gives' a performance, and his/her livelihood partially rests on its reception. Yet neither Signal nor Tickletext recognize Petro's specious addition to the giving/receiving model. Having learned to give the two are, not coincidentally, taught to graciously refuse Petro's generous offer of their own baubles back to them. Unlike Marcella's and Cornelia's replenishing jewel, the men's jewels, purely material commodities, are exhausted. When Tickletext asks Petro when they will learn to receive again, Petro happily picks up his cue: "Oh, Sir, that's always a Lesson of it self" (II, 341).

Before the men give any thought to this acting con, Petro offers another. He "act[s] a story" of transformation: "Makes a sign of being fat . . . Puts himself into the Posture of a lean Beggar, his hands right down by his sides, – and picks both their pockets . . . makes the fat bishop" (II, 341). And so forth and so on with the fat Bishop refusing the lean beggar, "Niente," over and over until Petro's slapstick finale, where he opens his arms wide to strike the two spectators in the face. Leaving his scene and the crime, Petro abandons the two men to their pathetic imitation and the act closes on the, much belated, discovery of the robbery and Sir Signal's words: "A pox on all silent stories" (II, 342). From a silent story one can collect nothing but knowledge gained by interpretation, and one's interpretation must be fluid enough to understand the mime as it is happening. At the end of the silent story, in which these two literal-minded characters have not partaken, they find themselves empty-handed; the product of performance in literal terms is nothing. Perhaps Behn implies those who come to the theatre for literal messages will be 'robbed' of their money, receiving no tangible product and having been blocked by their literalness from the experience of transformation.[27]

Behn's specific careful instructions created for Mr Leigh, who acted Petro, certainly would have taken Mr Leigh's acting prowess into consideration.[28] The visual spectacle of this mechanical's commentary not only rests on the customary cullying of the two fools, but on the physical sight of Leigh's body changing from greed, represented by the church and bishops, to need, the lean beggar. A satire on "giving" and "receiving" in miniature, the master at the close of the circulating act in the Garden of the Villa Medici is neither lover, nor rake, but signifying feigned pimp. The motion, the actor, the embodiment of movement and change runs a scam around that pillar of the community in his upright position with his suspended bluster, the clergyman. When Petro offers to teach silent storytelling, Sir Signal enthusiastically responds it "were an excellent device for Mr. Tickletext, when he's to hold forth to the Congregation, and has lost his Sermon notes" (II, 341). Improvisation, one assumes, is not the pastor's strong point.[29]

These two, actor and clergyman, share a mode of dependence different than a playwright or actor's dependence on performance; Tickletext must have his text, the comfort of the artifact from which to speak. The fat Bishop in Petro's story who refuses to give, like Tickletext in his wordy corpulence, becomes bloated, his stinginess an impediment to life-giving exchange. The too literal spectator cannot participate in the fluid exchange of the intangibles of pleasure, of knowledge, of reconfigured suppositions. The opportunity to act, to choose to give is bound by the temporal nature of performance, the mimetic miniature of life's motion, and can be missed or mangled by inaction. Behn's printed "Adieu" I mentioned at the outset of this chapter acknowledges the demands of ending; in a performance sometimes the "Adieu" is ritualized by the asking not of a formal goodbye, but of a conscious act of reception, applause.

Whatever an audience makes of the acting of a story – silent and not – the playwright and the actors offer a performance and must surrender, at the last, control over interpretation. The textual trace of Behn's scene, the italicized stage directions describing Petro's action, reinscribes the odd marriage of the text as silent record of an oral and visual performance. In some sense the story always waits in a space of silence for the collaborative catalyst of embodiment or voice. The silent – like the absence of motion necessary for evaluation as seen in *Epicoene* in Chapter 1 – lends itself to the collectible, the shelved playscript preserved as potential for an acted story. Although in the theatrical space the waiting has the dimension of an empty playhouse, on its vacant stage the text often will set the story in motion, ending, for a time, the silence. The psychic space between stage and pit and boxes expands while inhabited and shrinks when empty, the potent possibility for exchange enacted as the performance begins.

Behn's scene of roaming about the garden with characters speaking of revenge, love, money and words ends in a spectacle of plenty and famine. Petro cozens the men out of their money by tricking them first into participation, then into giving, and finally into its simulacrum, acting. "Gift exchange and erotic life are connected in this regard. The gift is an emanation of Eros . . . libido is not lost when it is given away . . . gift bespeaks relationship" (Hyde 1979: 69). Petro's freedom as well as that of Behn's female 'rovers' comes from manipulating the terms of commodity – in the end Petro improves on his actor's pay by pocketing the two men's jewels. In fact, at the end of the play Petro reveals that the money that has allowed Cornelia and Marcella to roam has been embezzled from the unnoticing Sir Signal; he has financed their play. Traders who know how to move their "libido," who hoard no sexual essence, and who take what they want when it is offered, in having little to lose, gain new mobility and power.

When the earlier scene erupts, it does so because Marcella steps fully into the role of the courtesan ("no rhetorick like ready money") who can be purchased another night, perhaps tomorrow. The world Behn creates on stage partakes of this erotic bounty, offers Marvell his mistress de-coyed. Behn s emphasis on movement and circulation suggests that the pleasurable, nay valuable, exchange offered different satisfactions than those gained by being admired for motionless artistry. These satisfactions, achieved in the fluid realm of the effect one has on the spectators, exist despite the lack of 'hard evidence' of textual success to substantiate and make permanent the claim. Widening the offer of pleasure and play beyond the usual traders, male spectators, Behn played to the women too who evinced a taste for circulation. Commodity carriers, like Cornelia with her little Ovid on display or Petro who trades his "acted story" for a jewel, defy the initial stillness required to become a 'transportable' commodity. Slipping away from the containers used to display wares, as if the barkers/traders suddenly turn to find the 'whore' or the 'virgin' absent, the cage the only motionless thing left on the block, these performers adapt the notions of looseness to fit their own freedom. Choosing with whom they will exchange jewels subverts imprisoned, enclosed, iconic passivity: once again performers (and performance) come, go and take, and come again.

5 Perpetually stilled

Jeremy Collier and John Vanbrugh on bonds, women, and soliloquies

THE ARGUMENT

Where the analogy of gender to forms of production consistently occurs in the writing of all the authors in this book, by the end of the century, marriage, discussions, and representations of it, begins to figure more overtly as a component in the duet of motion and stillness. Though in the works of Aphra Behn there are signs of the social construction of marriage being figured as a device to both control and define, by the end of the century in the work of John Vanbrugh and in the criticisms of the stage wielded by his contemporary Jeremy Collier, the domestic relation of husband and wife offers a basis on which to re-establish values of print and performance, of political relation of subject to ruler, of the behavior of women in marriage and out of it. The value of the still and preservable and that of the moving and ephemeral do not have exact correspondences in the distilled discussions of marriage at the end of the century. Yet the language used to worry over domestic hierarchy and the possibility of allowing for divorce as a choice made by husband and wife does incorporate the terms used throughout the century to determine value for conservation and change. The chapter concludes with a discussion of the use of soliloquies in Vanbrugh's play *The Provoked Wife*. The method Vanbrugh uses to stage soliloquies highlights the change in the nature of self representation on stage, taking up a liminal position between the printed and the performed, producing with the audience a set of equations about self and performance, the written and the spoken, the designed and the spontaneous.

At the turn of the seventeenth century, the self-conscious practice of Ben Jonson as author indicated a change occurring in authorship and theatre practice. Both Jeremy Collier's attack on stage practices (*A Short View of the Immorality and Profaneness of the English Stage*) and Vanbrugh's use of those practices give evidence of the different values being ascribed to the technologies of print and performance at the turn of the eighteenth century in England. As we have seen in previous chapters, the ascribing of value to these modes of production entails ascribing value for the still and the moving. At the meeting of Collier's complaints and Vanbrugh's characterizations, connections are made between representations of gender, of marriage and of property, of property and the self, of stability, and of political participation. In *Epicoene* (1609), Jonson's Morose seeks to establish his authority over Epicoene and insure her silence by "printing on those divine lips the seal of being mine"; in 1698, Collier urges playwrights to follow Jonson's example and control the unruliness of talking wives/women on stage whose voices threaten the established hierarchy (Collier chooses to ignore the critique Jonson makes of Morose's behavior in the body of the play). A husband/author's firm, silent stamp of fixity upon a wife or a female character, in this interpretation, provides a check to the danger and uncertainty of (female) movement. In each of Collier's preoccupied meditations on the representation of women on the stage, married or not, he equates a state of grace, of goodness to stillness (silence) and a state of transgression to the ephemeral, uncontrollable movement of the speaking woman. Even more volatile is the power a wife has to misrepresent her husband by her freedom of speech since she stands for him in public spaces. Collier's suggestions for control while firmly based on his religious authority reach out beyond the domestic to the value of modes of production and representation in flux at the end of the seventeenth century.

Jeremy Collier's reforming stillness

Regulation desires an audience; it is nonsensical if it is not created by demanding that something or someone be withheld or removed. A regulation carries little force unless it explains as part of its regulating power why the hands and bodies engaged in reception are harmed by the circulation of the wicked thing.[1] In his *A Short View of the Immorality and Profaneness of the English Stage* (1698), Jeremy Collier, while complaining of the treatment of clergy and the decadence of rakes, opens, dilates and closes upon the "immodesty" of the stage, the disgrace to and abuse of women in the audience, and the profaneness of conversing female characters on the stage. Collier articulates his confusion in a traditional form employed by male minds ruminating upon female behavior, the question: "Do the Women leave all the regards to decency and Conscience behind them, when they come to the Playhouse?" Collier, with what David Roberts terms an "air of a courtly sentimentalist," suffers "bafflement" at the contradiction of what a female is versus how she behaves (1989: 140). Such bafflement has, over the ages, proved more oppressive than overt misogyny. Mystery provides a convenient screen absolving its purveyors of the responsibility to listen to individual women dispel bafflement with facts. Cloaking oppression in a tone of concern, authors expend pages and pages of print in thoughtful inquiry about the nature of the "female" and the proper behavior toward 'them.' The creation of such an audience demands a contract of stillness and motion not unlike the one Behn criticizes in *The*

Rover where the idea of woman and the necessary absence of a specific woman (or various specific women) offer the still space for the moving pen to create its enshrined ideal.

For Jeremy Collier, as for many playwrights and writers at the turn of the eighteenth century, the creation of a section of the audience called "The Ladies" was as vital to his project of reforming the stage as his exhaustive production of evidence about the abuses of ladies as characters on the stage. The stage had long been acquainted with the ploy of creating a supposedly timid coterie of female audience members. Snug the Joiner precedes his halfhearted roaring in *A Midsummer Night's Dream* with a prologue writ expressly to "The Ladies" who might be frightened by his impersonated beastliness. In her preface to *The Lucky Chance,* Behn loses patience with a public adoption of primness by some group called "The Ladies," particularly because it is a primness not witnessed by the author herself when in private conversation with said ladies. For Behn, and later for Collier and the writers of pamphlets and periodicals at the turn of the eighteenth century, the creation of the entity of the "Ladies" was a printed phenomenon. By means of an invention necessarily dependent upon the regular dissemination and circulation of text, Collier in his reforming zeal, and periodical writers in their need to make and sustain an audience for their regular and regulatory publications, created what Kathryn Shevelow calls a "textual *projection*" (1989: 32).[2]

A form of print that considers itself in conversation with its readers must project (and therefore seek to define) an audience. Ben Jonson tried to establish an intimate relation to the worthy reader of his poetry while Milton hoped to convert his reader by the persuasive power of his printed drama. Yet in the early part of the century, as we have seen, this reader was most often a corporeal presence, addressed as a present auditor. In the theatre playwrights sought in their own way to "create" an audience, shaping an audience by content and presentation, but they sought to make that audience out of the bodies present. In Behn's prologue to *The Forced Marriage*, for example, a female actor interrupts the male actor and appeals to the "Ladies" in the audience (not as either a shy or modest crowd), a staged moment offering the actress the opportunity to seek out the female bodies and make eye contact or gesture toward them.

In the increasingly abstract world of the printed diurnal and late-century pamphlet, however, writers shape their audiences out of the idea of who *might* be the readers. Even if writers still encounter their readers from time to time, the task of imagining the readers is increasingly one of invention and construction set to work to encourage participation, but participation at a distance. The *gradual* framing in the construction of a somewhat distant audience of readers can be likened to the *gradual* displacement of acting bodies behind a proscenium frame in the theatre. Readers were imagined to be receiving the work no longer in the street or the coffeehouse but rather in the public/private of the home (see Epilogue). Though the addressed reader in the imagined public/nation is generally taken to be male, there are efforts to create a community of readers in the public sphere who are women and these women are usually sought after as potential regulators – voices for modesty and an influence for propriety.[3]

I do not link Collier's pamphlet to the new periodicals by happenstance. The project of Collier's several pamphlets, and the flurry of pamphlets in response, as well as the project of much of the new periodical writing, is one of reform or the rejection of reform.[4] The use in Collier's and other reforming writers address of the "Ladies" is an attempt to sculpt an opinion for a group who will identify with it when they read it, adopting ladylike views in accordance with one's sense of oneself as a Lady. In earlier decades such addresses to the "Ladies" appeared most often in prologues to plays, that is, as the poet's invitation for an exchange of masculine winking and nodding, "mere referents of sexual experience." Later invocations of the "Ladies" shine from the opening poem/prologue like beacons of a moral flame (Roberts 1989: 28). While addresses made to other factions in the audience – cits, wits, fops – also took place in the exceedingly tongue-in-cheek form of Prologue and Epilogue, the overwhelming use of the "Ladies" as a device to achieve moral homeostasis belongs to the particular trend of theatre in the 1690s. "Ladies" followed by a comma (potentially a pause on the stage) allows the poet (most often "he") to excuse himself as Vanbrugh does in the opening of *The Relapse*, to sue for good opinion, or to acknowledge his lack of access to what "they," this conveniently mysterious entity "Ladies," might find wanting in the play.[5]

The collective corrective entitled "Ladies" wielded an ambiguous power not unlike the eternal reference of 'Mom,' as in 'what would your mother say,' even if your own personal mother might very well say, 'bully for you.' Segments of the population who communicate and convey culture through predominantly oral means can be easily made use of in print by those who control the published medium. In this way motion can disempower because it disperses the opinions of a group whose presence is not represented by their printed, and therefore conserved, voices. Ironically, the "Ladies" become visible not out of their own attendance at the theatre and critical response to plays but because they are ubiquitously counterfeited in the playwright's Prologue, given substance out of the opinions attributed to them.[6] While the society of the "Ladies" no doubt includes those women who found the theatre an unfit place for themselves and their reputations, I propose that this particular address of the "Ladies" as a faction coincides with a social need to rein in the potentially anarchic stage, a cyclical desire played out in the earlier history of antitheatrical tracts (see Barish 1981 and Howard 1987). In order to take the strumpet out of the stage, and to distinguish between the strumpet actress and the proper "Ladies" in the audience, critics and reformers wielded what Behn wittily named "the old never failing scandal," the claim that the play "was not fit for the Ladies" (Preface to *The Lucky Chance*, 1915: III, 185).

Throughout Collier's complaining tract, he worries over the nature of woman as if the consummate representation of woman, silent and beautifully modest, would in turn produce a chaste theatre.[7] The theatre will be disciplined by some of its practitioners and its audience in much the same way in the coming century; Collier, though irritating and longwinded, did influence (or confirm) the opinions of his readers by collecting together their conservative sentiments about theatre in 1698. He fashioned an argument suggesting that simply by arresting the movement and speech of female characters, the theatre (and by extension society) would benefit, would become clean, proper, uplifting.

Looking to women in the playhouse, both players and fictional characters, Collier cannot reconcile his assessment of female comportment to the "use" of the "Ladies" (1698: 13). Collier and the audience he addresses recognize prologues and epilogues as a meeting between the play of fiction and immediate moment where "the actors quit the Stage, and remove from fiction into life" (13). In such moments, one suspects precisely because they represent a liminal space between fiction and the everyday, according to Collier "we have lewdness without shame or example" (13). Turning the "converse" to "address directly" the audience, the poets abuse the "Ladies," and what's worse, "Women are commonly pick'd out for this service" (13). The direct address on stage of an actress to the "Ladies" about the goings on between "Ladies" Collier finds "would turn the stomach of an ordinary debauchee" (13).

The potential offense in the delivery of self-assured, distressingly knowing and ironic prologues and epilogues by women can best be reanimated by using Susan Foster's model of the "choreography" of gender rather than the language-based term "performance". Foster's theoretical suggestion reminds us to imagine multiple bodies in the process of performing in gesture and sound, a multiplicity at the theatre Collier can imagine only in threatening terms (1998). The actress in her repertoire of motion and play moves vocally and physically when performing the suggestive text, her movements are received, perhaps interpreted and reinvented by other female bodies in the audience. There need be no more than 'minimal' choreography, a wink, a shift of the hip, a drop in the vocal register, but I suspect Collier worries over the tension (and attention) created between groups of women and a woman on stage, a community not commonly forged in public spaces. Collier recognizes a political danger more uncontrollable than bawdy plays; direct public communication between women on stage and in the playhouse might seriously undercut the spoken and written male 'authorities' who know better than women what "Woman" should be, and who want young women to be trained to dance that contained masculine choreography of Woman.

While a male poet's wrongheaded or vulgar abuse of women strikes Collier as profane and distasteful, the possibly vigorous and bawdy interchange between women in the playhouse does violence to his idea of the character of Woman. Even more violence is done to his idea of how women behave (particularly together), what they actually say and do. Even though the male poet writes the prologue so offensive to Collier's imagination, what is most wrong with this picture is that the "Ladies" in the pit and boxes are not being "used with respect" by the lady actress on the stage. Aphra Behn's declamation in her prefaces that women's private conversation runs to far greater randyness than the public avowals of their modesty suggests came from one who probably heard and participated in exchanges in private among women.

The return of the 'silent woman'

Collier harps repeatedly on the visible lewdness of a talking woman: "The old Romans were particularly careful there [*sic*] women might not be affronted in Conversation; for this reason the unmarried kept off from entertainments for fear of learning new language" (1698: 23). A woman unseen is unheard as Collier repeats the familiar correlation between visibility, motion, and the sound of a woman's voice partaking in conversation. The wise ancients denied their main female characters "any share of conversation upon the stage." A "share" in the conversation, in Collier's assessment, constitutes female "freedom," in fact "too much" a freedom "for the reservedness of a maiden-character" (20). To have a share in the talking renders a woman a linguistic property holder, her spoken opinion or response proof of a license to exchange talk, to converse.[8]

Worrying about the value of "shares" in the marketplace of conversation as it is represented on stage – and the possibility that the sight of women speaking freely might not just reflect a fictional dramatic world but produce those freedoms offstage – Collier shudders at the sight of a female talk merchant. Like Milton's Lady in *A Maske* who wonders if the freedom of speech she enjoys with Comus inevitably unlocks other chaste lips, Collier sees wantonness spread through the body of talking women who exhibit freedom: single ladies who speak suffer "under . . . disorders of liberty" (12). A woman who is free, both in the sense of unmarried and in the sense of unfettered, confuses Collier, who looks for the sign of her place in the world demarcated by the name of father or husband, or demarcated by her invisible silence, her acknowledgment of her lack of shares in public conversation. She is in Collier's universe placed firmly again upon the shelf, and one need only remember the coming portrayal of womanhood in Richard Steele's *The Conscious Lovers* where the frequently mute Indiana, emblematic of all collectible properties, kneels at the feet of Belville, Jr. to proclaim him, "my husband, my lord."[9]

The wariness with which speaking women have been received on the stage and in literature is nothing new: scolds on stage and scolds in the streets, talking women have been punished by bridles on their tongues, both fictional and real. However, in Collier's assessment at the end of the seventeenth century, speaking now carries weight in the world as a way of purveying personal status and *individual* property. More perilous than the shame or embarrassment a husband might suffer by his wife's words, the art of her speaking introduces her into a sphere of social business. Unlike 'manly' conversation, where two or more equal shareholders discuss business, a talking maid on stage displays "impudence," according to Collier, only infrequently mediated by her author's characterization of her as "sometimes . . . silly, and sometimes mad" (12). A maiden-character, like the silent woman, proves her unacquisitive virtue in silence. By not unduly fluctuating, giving voice to opinion and possible disagreement, she exists as a secure risk. Denying herself shares by remaining silent, she swells the coffers of her father or her fiancé by quietly investing in his own words the silent second of her obedience. Such female silence, thus invisible and modest, reinforces the hierarchy of the family Collier longs to [re]instate on stage.

Individual actresses, such as Elizabeth Barry, Mary Betterton, and Nell Gwyn, provided the post-Interregnum writers with models of particular force and energy; no doubt in rehearsal and in production the women might well have undone the stereotypes the authors themselves brought to the playhouse (Payne 1995). Many backstage anecdotes, Pepys' oft-cited lament about Nell Gwyn's disturbing freedom in her dressing room between acts for example, describe men shocked at how women really behaved. Even if briefly and imperfectly, the drama of the 1660s, 1670s, and early 1680s with its energy and multiplicity jostled the static position of looker and silently looked upon when bawdy, imaginative women moved about and a few male characters were willing to exchange the role of looker for the role of listener. Collier, and other like-minded reformers, by placing emphasis on the silence of woman, and interpreting that silence according to the whim of the speaking/writing male, reinforces the interpreter/interpreted relation of property. For Collier as later for Addison and Steele – those purveyors of the newest form of printed exchange – Woman exists to be observed, read, and interpreted.[10] If done correctly, the careful scrutiny and interpretation of text, of gesture and performance, like the interpretation of Woman, will, Collier argues, expose the immorality of the theatre.

In an unintentional *double entendre* his enemies must have loved, Collier names "show, music, action and rhetorick," "moving entertainments" whose "force and motion," while "things indifferent," can in use be like a "cannon seized" and "pointed the wrong way" (1698: 2). Disconcerted by performance – motion is a thing indifferent until *in use* – Collier treats plays as texts and his own work as critical commentary, citing page references to scripts rather than recounting memorable performances. Once under way, however, Collier finds the world of dramatic/literary criticism a bit cumbersome. Collier hopes "the reader does not expect I should set down chapter and page, and give him the citations at length" (3). To do so for

Collier would "be unacceptable and foreign employment." Lest you think Mr Collier a lazy scholar, he protests that the sentences from the drama are so vile to the touch, they "are in no condition to be handled" (3).

Print does not distance the hands or mind enough to keep them from contamination in Collier's universe. Collier's brief animation of language reveals what Julie Stone Peters in her essay "'Things Govern'd By Words': Late Seventeenth-century Comedy and the Reformers" calls the "heartfelt, reality-bound, literal language of the reformers" whose discomfort with the immodest is a discomfort with the "self-referential, involuted language of much late seventeenth-century comedy" (1987: 142). Peters figures the split as one based in the "Roman Church and the stage" whose "self-referential rituals" violate the "anti-figurative reform (no matter how High-Church Collier may have been) and the attack on the stage" (142). As Milton found to his dismay in the reception to his pamphlets on censorship and divorce, the space provided in a literary creation of the figural often gives the interpreter room to move. Thus multiple truth while conceptually invigorating is unmanageable in conservative, legislative terms. Collier gets caught in the paradox of the literal (certain, unified) and the figurative (suggestive, multiple) when he makes *double entendres* he cannot let himself 'see' and thus understand.

Collier's disgust at the shifting use of language, particularly fueled by the oral power of performance, must be understood in the context of his condemnation of the treatment of the "Ladies." When words are no longer "attached to the essential presence of reality," then women are no longer synonymous with Woman (Peters 1987: 142). As Peters sees it, "Collier, the reformers, and the dramatists of sentiment all refuse to accept a world of contradictions, [one made of] multiple and fragmented vision" (149). We return to the earliest troubled responses to theatre, that it is multiple, too quick to slip away, too various to categorize. Woman becomes many women in the audience and on the stage, one set of them not blushing enough, the other, not blushing at all, and too many of them to watch simultaneously.

With the help of Ben Jonson's maxim, Collier defines a "just writer" for stage or page as *he* who "will avoid obscene and effeminate language" (1698: 51).[11] Like Jonson's other equation, "a whore and so much noise," the "obscene and effeminate" are presumably the same thing. Obscene derives one of its meanings from the theatrical term scene – in French, *obscène*, in Latin, *obscaenus* – too much scene, too much show. Effeminate, an adjective usually reserved for 'aberrant' males, paired with obscene, designates inordinate display as an activity distinctly 'female.' Continuing the debate of show and/or tell taking place throughout the century, Collier and colleagues dress the questions of language and correct usage in the costume of gender. Fretting about the corruption of language, Collier sees the volatile lack of stable, culturally unanimous meaning as dangerous, read effeminate and obscene.

The proper(ty) wife and the provoked one

As if the instability caused by an unfaithful property, a debauching wife, is not enough, Collier weds the fear of property in motion to an old complaint made of the theatre: "But on our stage how common is it to make a Lord, a Knight, or an alderman a cuckold?" (24). Like the wicked theatre in which she plays, the talking, active wife endangers her husband's self-possession, self definition. Without his consent, she can steal away, love another and in so doing change her husband's nature from upstanding citizen to cuckold, change his social appearance, and give him horns. Collier equates this 'modwivery' with the serious business of careful objective calculation, cuckoldry "almost drawn up into a science" (24). Do the female practitioners turn scientists in their experiments? Certainly the plays excite the interest of the English male audience whom Collier fears will acquiesce to their own ruin, seduced by the innovation of these wives turned cuckolding theorists. He cites the alertness of the Romans who were "awake upon the theatre and would not suffer the abuses of honor and family, to pass into diversion" (24).

When attacking the behavior of wives in the drama, Collier worries less about female modesty at the playhouse than about male honor, an honor tied to family, an honor increasingly tied to money management and self promotion (Ketcham 1985: 2). Wives with the power to change the honor of a man, to mock his own notion of himself, were entirely too free, their plotting of a self-conscious nature at odds with "the distinguished thing, modesty." The Roman government, according to Collier, saw the threat to the nation in any abuse on stage that portrayed a skewed hierarchy of the family. And indeed many 1670s, 1680s, and 1690s plays supplied ingenious means to cuckold.[12]

Though no longer a sacrament modeled on the wedding of Christ to his bride the Church, marriage in late seventeenth-century England shored up the more earthly jointure of family and property.[13] Debauching wives and improperly behaved property have their lewd start at the marriage altar. In *Love Triumphant* Dryden writes "for virgin, for whore" into the marriage jingle, horrifying Collier in its blasphemous echo of "for better, for worse." To play with the sacred language of the marriage service, to play with Christ's infrequent pronouncements on the married state, undoes the mystical marriage of word and bond in the sight of an audience under the influence of the drama. Collier chastises Congreve, never at a loss for quips about marriage, because Cynthia in *The Double Dealer* turns Genesis and Jesus to her own purpose: "I am thinking . . . that tho' marriage makes a man and wife one flesh, it leaves them two fools" (1698: 82). One wonders whether Collier's already raised Christian ire suffered increase at the notion of a female character on stage who utters, simply, "I am thinking."

Though there are wives and husbands aplenty on the English stage in the early 1600s, at the end of the century the space of the domestic changes.[14]

Rather than a place where a secret desire for power might be whispered into a cowardly husband's ear, the representation of late seventeenth-century domestic space offers analogies and allusions to public life and one's place in it as property and property owner. In a gambling scene from Aphra Behn's *The Lucky Chance* (1687) Sir Cautious Fulbank – a name coined out of hard currency – handles his property Lady Fulbank recklessly, horrifying a growing class of critics whose sensibilities are too tender to witness even fictional property owners being careless. Behn's frank representation of two men haggling over the property wife perturbed the audiences in 1687, who, to Behn's annoyance, considered the play too bawdy. Behn's play, like Sir John Vanbrugh's *The Provoked Wife* (1696), had little smutty language, and, in general, less smutty action, than the out-and-out lasciviousness of many plays in the 1680s. However, both these vociferously denounced plays shared a performed view of the unfolding of property relations in marriage underscored by an obvious sympathy for the women who suffered the daily plight of a greedy and loutish husband, Sir Cautious, or a coarse and violent one, Vanbrugh's Sir John Brute.

Debates on the stage or in print about marriage and divorce, as in *Epicoene*, Milton's *Doctrine and Discipline of Divorce*, and *The Lucky Chance*, intermix language about (1) the strumpet *cum* speaking woman and property; (2) performance and the bond of matrimony; (3) print and the "binding" of marriage; and (4) print and the "broadside" of cuckoldry.[15] While talking wives rebel on stage by fashioning lives "accessorized" with lovers from the mid-seventeenth century on, the complaints against the avalanche of such "sex comedies," as Robert Hume names them, grew sterner in the 1690s, culminating in Collier's attack (1976: 333). To Michael Cordner's assessment in "Marriage Comedy After the 1688 Revolution: Southerne to Vanbrugh," that *The Provoked Wife* demonstrates "female modesty" as a "socially acquired skill" rather "than an inherent characteristic," I would add the play represents marriage itself as a socially acquired contract, reassessed (1990: 287). Cordner notes that this "exploration . . . is deployed with ingenious resource via a consideration of behavior in the playhouse," after which he footnotes Collier (287).

To explore marriage through discussing behavior at the playhouse is to yoke it to the notion that all social behavior can be interpreted as a form of acting. Both the choices available to and the strictures imposed upon a late seventeenth-century Englishwoman or man hint at the more subtle ways of, in Susan Melrose's words, "making do." Combining the theories of Pierre Bourdieu and Michel de Certeau, Melrose suggests the skilled author and actor will "have observed, and be able to embody, not just the contradictions of her or his formative lived conditions, but also the observed conditions of his-her social other" (1994: 89). Though Melrose writes of the twentieth-century theatre, her observations hold true for earlier periods. The "behavior in the playhouse" offers itself for consideration precisely because playwrights, actors and audience understand the "contradictions" in the social conditions in which they live and because they have observed the social conditions of each other, inside and outside the playhouse. The drama provides a forum where the playwrights question what is and is not a socially acquired skill or socially manufactured bond. The strategy of motion employed by Behn's wives and daughters becomes, as Vanbrugh transforms it, a strategy more contained, more suspended, proof of a more distanced address. Vanbrugh uses forms of tactical soliloquies staged so as to put pressure on the audience to interpret and participate in scenes and yet do so from a perspective both more reflective and distant.

As if he had a prescient notion of Collier's obsession with the profaneness of the stage and "the Ladies," Vanbrugh gives two women free rein to discuss "behavior in the playhouse" as seen in the dilemma of the theatrical blush. In *The Provoked Wife*, Lady Brute and Bellinda, having confessed to rehearsing the role of lady in public in front of their "glasses," discuss the problem of enacting 'lady at Playhouse.' Bellinda, while adept at most ladylike acting, knows not

> what face I should make when they come blurt out with a nasty thing in a play. For all the men presently look upon the women, that's certain; so laugh we must not, though our stays burst for it, because that's telling the truth and owning we understand the jest. And to look serious is so dull, when the whole house is a-laughing.
>
> (II. iii. 74–8)

This analysis goes a step further in Lady Brute's care: "Besides, that looking serious does really betray our knowledge in the matter as much as laughing with the company would do; for if we did not understand the thing we should naturally do like other people" (III. iii. 78–87).

Meta-theatrical pleasures form a particularly self-conscious exchange. An actor can address the audience who simultaneously recognize that they are following a story in performance while being made acutely aware of where they are and how they behave at the theatre, as an audience. Even though Bellinda and Lady Brute (and the actresses playing them) portray a knowing intelligence about being observed and interpreted, there is a coolness to Vanbrugh's playing with the audience, an acknowledgment of the world weary status of social self-consciousness. Unlike Behn's characters who reveal the lover hidden under the tablecloth only to kick the table over and start the action again, Vanbrugh's characters know, reveal, but don't seem to be able to do; a frozenness that serves in the play to "show" the audience the injustice in a society without recourse to divorce. The arresting of motion Vanbrugh employs in his emphasis on language (not enough of course for Collier's satisfaction) proceeds from a world of representation inevitably influenced by the technological advance of printed production and its reception during the century, as well as a society that has moved from an intact monarchy, to Revolution, to Restoration, to Glorious Revolution, and the advent of Whigs and Tories.

In mock seriousness Lady Brute and Bellinda investigate the dilemma of the specularity of Woman in the playhouse audience. They discuss the dilemma of the "blush" with a complete understanding and sophistication Collier cannot stomach. Blood to the face signals modesty or in certain cases too much knowing; marking such signs of modesty are the male watchers of the female visage. In Vanbrugh's play learning by the senses has been disrupted by an *a priori* intrigue of awareness. Between apprehension and comprehension, Vanbrugh's characters imply, is now the distance and delay which becomes interpretation, a mode of social being reflected throughout the drama of the eighteenth century and beyond. In articulating the terms of being watched and being 'read' in the face, the two women debunk any cherished belief that the "Ladies" respond by instinct, rather they deftly employ collection and invention, to use the formal terms of Rhetoric. Bellinda describes playhouse behavior befitting the refurbished tennis court theatres in which the plays were staged after 1660. The audience watches the stage until a bawdy remark turns male heads back to observe "the Ladies'" response ("for all the men presently look upon the women, that's certain"), to examine the face for clues about the virtue of the spectator. Since most plays abounded in smutty witticisms, the heads of much of the audience must have resembled the rhythmic following of point, set, and match.

In her earlier soliloquy in Act I, the debauching wife Lady Brute, like the talking maid Bellinda, speaks reason in methodical argument, a scandal to Collier, who denounces the play in his pamphlet. Representing at first what Collier denotes a struggle "between conscience and lewdness" (1698: 147), Lady Brute shortly concludes "the part of a downright wife is to cuckold the husband . . . tho against the statute-law of religion, yet if there were a court of Chancery in heaven, she should be sure to cast him" (I. i. 83). Such a soliloquy by a female character placed almost at the very beginning of the play surprises since those innovations went the way of all Behn plays several years before (Skantze 1994). Standing alone downstage in 1697, Elizabeth Barry would have captured her audience's attention as she considers her character's position, ascertains the consequences, canvasses her heavenly judges, and finds herself acquitted of any but a just form of action. At work in this performance would be what Marvin Carlson calls "ghosting": the presence in the memory of the audience of previous parts an actor has played on the stage (1994). Against the spirit of Barry's years past when she played the witty, intelligent, unrepentant rovers in her younger days, here in her forties, she uses wit and motion to create a sinuous argument for divorce by mobile and performed thinking aloud.[16]

The passages Jeremy Collier cites to give evidence of Lady Brute's questionable, talkative character all appear in the powerful soliloquy she speaks near the opening of the play. Vanbrugh stresses the trouble in the marriage by having Sir John enter solo to open the play and leaving Lady Brute solo at the end of the same scene. No happy repartee between deftly sparring couples here. Sir John speaks immediately in characteristically irrational bad temper of his conjugal dissatisfaction: "My lady is a young lady, a fine lady, a witty lady, a virtuous lady – and yet I hate her" (I. i .8–9). Reason not the need. Lady Brute then enters, asks a considerate question and receives a barrage of mean-spirited responses. A comic problem at the opening of a comedy surprises no one, but a comic dilemma between a couple already in the indissoluble state reserved for the end of comedy presents an unsettling beginning. Will the play reconcile the two? How, with a new understanding? With a (not legally tenable) divorce?

Lady Brute addresses the audience in a thirty-line soliloquy regarding marriage, husbands and wives, and her particular marriage. Collier's fury possibly owed much to the central position of this talking lady, her freedom of thought, her liberty of choice and decision, displaying all the indecency he rails about in his tract. Even more threatening to the sovereignty of husbands and fathers is the obvious sympathy Vanbrugh nurtures in the audience for this mistreated wife. Betterton as Sir John Brute would, according to all reports, have played the Brute full brutishly; the public's love of Elizabeth Barry and her happy sidekick Anne Bracegirdle as Bellinda would have secured the audience's sympathies.[17]

How hard to reconcile "the precious Ladies" vulnerable to ill usage with such strong representatives of a different "type" of woman – both the character of Lady Brute and the actress Elizabeth Barry – clearly aware of the unequal terms of the marriage/sexual contract: "I thought I had charms enough to govern him, and that where there was an estate a woman must needs be happy" (ll. 48–9). What else could she think, since to be married well was her highest achievement? Yet she understands her part, her "vanity" deceives, and "her ambition" made her "uneasy" (ll. 50–1). Barry might have moved across the stage in thought, gesturing toward her own charms, indicating the trend of her thoughts by the play of her features. If an actress chooses, she could turn this reasoned speculation into a flighty occasion for showing the quick changes in the female mind. But the speech itself shows a relentless movement toward reasoned action.

Considering the paucity of choices left her, primarily to take a "gallant," Lady Brute thinks upon her husband's brutishness and wonders "how far he may provoke me" (l. 55). She admits she "never loved him," yet has been "true to him," though sorely tried by the presence of her appealing suitor Constant. The thought of the appealing lover gives vent to a startlingly different interpretation of heaven's intent: is her husband's ill usage heaven's retribution for her "cruelty to" her lover? Now God stand up for adulterers.

Querying herself in the faux objective stance of barrister or scientist, and one imagines Barry cross-examining herself with relish, the Lady enunciates the contract: "What opposes? My matrimonial vow? Why, what did I vow? I think I promised to be true to my husband. Well; and he promised to be kind to me" (ll. 65–7). Lady Brute brings her audience along this train of thought, and her author has employed no characters in a previous scene to report upon her, to undercut the dignity of her speech. In fact Vanbrugh's opening with Sir John's brutishness and Lady Brute's calm consideration upends the expectations of "reasonable man" and "irrational woman." Continuing to puzzle out word and bond, Lady Brute concludes, "But he han't kept his word. Why then I'm absolved from mine. Aye that seems clear to me" (ll. 67–9). And should be clear to us in the audience.

Soliloquies and the aesthetic of stillness

It is possible for a critic searching for representations of a thinking and self evaluating character to follow the soliloquies of this century from the beginning with 1600 and *Hamlet* through to 1697 with the soliloquy of Lady Brute. Such a course would take one from "table books" and self query by way of familiar maxims to a linguistic shift in the understanding of the word "soliloquy" itself, a word which, Raymond Williams suggests, after the Restoration, "became a dramatic term for what only then seems to have been recognized as an exceptional kind of speaking" (1954: 75). The performance of a soliloquy on stage has much to do with the aesthetics of stillness and motion, of the supposedly "internal" workings of the character and the external performance of action. Margreta De Grazia suggests the staging of *Hamlet* calls for Hamlet to be reading "upon a booke" for the "to be or not to be" soliloquy, complicating the play of influence and thinking represented, according to De Grazia, not as original, sudden ideas, but as remembrance of common knowledge, a thinking in common rather than psychological invention (1995: 74). Importantly Hamlet *appears* reading upon a book in stage directions as well as in De Grazia's gined staging.

An attempt to draw an analogy in order to distinguish the status of playing, reading, stillness, and motion at the beginning and at the end of the century runs the risk of reducing an ongoing transition into a sudden change. Yet a transition can be discerned where a character speaking a soliloquy on stage no longer reads 'upon' the book, shares common thoughts, but must in some sense become the book speaking, as if dictating a written text to him or herself. Though the audience receives the speech as spontaneous, the shared sense of common knowledge, of audience and character thinking in common, recedes. The performance of individual thinking becomes its own staged *tour de force*.[18] In the soliloquies of Lady Brute and Constant (discussed below) the working of 'textual speech,' speech made not of bits of remembered texts but speech written as it were into a text, creates the staged scene.

Lady Brute, property of her husband, assesses her 'owner.' If he defaults, she can be absolved. The bawdiness Collier finds in her speech is wanton not because of its sexual looseness but because of Lady Brute's intellectual agility. When "ill used," ladies at least can be pardoned, but when they take the property of their marriageable bodies into their own hands, assess their "rights," and act accordingly, then they exist independent of modest, inventoried property, collected and labeled a wife. Lady Brute moves from domestic to political spheres with ease, opening the case to bear even more on the citizens sitting in the playhouse. On the heels of her absolution comes her wider reasoning: "The argument's good between the king and the people, why not between the husband and wife?" (I. i. 70–1).

In her discussion of *The Provoked Wife* in *Players' Scepters*, Susan Staves notes that "the play toys with the issue of how far an argument likened to that between King and people might go to justify the rebellion of wives, though Vanbrugh is unwilling to press it so far as to allow his heroine to commit adultery with her gallant" (1979: 180). Yet I suggest that Vanbrugh "presses" the matter by theatrical argument rather than through his character's speech and actions. *The Provoked Wife* is ingenious in the way it works to leave the *audience* dissatisfied with Lady Brute's marriage. This potential longing (taking into account not all audience members might have responded in the same fashion) in the spectators to see Lady Brute shunt off her awful husband, a longing based not simply on her attractive intellect or the goodness of her lover but upon the reasonableness of her cause, is *strengthened* by Lady Brute's 'innocence.' Had she cuckolded Brute, he would have got what he deserved and there's an end on it, but as it is, she remains stuck to a brute and the curtain falls. When theatre productions work as a political catalyst, they can work by the 'how' of what an audience experiences as much as by 'what' an audience hears. Rebellion usually is fomented precisely because the weight of injustice without release presses down until something must be done. Where a playwright holds the action still – for example, Vanbrugh freezes the potential motion of the love story between Lady Brute and Constant – the representation he or she creates can have a moving affect upon the audience who in turn long for change to the conditions of injustice portrayed before them.

Continuing to imaginatively dismantle legal hierarchies, Lady Brute refines her argument of marriage via monarchy. She amends her understanding of "absolution," for a monarch who has been false to promises made to a subject, to include her recognition of the power of common, nay national, understanding which supersedes the evidence of documentation: "O, but that condition was not expressed," meaning not printed, "no matter," she says, "'twas understood" (I. i. 71–2). Like Behn's female characters in *The Roundheads; or, the Good Old Cause*, Lady Brute refines a model for marriage and choice in light of recent transactions between the monarchy and the people. The sovereignty theory circulating during 1688 – if a King does not fulfill his promises the people cannot be bound to theirs – while perhaps not ratified and made permanent in a printed contract, still held sway in opinion and action (Vanbrugh 1969: 7).[19] If Raymond Williams is right and soliloquy began to take on its changed meaning in England after the "Restoration," I suspect it did so not simply because of technological changes in production and philosophical changes in calculating the location of the self, but in the political/national changes whereby contested commonplaces like divine right were held up to the light of human action. (Milton's charge leveled at Charles I in his role as King already suggests the subject's role as critic, see Chapter 3). Staged rumination, while arguably a quintessentially solitary act, when taken up across questions of fidelity and duty becomes a participatory phenomenon, one fundamentally moving between internal query and external proof. Thus can Lady Brute look to her "monarch" with the confidence of a female subject loosed from her ties by her sovereign's broken word.

Coming to the end of her contemplation, Lady Brute finds this self assessment powerfully influential. If she "argue the matter a little longer" with herself, she will find fewer obstacles than she once assumed. In fact those "old foolish philosophers," upon whose credit women take "fine notions of virtue," look downright wrong in the wake of the Lady's pondering. Enumerating old rules in a singsong fashion (perhaps delivering them in a singsong voice) turns these rigid products of a disciplinarian, oral culture into nonsense: "virtue's its own reward, virtue's this, virtue's that." Lady Brute finishes her list upon Collier's hated note – "virtue's an ass." Collier drops his condemnation of this line in an aside in the midst of a discussion of female obedience to fathers and respect of "duty," thereby omitting the preceding lines where Lady Brute subverts those exact terms of virtue (1698: 147). In rejecting old maxims – she is *not* reading out of an imaginary commonplace book though she is rehearsing (and rejecting) common knowledge – Lady Brute takes the staged opportunity to redefine "virtue," the indelible mark of a good woman, as an "ass," tradable for a "gallant," who's worth forty times more.

With an air of mock courtliness Vanbrugh in *A Short Vindication of The Relapse and The Provoked Wife from Immorality and Profaneness* suggests Collier's conviction that Vanbrugh's play caused havoc in the hierarchy of marriage and family comes from Collier's too serious reading of the Lady's speeches. In light of the printed residues of the conversation between Collier and the reformers and those playwrights who responded to them, I might be unhappily placed in Collier's camp by Vanbrugh himself.[20] A warning not to be taken too lightly by anyone interested in how theatre works, the over reading of the meaning of lines can divorce the text from the play of its performance. Yet even Vanbrugh sees the need for muting the reasonable sound of Lady Brute's voice as he has her abruptly disavow all she has argued in her soliloquy after Bellinda enters the scene. In a theatre deluged with the representation of the domestic in public, this shift between the 'truth' of Lady Brute in private and the mock play of her conversation with

Bellinda can influence an audience's reception. Importantly Vanbrugh did not edit out Lady Brute's soliloquy, and thus the audience hears her words echo in the memory as the play alternates between arguments for freedom and conventional love scenes. As importantly, Vanbrugh is staging a highly self-conscious social intercourse so that Lady Brute 'in private' may be understood to be telling the truths she then pretends to dismiss.

The Provoked Wife reads (and would play) more powerfully as a frustrated argument for mutual freedom than Vanbrugh allows in his pamphlet response to Collier. The very weakness in Vanbrugh's play writing, lack of action and momentum, creates a more persuasive argument than, perhaps, even he desired. Like debating teams, the characters take up the question of marriage, divorce, and cuckoldry, with reason on the side of the Constants and Lady Brutes who out-argue the drunken, discombobulated rants issuing from Sir John and his friends. In Vanbrugh's play, as in those of his contemporary Congreve where "print freezes motion, it also allows leisure for characters to engage more in complex thought and to put themselves through elaborate self examination" (Peters 1990: 25).[21] With the exception of an outdoor meeting and Sir John's drunken effronteries, and an anemic scene of hidden lovers, the 'movement' of argument and elaborate self-examination constitutes the action of the play. The varieties of motion can be seen in the extremes of festive license and in the motion restricted, though not utterly stilled, which transforms into a plea made by inaction and overmuch conversing.

Collier's ire about Vanbrugh's play, I argue, gives us an understanding of the dissension alive in the culture in 1698. And what we come to see as the wellspring for the outrage Collier expends is something Collier himself allows to show through his sentences, though it is not the argument upon which those sentences are based. A woman 'cross-examining' herself can find no place in a world where Woman and "modesty" must, according to Collier, right themselves again into the single, staunch, cultural supports that he deems them. Where separation of language and meaning causes in Collier a flurry of horror, articulated in his desire for reform of female conduct and the conduct of the players in the theatre itself, the more subtle aspects of Vanbrugh's rebellious play undo the linguistic stays that hold Woman still and virtue true. Such an 'unlacing' happens when Lady Brute and her lover Constant conduct an instructive *performed* dissection of "virtue" in Act III.

Working an airy analysis upon reputation, that outward show of honor, Constant speaks his tender regard for Lady Brute's position and the necessity of "secrecy." Using the same reason she showed in analyzing the marriage vow, Lady Brute sends Constant's 'conversational missive' back to him with an addendum. "Secrecy indeed in sins of this kind is an argument of weight to lessen the punishment," Lady Brute concedes, but no full "pardon" can be gained without "sincere repentance" (III. ii. 333–5). Standing across from her, Constant receives this newest rhetorical message, responds by repeating the phrase "sincerity of repentance," announcing himself "a true penitent" if repentance means "sorrow for offending," but distinguishes an offense to virtue from the non-offense of love "where 'tis a duty to adore" (ll. 336–8).[22]

A modern audience would do well to remember that the representation of the process of learning by staged dialogues, as discussed in earlier chapters, was still the method of instruction at the end of the century. As we have seen in Jonson and Milton, in pamphlet writings, not only did the writers borrow the well-known ancient tradition of Socratic dialogue, but also the basic schoolbook style of writers like Comenius who 'stages' the debate between old and young in order to teach the virtues of knowledge. In this kind of demonstration we see the vestiges of pre-Ramistic training when oral compositions included, as components of the art, invention as well as delivery. Thus learning proceeded through aural attentiveness and discovery. Parts of the discussion between Lady Brute and Constant are reminiscent of the boy's school language of characters in *Romeo and Juliet*, where everyone shows off his/her talent for rhetorical tricks to display virtuosity rather than clarification. Yet in the main this conversation between Lady Brute and Constant owes much to the increased role of the reception of print and the reasoned world of interrogation more reminiscent of Milton's printed/performed dialogue in *A Maske*.

Back and forth the orderly exchange between Lady Brute and Constant moves like an 'oral epistolary' engagement with the parties composing their replies in the air; replies so set, the lines sound wet with ink. Constant, his name a moniker of fidelity, takes the role of true and faithful lover to Lady Brute, more husband than seducer. We have come some way from the attraction of Behn's 'inconstant' lovers whose erotic claim is to motion and to energy. Earlier in the century, seducers, particularly malevolent ones like Richard in *Richard III*, move themselves around the object of their hunt, wooing or trapping according to their motives. The late seventeenth-century predators through trickery (Wycherley's Horner) or through wordy patience (Congreve's Mirabelle) must win consent to show the notch upon the intellectual bedstead.[23] Constant's lack of physical movement reinforces his purpose; his abstract, capable wooing judiciously delivered. Both members of the conversation can therefore remain still. Long-suffering and yet blind to all other women's attractions, Constant only breaks the mannered seal of exchange in his wooing twice, once to turn upon the word "virtue," and once to turn toward the audience to 'meta-soliloquize' the very conversation in which he is engaged.

On "virtue" – that term Collier interchanges with modesty and women – Constant loses his poise, railing on for ten lines, breaking the balance of his patterned two-or-three-line response to Lady Brute's two or three previous lines. Lady Brute, who earlier turns virtue into an ass, now names it an item for a lover's adoration, what women "ought to be adored for" (III. ii. 341). Chastising Lady Brute by exposing her shift into antiquated methods of discussion where virtue has only one meaning, Constant rejects simple definitions, those catchwords that were once a banner for a lover to ride under. "Virtue" in its earlier manifestation "is no more." No more "like the thing that's called so, than 'tis like vice itself" (l. 342). Instead Virtue becomes a category, "consists in goodness, honor, gratitude, sincerity, and pity" unlike the dissimilar group, "peevish, snarling, strait-laced chastity" (ll. 343–4). Throughout this somewhat fretful argument the lovers would convey the disjunction between the supposed inconsequence of what they are discussing and their fervent desire (perhaps conveyed through the tension in the body) that the other might understand the deeper significance of the social contract of virtue.

Pretty though Constant's elucidation is, even he recognizes "true virtue wheresoe'er it moves still carries an intrinsic worth about it." Lady Brute brings virtue's intrinsic power in line with the social usage of the term. If, she wonders, virtue is overrated, "why do you so earnestly recommend it to your wives and daughters?" (ll. 351–2). Constant replies with an honesty that probably sent Collier round the bend: "We recommend it to our wives, madam, because we would keep 'em to ourselves . . . to our daughters, because we would dispose of 'em to others" (ll. 353–5). Like the guardian blush, the guardian term "virtue" keeps a watch over property, maintaining wives private to their owners and making daughters sound public offerings.

Lady Brute breaks etiquette with Constant further along in this discussion proclaiming his "sophistry" "puzzles, but don't convince" (l. 370). Her breaking off the spoken 'correspondence' encourages Constant's second loss of poise. In fact interruption plays the role of temporal partner in the work of this scene. Like the intrinsic artifice of staged privacy, a planned interruption occurs as a false break in the temporal space of the play, being *like* an interruption even though it cannot be genuine anymore than the lovers actually conduct their scene in private. Unlike Shakespeare's representation of improvisation in *Measure for Measure*, where Lucio and the Provost play stand-in characters for the audience and thus heat up the immediate sense of risk and power in Isabella's words by prodding her to go farther, here the 'witnessing' of the audience remains at a certain distance. Without urgent proddings from onstage characters, the faked nature of the interruption simply opens a wider space for the audience's intellectual participation in understanding the private code.

The code the two lovers have been examining, holding to the light, has not brought Lady Brute the illumination she wants, or she wants Constant to have: "you have a worse opinion of my understanding than I desire you to have" (l. 375). On stage this sentence would act as a spoken breach between Lady Brute and Constant, not unlike the one between Comus and the Lady in *A Maske* that signals the end of intimate dialogue when both parties begin to speak of the other in the third person. Yet rather than move toward his lover in an effort to heal the breach – as might be portrayed both physically and rhetorically – Constant, in response to Lady Brute's comment, addresses a third party conspicuously ignored in staged seduction, the audience. He would probably walk downstage of Lady Brute, breaking the dialogue and to deliver his 'aside' of discovery to us. Constant correctly interprets the confusion between the lovers: "she would have me set a value upon her chastity that I may think myself the more obliged to her when she makes me a present of it" (ll. 376–8).

Because the audience rather than Lady Brute becomes the first recipient of Constant's understanding, the consummation of the scene occurs between 'man' and his own virtuoso understanding. It could not help but be an awkward moment for the actress playing Lady Brute; she must stand and wait for this cool deliberation happening downstage of her instead of receiving the kneeling, penitent lover we have come to expect. Constant's response instead suggests that the social recognition of the implied terms of virtue and their relation to the position of public and private woman supersedes the consummation of understanding between lovers – this particular man and woman. Constant's interpretation of his scene with Lady Brute and his commentary about it to the audience make up all the action of the moment: it is a completely intellectual and, for a moment, individual drama. Finally, Constant understands that the signifier "virtue," held at a distance to be examined, suddenly becomes a substance closer to the body when Lady Brute puts *her* virtue at risk. That which he insisted at first to have no value, must now be reappraised in order for him to deserve its "sacrifice" (ll. 384).

The word play and self-examination in late seventeenth-century drama differed from Shakespeare's meditative soliloquies and wooing scenes in which the words originate out of the characters' mouths in a seductive game. Richard's slow torture by language of Anne in Act I, scene ii of *Richard III* comes from the throat of a speaker whose language strains his body toward or away from the other, a conduit of the self, false or true. Anne's increasingly deadly stillness, her surrender marked by fewer words and less movement, matches Richard in its physical intensity. Thinking in terms of the soliloquies at the beginning of the seventeenth century, one can look back in order to see how at the century's end the theatre will come to stage speech fractured by the 'action' of self assessment. One direction the drama moves toward is the staging of intellectual discovery, a direction clearly foreshadowed in *Othello* where the characters use the word "think" more frequently and more confusedly than in any other Shakespeare play. In fact the word "think" carries a weightiness in sound and in outcome, perhaps because it is used by characters whose production and reception of meaning occurs in a theatre of sensuous attention. Tragedy can come in an instant – simply by thinking Desdemona is unfaithful, Othello shatters a noble sense of self. The intricate shifts and shapes of the operation of thinking and those who would manipulate it in others goes some way toward foreshadowing the coming distance between language and its negotiated meaning. As I argue in Chapter 3, post-Interregnum drama is marked by a distrust of the certainty of meaning, a growing fissure in the contiguous space between the signifier and the signified. I do not mean to suggest there was a 'naïve' use of language in earlier periods, but rather that the uncertainties under discussion were for the most part not the *very terms* in which the discussion was taking place.

In the exchange between Lady Brute and Constant – a discussion intent on moving bodies, yes, but only as a secondary purpose – the characters seem to hold the language away from them, to catch the light of definition. Turning words like "virtue" and "reputation" to the left or upside down until the colors appear refracted as if by a prism held by the speakers, the two characters move neither closer together nor farther apart. (Chances are this coolness of speech communicated through the body would be reflected in the bodies of the audience receiving it.) In *Richard III*, the motion of language as a vehicle, for the body, for laughter, even for skepticism, differs from the stillness of language, language incapable in *The Provoked Wife* of transporting so much weight, its meaning no longer trustworthy enough to bear so fierce a purpose.[24] An actor or an actress would find him or herself hard-pressed not to mimic in voice and action the "coolness" of Lady Brute's and Constant's detached debating, a different method than the body and language unified in the purpose of cuckoldry, seduction, or entrapment.

Collier's ire should have fallen as harshly on this scene in *The Provoked Wife* as on any other. For here are the seeds of the ruination of family and country. If things are truly "govern'd by" these most malleable words, then the "governance" of the words of marriage and fidelity can be readjusted to suit the governed, in this case a married woman and a single man. And yet here too Vanbrugh reaffirms the male trade of an abstract code "virtue/Woman" in his staging of Constant's individual understanding; Constant's cognitive awakening is more stirring than any relations between woman and man. Following Vanbrugh's display of masculine awareness, Richard Steele in his *The Conscious Lovers* was soon to design an entire play around a scene where "our hero" (Bevil, Jr), one of two principal male characters, while engaged in a fight prompted by a jealous misunderstanding, visibly and verbally masters himself in order not to provoke a duel. His accomplishment, and here we return to the Lady in *A Maske*, is not to act, though unlike the Lady, Bevil Jr becomes an imitation of a social savior rather than a divine one. The 'show' of his mastery is offered to satisfy what Steele represents in the Preface to his play as a misguided, crude thirst from the audience for the action of plot or the sudden eruption of violence and revenge.

One cannot help but see how like a David painting the description of Steele's *The Conscious Lovers* 'reads': the upright man, the enraged friend, a bit of drapery to frame the potential moment always about to happen, frozen into a tension never to be released by oil and canvas. Like the printed display of the role of the spectator Steele created in the magazine of the same name, in his 'masculine' intellectual *mise en scène*, that 'show' of reason, he seeks to regulate an exchange of observation and representation with the intent of improving the audience. In some sense regulation would seem to have found the audience it desired and that audience is male. By turning the drama's attention to the portrayal of the male stoic, Constant and Belville, Jr, the authors bypass an address to the "Ladies" using courteous men to display the proper comportment to the men watching them. Most importantly, regulation or resistance could be staged itself as dramatic tableau; this mastery of emotion, the very stilling of free words and movement Collier argued for, could be said to discipline the loose flights of passion, and those moving women always associated with them, in the preceding years of the drama.

Epilogue
Making space

Architectural containers

Critics tend to condense the complexities and idiosyncrasies of the periods preceding and following their own in order to mark a stable (and necessarily reductive) boundary against which the ambiguities and nuances alive in their own period can be read. Like the shorthand term "Restoration," adopted to provide a link between a political event and the literature produced in the wake of it, so the shorthand for the advent of a "proscenium theatre." The enclosure of the proscenium was erected in the scholarly mind as a not-so-triumphal arch through which theatrical production passed from a vibrant, messy, egalitarian space (pre-1660) into a distanced, iconic, bourgeois space. But the nuanced performance practices taking place in front of and then behind the proscenium in the period from the 1670s well into the 1800s are intricate, dynamic, and *gradual*. This architectural innovation demanded adjustment and re-evaluation from practitioners of theatre just as the innovation of print demanded an effort by writers and makers of theatre to combine the aesthetic pleasures of comprehension in the circulation of the printed word with apprehension in the dynamic force of performance.

Prosceniums (*pro-scena*) have a much longer history indoors and out than granted by the too much used shorthand term, the "picture-frame" stage. This term of convenience usually portrays the proscenium as a boundary first put in place after Shakespeare. In this widely accepted version of theatre history, the players were kept behind the proscenium frame until the advent of experimental theatre in the mid-twentieth century.[1] Yet, a proscenium designed and employed for a fifteenth-century Medici festival or a seventeenth-century masque by Inigo Jones functioned in those ephemeral works very differently than the architectural structure erected in the "new" Drury Lane Theatre of 1674 or Lincoln's Inn Fields (Leacroft 1973). In 1696 at Drury Lane changes in the design of the apron stage, the eradication of two of the onstage doors where previously actors entered directly into the audience rather than appearing "behind" the proscenium, signaled to the audience a reorientation of spectatorship and reconstituted the formal relations between stage and house. In this Epilogue I move forward in time just far enough to remind the reader both of the architectural changes in process in the indoor theatre and of the moment in English history (1710) when the container of print became legally labeled as the property of the author. The creation of the aesthetic of motion and stillness upon the stage changed in response to the increasing identification at work in late seventeenth-century English society of property, its holders and its collectors, as evidenced in Vanbrugh's play and Collier's tract (see Chapter 5).

While taking care not to conceive of the space of the proscenium rigidly, one can still juxtapose an analysis of how early eighteenth-century theatre worked against something that came to look like a frame over the course of one hundred years or so. This conjunction helps give a sense of the increasing anxiety about the responsibilities in the care of property and in the evocation of a communal world where property came more and more to decipher and define the self.[2] In some sense the architecture of the stage and the architectural structures of legal property made for a revised socio-spatial mandate. In her opening essay to the collection *A New History of Early English Drama*, Margreta de Grazia makes a provocative call for a history demarcated by the development of spatial innovations in the theatre in contrast to the habit of the periodization of drama (1997). However, she herself then employs a static notion of the unchanging space of the proscenium to demarcate "early" from "not early" theatre. In this book I have tried to follow the arc of a transition to chart the way in which a shift that calls for adjustment – technological, aesthetic, political – leaves behind telling traces of that which has gone before and that which is to come. So the pairing of architectural innovation and print/property legislation offers one point on the arc of this transition with residues of before, during, and after.

Another pairing might be what Deborah Payne, quoting John Dennis (1698), notes as a striking conflation of the two innovations on the "Restoration" stage – "scenes and women" (1995). Using theories imported from film, Payne accounts for the position of the looker and the looked at on the Restoration stage. Since Dennis' couple (scenes and women) supposedly comes under the category of the "looked at," the container in which they are placed, the stage, is designed with an eye to taking in. But Payne wisely corrects the assumption of the single viewer to the singly viewed, reminding us that in the immediate moment of performance the actresses could actively return a spectator's look. I would take us further animating the several senses at work for the spectator whose perspective *is in the midst of being* shaped by architectural design and innovation in scenery. Importing theories of the position of the spectator at a film into that of a spectator at the theatre risks forgetting that a spectator at the theatre has the freedom to look where and at what on the stage he or she chooses; the movement of several bodies in dimensional space, a dimensional space the spectator shares, disturbs the framed containment that is an essential part of film, even though within the frame of film there is movement as well.

To return for a moment to architectural innovations, the designs for Lincoln's Inn Fields and Dorset Garden theatres suggest an apron stage extending into the audience approximately thirty feet. The actors, then, would enter into the audience and play in front of the framed section of the stage or thrust themselves very close to the spectators. The playing could engage an intimate actor-to-audience compact on the edge of the apron stage. Managers could also set the racy, bawdy bits all the way to the back of the stage between the movable scenes: this would force the audience to lean forward, to patch together out of what they could see and what they could hear an idea of what the actors were doing. The movement of the bodies watching then shifted in response to the placement of the scene at the back of the stage; in particular those in the boxes who had to lean out to have a full view of the side on which they were sitting.[3] Though the perspective might have been best from the King's box, the majority of the members of the audience sitting or standing would correct their own sight lines by adjusting their bodies.

The textual nature of reports exploited by scholars of architectural, technological, and publishing changes over the centuries unwittingly conceal the necessary sensory adjustments made by audiences in the presence of new forms of production. For example, when the shift began in the late fourteenth century from reading aloud to reading privately, it was a change signaled by the change in sound: from chanting and intoning to reading aloud as a rhetorical performance to murmuring quietly while reading.[4] Similar shifts in sound accompanied architectural changes in stage design as well. Colley Cibber lamented Christopher Rich's too sudden, too drastic change in the forestage of Drury Lane. Rich "increased the seating capacity by trimming four feet from the depth of the apron and reducing its width, in order to install boxes in place of the original stage doors." The actors were "drawn some ten feet further back from the audience than before" (Trussler 1994: 149). Reminding his reader how much more effective the stage had been before Rich's emendations, Cibber writes: "When the actors were in possession of that forwarder space . . . the voice was then more in the centre of the house, so that the most distant ear had scarce the least doubt, or difficulty in hearing what fell from the weakest utterance" (cited in Trussler 1994: 149). Where the voice dominated, the other senses participated in making the scene with the performers, a scene aurally powerful whose visual power was indeed dependent upon its aural clarity: "All objects were *thus drawn nearer to the sense*; every painted scene was stronger; every grand scene and dance more extended . . . nor was the minutest motion of a feature (properly changing with the passion, or humour it suited) ever lost, as they frequently must be in the obscurity of too great a distance" (149).[5] According to

Cibber, this architectural change resulted in a change in the sensuous reception of the audience.

Many actors complained of not being heard as they were moved further and further back from the point of power in the midst of the spectators – the "centre of the house." More subtle shifts in sound also affected the playing. With fewer onstage doors, an actor's entrance was no longer concrete. While an actor entered through the door on either side of the stage, the sight of the door opening, the sound of it closing, the sight of the character, the sound of his or her voice all made up an entrance. As actors began to enter from the wings, the body of the actor would enter quietly from a place to which the audience had no access. For a theatre that would someday begin to play in the fantasy world of the fourth wall, this silent gliding fostered an illusion of the player materializing from nowhere.

During the century passing from 1680 to 1780 the bodies of actors were pushed closer and closer to the proscenium frame, but not until the conception formulated by Goethe – that the bodies which "broke" the "frame" ruined the "picture" – did there exist a mandate for acting to take place permanently framed. David Garrick finally banished audience members from the stage itself, but not until the 1740s. In fact Peachum's lads, if they so desired, might while away their time waiting for their cues by cutting purses, since productions of *The Beggar's Opera* were famous for crowding in as many people in chairs upon the stage as possible. Obviously the relation of stage to house when the house was on the stage made the barrier between the acting and the watching thin indeed. I am reminded of Dutch genre painting in which a figure might be portrayed seated in the window, the frame a doubled one from the picture itself, but at one corner the sitter's elbow and arm extend beyond it, a visual reminder of the permeable nature of a frame.

In the London theatres of the 1690s, the old and the new coexisted architecturally. The actors were on a shorter thrust stage and yet they still played to the pit; the proscenium was a movable feast where the figures could choose to recede behind the arch and thus be seen against the scenes or come forward of it to play inside the space of the audience. The actors of the 1690s were the aging veterans of the Restoration stage who might tell the tale of starting from scratch after the re-opening of the theatre, having developed a style that mixed the remembered public playhouse delivery with a new form of delivery designed for refurbished tennis court interiors.

The Copyright Act and the author's name

At first glance, the terms adopted by early twentieth-century critics by which one might follow the evolutionary march to the orderly eighteenth century in England look unavoidable. The hardening of the binaries created by theories of male and female behavior, of the arrangement of sets of things into columns labeled "this" and "not this" can be seen to shape the possibilities of a culture on the brink of the Enlightenment. In print studies the date which continues this march toward order and social regulation, the date most often cited after the Gutenberg's invention of moveable type is 1710, the passage of the first Copyright Act in England. It's a handy date poised in the midst of a self-conscious revolution in periodical print culture and in the ongoing development of its private printed companion, the novel. What interests me here, however, is the relative chaos in publishing at the end of the preceding century. While there are clear indications of a more regimented relation to the printing of texts and the creation of boundaries for the authors and players, there are also new uncertainties making the boundaries seem still very permeable and undefinable.

If the spatial relations of author to audience is one forged by circulation, and if the anxiety of the author about circulation includes watching his or her mature work make its own way into a harsh world, then the spatial relation of property owner to property involves some of the same pleasures and dangers. Whether a fond parent or a despairing guardian, authors throughout the seventeenth century figure their relationship to the book as one of progenitor to progeny. Continuing this analogy, a child at the breast not yet walking has a spatial claim on its mother or wetnurse which fundamentally changes when the child can move and eat on his or her own. In a period theorizing property in the self, the need arises to create a 'sign' of ownership on those properties circulating beyond the space of the owner's body and as importantly beyond the limited social space of a small village.

Surveying the 1690s from the vantage of the twentieth century's end, it is easy to collapse millennial anxieties from the twentieth century into those of the seventeenth century. The end of the seventeenth century in England produced the first paper money; money as Julie Stone Peters reminds us was indelibly related to the distinction between script and print (1987). Where handwritten promises signaled a fictive human body – the promise bound by the corporeality of the body receiving the note from the body giving it – generic, printed paper money passed through anonymous hands in a new exchange that left the receivers often feeling queasy about the worth of a piece of paper not attached to a thing.[6]   Meanwhile the Licensing Act expired in 1695 leaving a limbo of legal proof governing the ownership of printed work. The tug of war between author and bookseller became fiercer, and the fear of *copia* in the non-restricted world of unlicensed printing, a familiar fear voiced about the proliferation of pamphlets in the Interregnum, returned.

Copyright and the discussions of it, as now in discussions of intellectual property and/or genetic research, hovered about the idea of how to define what was being owned apart from who the owner was and where the property and its increase resided. Property theorized to reside in the self, as Locke proposed, did not necessarily set in motion a generation of self promoters. Locke's dictum allowed for a certain insubstantiality. One can imagine Hamlet's response to the news that he owned property in himself. A long soliloquy, perhaps, turning upon the exact location of the self that one owned. Locke's imagined corporeal freedom from fealty and bondage – no one owned one's own body if the body was male and not a slave – did not immediately translate into corporeal security. While the country gentleman could prove to himself by riding out upon his estate that the property he owned did exist, the self one owned and the labor of the body that confirmed self ownership existed uncertainly in a world making an uneasy transition from tangible things to abstract ideas of property such as credit (see Arendt 1958). In some sense we might see the desire to collect objects and to catalogue species as a subset of the anxiety caused by the shift in self-definition, accumulation, and display. Collecting might give visible proof to the wealth that otherwise exists largely in liquid assets.[7]

In the less abstract practical world of daily exchange, the unsettling effect in the rise of credit, the use of paper money, and the lack of licensing laws met with individual practical responses. As the accumulation of hedge funds or the inexplicable rise of the Stock Market at the end of the twentieth century did not have an immediate material effect on the modest balance in the checking accounts of those who live from wage payment to wage payment, so the moneylenders and the booksellers at the end of the seventeenth century continued to practice their trade with a mixture of tactics drawn from tradition and created in the face of innovation.

Indeed in "the decade that followed the lapse of the Licensing Act," according to Mark Rose, "the stationers, who were concerned about their properties, collaborated with those who favored censorship on ideological grounds in repeated attempts to restore the old system of press regulation" (1993: 34). As an action taken because of the social perception of too much license, censorship was, as Rose theorizes it, an outmoded response. In the late sixteenth and early seventeenth centuries, the text was conceived of as an "action" not as a "thing." Thus the control of actions necessitated regulation: "thinking of texts as actions, valuing them for what they could do, was commensurate with the regulatory system in which censorship and the privileges of booksellers were conflated, just as, later, treating texts as aesthetic objects was commensurate with a system of cultural production based on property" (13). (One might say that in this formulation actions must be apprehended where objects came more and more to be comprehended.) Further the role of paper money as action in exchange echoed that of the playtext, standing in for a thing, needing to be regulated and readjusted for value.

So the instinct to censor or regulate fell most heavily in the seventeenth century not upon the printing of playtexts, though there as well, but on the performances and the actions of the players when embodying those texts. In a time of shifting values, of arguments from philosophers – Locke in particular – and writers – Defoe and Addison – for the length of an author's right to his/her own property, censorship took its form in an old guise, the control of the behavior of women. What is clear about metaphors of gender and how they affect the laws placed upon female bodies is that these metaphors shift according to use and value. While the published text and the process of its writing, as discussed in the preceding chapters, had been for the most part clothed in manly garb, Daniel Defoe in his pleas for authorial control over the abuse of having one's work stolen and printed by another suddenly shifts the gender of the printed book: the abuse of "printing of other Mens Copies, [is] every jot as unjust as lying with their Wives, and breaking up their Houses" (from "Essay on the Regulation of the Press" as cited in Rose 1993: 35). Not since Cutbeard's "cum privilegio" in *Epicoene* when he likens the taking of a wife to the marking of a book as one's own has the relation between book, wife, property and author, husband, owner been made so clearly. In light of the discussion of Vanbrugh and Collier on marriage in Chapter 5, the child book from Milton's time has grown into the book wife, an outward sign of the husband's labor, evidence of his property. In fact, the language of rape and domestic dissolution fuels Defoe once again as he rails that there are laws against robbery and ravishment but not for an author whose "goods" can be "stollen, his Pocket pick'd, his Estate ruin'd, his Prospect of Advantage ravish'd from him" (as cited in Rose 1993: 37).

If there exists any consistency in the cultural use of Woman to attribute value to an object or an idea, it is in the consistent feminizing of the unprotected thing and the assertion of the masculinity of the protector. Even printers, writes Rose, "couched their pleas and petitions to Parliament in pathetic domestic terms, complaining that they, their wives, their children were being utterly ruined by piracy" (1993: 40). As Chapter 5 narrates, in Collier's angry text and Vanbrugh's pseudo-reasonable play this particular conjunction of owner to property collides: (1) in the unruliness of owning property who can by her behavior undo the power of the keeper; and (2) in a printed book which through reader interpretation can become a misrepresentation of the owner's intent.

Reasserting domestic hierarchy manifested through the fidelity and the steadfastness of wife to husband offered an anchor in an uncertain world where monarchy after 1688 was an even more negotiated principle than in 1660. Fine feeling seemed not to follow a solemn oath so surely as in the earlier part of the century. Many there were in Jacobean and Carolinian England who were skeptical about monarchical right, but traitors and treason tended to be set forth as a recognized form of evil. Now the language of obedience, at least in terms of subject to monarch, was a negotiated language, words chosen carefully affixed as they were to shifting values.

* * *

The ends of plays like the ends of books often seem to let every closed door fly open to reveal the lurking figures one sought to keep (partially) hidden behind the door of nuance and precision. The gradual separation of stage from bodies surrounding it, the regulation of printed materials, the cyclical cry for the reform of sensibilities – usually female – in order to reorient the social picture all have their origins in the works being performed upon the stage. But the happy inclusion of a healthy messiness in our once too-pat critical understanding of the eighteenth century suggests the aesthetics of the still and the moving, the receivers' and the maker's consubstantial desire to thrill to action and to cherish the vibrant evidence held still for recognition and savor, continue to dance in their differences. Such stuff are the negotiated shoals of comprehension and apprehension made of: the sweep of sensual knowing and the kind clarity of perception and understanding.

Notes

Introduction

1   From the *Advancement of Learning*, "certain it is, through a great secret of nature, that the minds of men [*sic*] in company are more open to affections and impressions than when alone" (Francis Bacon 1605).

2   I am indebted to the last decade of performance studies work specifically focused on 'how' theatre and performance works, particularly that of Joe Roach, Susan Leigh Foster, Mark Franko, and Susan Melrose.

3   In his Introduction Fox corrects the inherited theory of thinking of oral and literate as a binary: "England in the sixteenth and seventeenth centuries, therefore, was a society in which the three media of speech, script and print infused and interacted with each other in myriad ways . . . There was no necessary antithesis between oral and literate forms of communication and preservation . . . the written word tended to augment the spoken . . . any crude binary opposition between 'oral' and 'literate' culture fails to accommodate the reciprocity between the different media of this time (2000: 5–6).

4   Thinking about the object as an object, the hands holding the object book, reminds one of Peter Stallybrass' supposition in his delineation of "objectness": "the object then takes on inestimable value. For, in working upon it [or holding and reading it], the bondsman [reader] comes to recognize her or his identity as an objective being or 'objective personality' – that is, a being in need of outside objects and in need of being an outside object to another" (1999: 4). See the Prologue for a discussion of the paradox of book as object in hand but not always an object in reception.

5   As M.T. Clanchy reminds us, one of those traces is to a time when evidence was trustworthy because spoken by a human being. When no one could be found who could remember, the court could not resolve the case because it was "time out of mind" (1993: 152).

6   "Customarily it was three trumpet blasts, filling all the 231,028 cubic feet of the acoustic space, that signaled the start of performances at the Globe" (Smith 1999: 218). In the private theatres the audience heard "consort music" (222).

7   Readers will hear an echo of Elin Diamond's phrase, "a thing doing and a thing done" (1998).

8   Mark Rose makes an important distinction in a discussion of censorship between the beginning of the seventeenth century and the end of it when he suggests that in the early part of the century texts were thought of as "actions," valued "for what they could do . . . later, treating texts as aesthetic objects was commensurate with a system of cultural production based on property" (1993: 13). See Chapter 5 and Epilogue for the increasing influence upon the values of the still and the moving made through the language of property.

9 See Orgel (1993) and Barroll (1996) for discussions of what this two hour playing time actually meant, how theatre managers might have cut the text to serve different audiences.

10 Douglas Bruster in "The Structural Transformation of Print in Late Elizabethan England" notes that as early as the "1590s, publishers found that readers were eager to buy the plays they had seen and heard in London's theatres . . . [in] the first decade of the seventeenth century, published plays constitute over 20 percent of all literary publications, and over five percent of all titles published" (2000: 65–6).

11 Obviously this book rests upon the texts published over the last two decades reinventing our understanding of print culture. Roger Chartier (1987) and Elizabeth Eisenstein (1980) brought to our attention the powerful impact of print not simply upon the production of the book but also the manner in which ideas were conveyed, stored, and retrieved. From various perspectives Wendy Wall (1993), Margreta De Grazia (1991), and the writers of the essays in *The Practice and Representation of Reading in England* (1996) bring print culture studies to bear on specific authors and the cultural production of them as authors for a reading public. Joyce Coleman (1996) and Adam Fox (2000) allow the sound of reading aloud to enter into the discourse of print and author, bringing the performative aspects of reception to light as well as the cultural place of reading as it evolved in the early modern period.

12 See Sherman, "The Place of Reading in the English Renaissance: John Dee Revisited" (1996) for a discussion of the library as a sociable space more than a place of solitary contemplation. Sherman's suggestions carry an interesting echo of Paula Findlen's description of the early museum as a place where civility was practiced among groups of gentlemen.

13 See Chartier (1994), Darnton and Roche (1989), Kernan (1987), Peters (2000), and Wall (1993) for various discussions of the relation of the "author function" to the material production of the book. Circulation, the "lifeblood," as it were, of the book as property offers a little explored aspect of the author and his or her control over the published book, the reception of the physical artifact of the book, and metaphors about property holding itself. See R.A. Shoaf's "'Unwemmed Custance': Circulation, Property, and Incest in the Man of Law's Tale."

14 The clichéd notion that those things a writer scorns are those things he or she secretly desires obfuscates the complicated temporal tensions in reverence and disdain. Antitheatricality flirts with Midas' bargain, what must be kept close may by the closekeeping be drained of life, the living thing cannot abide the memorialization of a hardened case. This study owes much to the work of Jonas Barish, though like its debt to Foucault, the imprint of influence is not drawn in quotation but spread throughout the book. Without the powerful influence of *The Antitheatrical Prejudice*, I could not have begun to trace the longing moving like an undercurrent in the antitheatrical complaints that seek to still the uncontrollably moving (1981).

15 In a work not coincidentally on gift exchange, *The Logic of Practice*, Pierre Bordieu makes a critique of the way scholars have studied rituals and practices (in which I would include performance) which "derive some of their most important properties from the fact that they are 'detotalized' by their unfolding in succession." The tools of analysis often miss properties of such practices because "detemporalizing science has [the] least chance of reconstituting" such practices "constructed in time." In fact, by losing the ability to follow the "order of a succession" theories can arise from the misguided "absolute gaze of the omniscient spectator" (1990: 190). Though Bourdieu will develop much more skeptical conclusions about the possibility of gift than those held by other critics

I cite, his astute critique of "detemporalizing" bears upon all the practices discussed in this book. One comes to look at practices which unfold with the omniscient sense of all of it before one because print produces it there before you as a whole; the performance scholar must reconstitute for the reader the process of unfolding as if she or he did not know the 'end'. See Lepecki for an elegant treatment of the conundrum of gift and time in dance (1996).

16 Wolfgang Iser's *The Act of Reading: a Theory of Aesthetic Response* (1978) is one of the foundational texts for theorists of reader response.

17 I hope the variety of possible audience responses – the communal spirit of the audience in the context of certain performances, the difference in reception according to class, height, gender, health – will inhabit my reader's mind while remaining as fluid as printed text can allow in these chapters.

18 My interest in using theories about gift exchange and performance is based generally on the work of readers of Marcel Mauss who reconfigure anthropological theories of gift to include the aesthetic (Hyde 1979), the performance of comedy (Serres 1982), and the spectator's space of resistance and strategic choice (de Certeau 1984).

19 The reputedly raucous audiences to public theatre could get caught up in the power of the performance, responding emotionally to Jack Cade or shouting a warning to the hero in peril. See the Appendix in Gurr (1987) for contemporary descriptions of various kinds of reception.

20 Discussions of rhetoric often recognize the collaborative performance of the still and the moving as when Kenneth Burke, writing beautifully about speaking beautifully, encapsulates the dual task of the orator to move and to captivate: "though it aims ultimately to move the audience by a sweeping appeal to the emotions, [oratory] can only do so if it holds their interest" (1969: 74).

21 Of the small number of critical works attempting to relate Hyde's theory to artistic exchange, each either considers poetry (Romantic) or drama. (Ronald Sharp on "Keats and the Spiritual Economies of Gift Exchange" 1989 and "Gift Exchange and the Economies of Spirit in *The Merchant of Venice*" 1986.) Hyde, in the second half of his book, turns his anthropological discussion to two writers of poetry, Whitman and Pound. Poetry and theatre share orally performed antecedents. I suspect the unexamined but consistent connection between gift exchange and these particular modes of writing/performance indicates that, like the gift itself, such rhythmic, performed practices "must always move" or they diminish (Hyde 1979: 4).

Hyde's book published in 1979 was unique in positing the use of Mauss to understand the unquantifiable in the exchange based on folktale as well as cultural traditions and as an exchange between makers of art and receivers. Derrida's influential lectures on gift have made the language of gift exchange more familiar in the critical world (1992).

22 Michael Bristol argues that "gift exchange rather than monetary circulation is one of the central categories necessary for an understanding of Shakespeare's plays both at a thematic level and at the level of their historical reception" (1996: 142). According to Bristol, giving "increases the authority of the donor; reception obligates or binds the recipient. There is a deep ambivalence in the binding character of the gift . . . Reception is not always, and indeed not usually, voluntary" (1996: 142). And yet audiences usually have a remarkable autonomy in the exchange, being able to leave when they choose or reject the gift in the response. It might be the actors who are most burdened by the demands of giving a performance.

23 The power of oratory and of performance to bind a crowd together, to move and persuade cannot of course be separated from the history of such moments used in the service of great evil. The give and take of speaker and listeners can be

corrupted into the taking of manipulative language and naïve, or worse, eager, reception, turning an audience into a mob, as the history of the twentieth century shows.

24 Ben Jonson's career, according to E. Tribble, "can be read as a series of attempts to exploit the potential of the press to order and contain" (1993: 130).

25 There is a scholarly component to the practice of collecting embedded in such questions. Work is most definitely shelved under a certain methodology or a certain set of critical ancestors. In the current climate of publishing it is often a response to overwhelming amounts of text to be read and to be responded to, but it seems to me important to question the approach in light of a desire for interdisciplinary studies which at their best should defy single categorization. I take Joseph Roach's work as an example of important work which cannot easily be categorized: he works at the intersection of performance, history, philosophy, cultural anthropology, and literature.

Prologue

1 From many different perspectives, there have been recent attempts to theorize, awaken, and reanimate the body as site of conjoined reception and cognition. Jacques Derrida, according to Gary Ulmer, seeks to use pictographic writing to stimulate a response more complex than the flat reception of words on the page. Kristin Linklater posits Shakespeare's language as one made with words whose syllables and sound conveyed meaning in the process of its saying. In her work Linklater calls upon actors to again learn with the senses the power of sound and experience. In the last decade many contemporary theatre companies distinguish their work from traditional theatre by naming it "physical theatre," a combination of dance, mime, and physical movement as if the theatre of words had somehow drained the corporeal intelligence from the playing.

2 One can of course trace the history of binary separation between the body and soul from ancient to medieval philosophies comparing Platonic and Aristotelian enthusiasts, but the public discourse of this separation, the influence of its effects (the reorganization of public space and private property, for example) begins to be felt more widely toward the end of the seventeenth century.

3 Straker suggests that even if Yolton is only partially correct, this theory suggests the seventeenth and eighteenth centuries retain much closer ties to the Scholastic "participation theory" in early modern thought (1985: 269).

4 Emblems function powerfully in the interstices of stillness and motion. The counterbalance in the play is everywhere mirrored in the evocation of scales, "Escalus" being the first word of the play (in my discussion of the play, I remain indebted to Ted Taylor for a seminar in Shakespeare he conducted at Columbia University). Scales themselves perform a powerful conjoining of stillness and motion whose interpretation can be death – a pound of flesh – or whose emptiness can mean both poverty and mercy. They move until they stop and the value placed upon the goods in them or the method by which they are weighed rest upon motion and stillness.

5 See Skantze 2000.

6 I don't think the verb "to breathe" here is a linguistic nicety. Mercy indeed does let the breath – the breath held in anticipation – out in relief; it is a release emblematically, physically, sensually, practically. Throughout the play the mouth performs actively in time with decisions; Angelo accepts the distance between intent and deed using the verb "chew" when in II. iv he acknowledges God is "in his mouth/as if I did but chew his name" (4–5). Dangerous to talk of

chewing God in a world arguing over transubstantiation as if belief in it or denial of it were a test of national fidelity.

7 It is worth noting that to improvise in Shakespearean terms was to use the very discipline of rhetorical speaking to "collect" one's ideas and display. So this collaboration too made for a mix of stillness, the learned art of rhetoric, and motion, the use of the art in active, immediate interaction.

8 From Merleau-Ponty to Bert O. States, phenomenology has been an important philosophical influence for the language of performance studies.

9 "Even if people could not read themselves, they bought printed texts and books in the expectation that they would be read aloud to them when the opportunity arose. The Bible was the supreme example of this" (Fox 2000: 37).

10 In an article whose title asks "Why Isn't the Mind-Body Problem Ancient?" Wallace I. Matson reminds the reader that the lack of "explicit statements" about the inseparability of the mental process from the bodily in Greek literature "is so because the mind-body identity was taken for granted" (1996: 93).

1 Permanently moving

1 See Findlen for a description of the collector's desire not only to produce wonder and awe in the spectator at the museum but to produce that response by way of setting the objects in motion. A static magic lantern whose parts can be separated and analyzed has none of the affective power of the working one set in a case along with a puppet holding a pendulum against the "tomb of an Egyptian mummy" in order to "'demonstrate'" the "'facility of motion'" (1994: 47). Here is a clear instance of the interdependence of stillness and motion, one is used to heighten the awareness of the other.

2 "Dee's library was the centre of his life and livelihood. It was the site not just of his reading and teaching but of chemical experiments and a fascinating range of astrological and medical consultations . . . Dee's library should also be considered in some senses a museum and an academy . . . a place where court, city and university could meet" (William Sherman 1996: 65, 69). For descriptions of the arrangement of collections for display, see Findlen (1994) especially chapter 1.

3 In fact, Jonson often refers in his writing to what he witnesses while at plays, his own and others, as in *Everyman Out of His Humor*: "You can espy a gallant of this marke . . . sits with his armes thus wreath'd, his hat pull'd here,/Cryes meaw, and nods, then shakes his empty head."

4 In keeping with the aims of this study, it bears noting that Barbour himself uses language employed from the early modern period until now to subtly distinguish the literary ambition from the performed: "firm" as an adjective like rigorous and other words of fixity continue the dichotomous understanding of firm aspirations as literary versus the softer desires to "serve" personal relationships. As is clear from the words themselves, the terms offer a commentary on the gender attached to these values, "firm," "serve," etc.

5 Obviously forms of reading differ according to the intent of the publisher. While ephemera such as plays, pamphlets, ballads, closet drama were often read aloud in company, the model for 'solitary' scholarship had been established much earlier, for example in the Laurentian library where manuscripts and codices chained to stands were pored over and copied from, one body to one book. Yet even here Michael Camille might argue the multiplicity of voices dwelt in the marginalia, with its audience of figures, monsters and wonders making commentary down the sides of the manuscript (see Camille 1992 and Chartier 1994).

6 That Jonson in the last two decades has become such a figure of the author for print studies rests partly, I suggest, upon his articulation of this "comfort," the relief of being received in print – a prejudice of scholars shows itself here, the expectation that any self-respecting artist would be relieved to be an author rather than a producer of live performance.

7 Though he seemed to argue constantly for the safe position of a singular truth, Jonson's work unfailingly produces multiple, often contradictory ideas. That the frontispiece for *The New Inn* can make a statement that reads like a clear preference for readers while the play, according to Julie Sanders, expounds the "politics of the theatre itself . . . within its acts and actions" confirms how Jonson collapsed the performed and printed, seeking to correct them both (1996: 545).

8 Susan Stewart contends in *On Longing* that "the collection seeks a form of self-enclosure which is possible because of its ahistoricism. The collection replaces history with classification, with order beyond the realm of temporality" (1993: 151). This seems particularly apt for Jonson since fame is in some sense profoundly ahistorical, that is, existing beyond time and at the same time dependent on it.

9 In trying to account for Jonson's ambivalence, his desire to at once thoroughly dismiss his audience and yet be in their company when they acknowledge his poetic powers, I do see a longing that perhaps many scholars have underestimated. Richard Helgerson charts Jonson's desire to be in print as one based on the binary of soul and body, which brings with it the traditional attributions of gender, soul-man and body-woman. "For Jonson, the fixity of print offered a way of transcending the mad mimicry of the stage, a way of representing a stable and centered self superior to the mere contingency of the playhouse world . . . the abstraction of soul from the mortal body . . . into the unchanging body of a printed text, betokened the achievement of absolute goodness . . ." (1987: 5). The vision Helgerson describes of the removed poet laureate depends upon believing print redeemed the soul from the messy bodily world of stage performance, but only in that world or a printed world based on the body could Jonson have the satisfaction of sensuous exchange.

10 "With the players, dramatists did better, averaging at the turn of the century 6 [pounds sterling] per playscript, their fee doubling or tripling by 1614 . . . Jonson might make 40 [pounds sterling] for a masque" (Barbour 1998: n. 11).- See Riggs (1989) and Womack (1986) for theories of Jonson's financial considerations in writing for the stage.

11 The longing always at work in the hope to keep something still has been powerfully articulated by Susan Stewart in her work on collecting and souvenir *On Longing* (1993), see Introduction.

12 Elements of gift exchange first theorized by anthropologists Marcel Mauss (1967) and Claude Levi-Strauss (1969) take on economic, social, and philosophical dimension in Jacques Derrida (1992) and Pierre Bourdieu (1990). Lewis Hyde (1975) posits an aesthetic gift exchange engaged in by artists. In the last decade gift theory has flourished in many different disciplines, inspired by the French theorist mentioned above as well as by the work of Georges Bataille (1988). See Introduction for a description of gift exchange in relation to performance.

13 Jonson's shifting allegiances from Protestant to Roman Catholic would suggest he was familiar with the tenets of both faiths about acts of giving and the grace of receiving.

14 While 'wistful' might seem too mild an adjective for the playwright who gives us the animal appetites of Mosca, Volpone, and their crew, I am not ignoring the cold courtesy and harsh demeanor of the author. Rather I am suggesting that

when faced with a particularly well-made performance, Jonson sees what he wants to endow to print, to preserve, and sees that he cannot.

15 In *A Director Prepares* Anne Bogart describes the "violence" of even the smallest decision made by a director. She recounts a story of director Robert Wilson entering a studio where he was to direct a play, sitting for a long time looking at the stage, and then going on to the stage and moving a chair a fraction of an inch (2001: 43–4). This deliberation signaled an acknowledgment of choice and finality; the chair became a part of a carefully designed scene.

16 Denis Diderot's *Encyclopédie, ou Dictionnaire raisonné, des sciences, des arts et des métiers*, to take a famous example, illustrated knowledge through plates that showed the processes of manufacturing and artisanal fabrication – making bread or forging iron – as well as illustrating the social practices of aristocracy, for example, plates illustrating steps of a dance or showing the well apportioned kennels for the royal dogs. Diderot was of course also a dramatist and as adept at dialogue as illustration. See Will West's "Spaces for Experiment: Theaters and Encyclopedias in Early Modern England" (1997) and Roach (1985), especially Chapter 4.

17 See Jonson's (1966: 6) "Dramatis Personae" page taken from the 1616 Folio edition.

18 It is important to remember that the audience for Jonson's work in 1609 had no stake in keeping the fiction of the play as an isolated, protected performance in which the audience pretends to be invisible. Unlike twentieth-century theatre etiquette, where an audience not only colludes with the fiction but often chastises fellow members who try to break it (by noise, crying out, etc.), in the Blackfriars Theatre a curtain of darkness did not hide the audience from the players. The "pretend" of privacy or hiding depended upon the willing play of an audience who allowed the pretence to remain in place by their own attention.

19 Blackfriars Theatre was an excellent venue for such play with volume according to Bruce Smith: "the Blackfriars theatre, like the Globe, shapes up as a space in which individual auditors enjoyed a listening space exceeding modern standards" (1999: 215).

20 For example, in a 1692 Folio version of Jonson's works, the pages where Morose conducts his controlled scenes appear to introduce prose onto a printed page otherwise marked by dialogue, by exchange.

21 Several scholars from varied perspectives have helped us imagine the reader as listener and the reception of meaning in sound. Joyce Coleman writes persuasively about the coming of silent reading and how the practice of reading aloud lasted well into the sixteenth and seventeenth centuries (1996). Roger Chartier builds upon his own foundational work on print, enlarging our understanding of the freedom and the diversity of the reader (1992, Chapter 1 especially, and 1989). Kristin Linklater in her Introduction to *Freeing Shakespeare's Voice* discusses the possibilities for meaning and interpretation for readers who were still thinking in sound (1992). John Russell Brown's editions of *King Lear* and *The Tempest* give us essential cues about when the actor's breath must change, adding the time and pressure of the breath as a part of the meaning in the lines of the plays (1996). Most recently, Bruce Smith (1999) explores sound as cultural phenomenon in the early modern period.

22 The primary castration of course is that of the boy turned to girl in *Epicoene*, but the figurative castration will be the loss of power for Morose, both sexual and monetary, at the end of the play.

23 What would have happened, I wonder, if Morose turned to Epicoene in the presentation scene and identified her as a boy? Or if her wig blew off, her voice cracked, her walk grew unwomanly? The play is at risk when delivered into the hands of actors. David Henry Huang's *M Butterfly* like *Epicoene* bases its

depiction on a man who is taken for a woman. The play carefully portrays the masculine Western culture blinded by its desire for the secret erotics of the Orient. So blinded is the diplomat that he lives for years with a man who is a woman, the perfect woman, demure, loving, obedient, and self effacing. If the audience does not know ahead of time – theatre critics serve the same function these days as Jonson's Dramatis Personae page – B.D. Wong's transformation from geisha to young man is unexpected.

24 In John Northbrooke's *Treatise Against Dicing, Dancing, Plays and Interludes* his fictive character "Age" tries to instruct "Youth" about the evils of entertainments, telling the story of the "Beniamites" who stole away the daughters of Israel by "watching them in a special open place" where in festival they danced and disported themselves "wantonly" (1845: 86). The usual conjunction of theatrical display and female display becomes more dangerous because of the ease with which the 'show' could be seen, in an 'open' place. The vulnerability of the "open," of the penetrable, of the talkative for Dauphine in *Epicoene* is controlled by withholding, keeping mum, playing with notions of silence. While those who equate "open" orifices to shameful wantonness usually mean either female orifice, the most exposed orifice of man or woman is the ear. A reader can independently open and close a book, his/her eyes, but the spectator who closes his/her eyes to the sight of performance must rather awkwardly, and finally incompletely, close the ears by covering them with the hands.

25 According to Adam Fox Jonson's audience would not have been surprised to hear the barber speak a term borrowed from printed books: "Barbers provide one example of a group who seem often to have been readers: their shops acted both as centers of news and gossip and as places where newsletters or pamphlets might be seen" (Fox 2000: 39).

26 Mario DiGangi suggests the "fates" of Dauphine and Morose are determined by "the Renaissance epistemology of sodomy" because Morose in his "disorderly marriage" to Epicoene is marked "as a sodomite," whereas Dauphine even if "he *has* had sex with Epicoene" is not "marked as a sodomite" (1995: 186). The orderliness of Dauphine's "relationship with Epicoene," is proved through the "effect" of Dauphine regaining his inheritance. When the two buffoons are proclaiming triumph over the "virginity" of the 'maid' at hand, it is not that the taking of a boy's 'maidenhead' is not possible, but that their triumph is one of property, being the first to usurp. The reading audience knows this is impossible because the terms of ownership do not apply in the same way to a "gentleman suppos'd the silent woman." DiGangi's argument may be augmented by speculation about the agency of the boy actor. While there is no doubt that Dauphine "wins," the terms upon which he has won depend upon not only the "faithfulness" of his "young companion" but also on that companion's ability to improvise his master's lines.

27 I came across Douglas Bruster's use of the term embodied writing after I had completed this chapter: he defines embodied writing "as a kind of text and textual practice that, increasingly during the 1590s, put resonant identities and physical forms on the printed page. Embodied writing aggressively drew real and imaginary figures into print for indecorous handling" (2000: 50). Bruster takes up writing between the 1590s and the early 1600s, seeing in it an expression of the body which owes its vividness to change in authority, writers eager to take up the new form of print and writers under the influence of the playhouse. I see this writing as a marker of the transition between a print culture made vivid by the bodies evoked in texts but also by the bodies receiving the texts through their senses.

28 See Karen Newman (1989) for an analysis of Jonson's consideration of gender, consumption, and commodification in *Epicoene*.

29 A frequent connection made in this century, and present in most of the works discussed in this book, is the uncontrollable motion of sound and its likeness to the female, the wanton, the uncontainable. See Anne Carson (1995) for the origins of this connection in the ancient world and Patricia Parker (1987) for the likening of wanton women to that wandering trope, the metaphor.

30 See Gossett (1988) for a description of a masque at court where drunken Hope, retching Faith, and unsteady Chastity mar the performance.

31 For circulation of masque texts, see Leeds Barroll (1996) and for Jonson's particular interest in publishing his masques, see Stephen Orgel's introduction to *The Complete Masques* (1969).

32 Masque studies since Orgel have been influenced by studies in gender since the form invited female participation, albeit usually silent, well before women were on the stage in England (Gossett 1988); studies in dance with attention to the performed power of dance and its meaning (Franko 1993, 2000); and studies of festival and spectacle which attempt to understand the national, political, and aesthetic components of the masque (Strong 1984; Peacock 1995).

33 Dances in masque performance intersected with texts in a quite literal way when the choreography instructed the dancers to stop in patterns of letters and words that the audience could read (Franko 1993). Another source of dancing inspiration for a collaboration of stillness and motion was the garden as Jennifer Neville writes: "there were close similarities between the static choreography of the formal gardens of the nobility and the moving choreographies performed by members of the court" (1999: 819). Neville observes that in masques the design of the stage and the dances changes from orderly geometric patterns to a more flowing choreography reflecting the change from geometric shapes to circular paths in gardens from the sixteenth to the seventeenth century.

34 Jonson's instructive scenes in *Epicoene* follow a cruder formulation of this idea. The spectator experiences the play as one plot cast with expectations of gender and sexual intrigue only to be surprised and overpowered by the author's revelation that one didn't "get it." The surprise shocks the senses rather than soliciting them. In the masque, as in the text of *Epicoene*, Jonson invites spectators to participate in the unfolding.

35 One need only read Jonson's textual apparatus for the masques to see how in this case print seems to lack the self-evident power of the performance, and the poet must fill in the gaps by frequent notes about the stage, about the intent of the dance, etc. See *The Complete Masques* (1969) and Howard (1998).

36 In a masque this reception was complicated, including a self referentiality made of the close connections between court figures playing in the masque and the gossip circulating in these closed communities about intrigues, betrayals, and changes of fortune.

37 The Duke of Buckingham enjoyed James' favor as a performer as well as a subject. Known for his dancing, the manly "bounding" James preferred according to Jean McIntyre, Buckingham as masquer combined the aristocratic place with the professional talent of a hired dancer (1998). McIntyre also notes the unusual choice Jonson made to give "anti masque-like speaking parts to normally unspeaking masquers."

38 Jonson, as John Demaray reminds us, makes a "surprising confession" in his reminiscence of *Hymenaei* about "the excellence of dancing . . . when the main masquers descended to the ballroom floor and first began to dance, he wrote that their dances were so 'excellently performed, as it seemed to take away that Spirit from the Invention, which the Invention gave to it: and left it doubtful, whether the Forms flowed more perfectly from the Author's braine, or their

feete'" (Demaray 1968: 24). To the wistful Jonson who wants an intimate, immediate relation with the reader we might add the insecure Jonson who upon witnessing the masque in performance sees the fulfillment of the meaning of even the most evocative of words made manifest through corporeal performance.

39 This is not to suggest that we forget that the work of Stephen Orgel (1965; 1975) and Roy Strong (1984) have made scholars see the masque and spectacle in entirely new ways. However, while advances have been made in interpreting the masque according to new innovations in critical analysis, we still lack work on "how" the masque had the effect it did, what in the performance itself produces the effect.

40 See Butler (1991), as well as Rebecca Ann Bach (1995) who makes an analysis of the language of "savagery" and Jonson's transformation of such colonial language into "theatre" in *The Gypsies Metamorphosed*.

41 Considering the masque form as a theoretical puzzle without thinking about how it conveys ideas through performance hinders our understanding of colonial relations. "Colonial logic," to use Rebecca Ann Bach's phrase, depends upon performance – of submission, of authority, even of ambivalent cooperation (1995). The theory of colonial relations cannot be separated from an understanding of performance, and of the potential resistance made through performance. Such performances also offered space between, as Johannes Fabian has attested in his work on performance in Africa; the mimetic could open a space for resistance as well as reification (1990: 56).

42 Though the word curator is an anachronism, I think it helps to communicate to a modern audience Inigo Jones' arrangement and display in the masque. Masques were often settings for collectors to show their wonders, either in the set design, in the costumes, sometimes in the reproduction of precious objects on the stage. The masque itself could also function as a microcosm of something collected since the power of the patron was shown in the demonstration of this miniature, beautiful, moving world.

43 The Collector of Collectors honored by masques was James' son, Charles I.

44 The circles implied by the rhythm of the language and the movement of give and take might be mirrored in the dancing of the masques since *The Gypsies Metamorphosed* was performed at the crux of a transition in choreography from the "rectilinear" patterns toward the French passion for "scroll-like patterns and 'S'-shaped curves and arabesques" (Neville 1999: 820).

45 The bonds of obligation extended beyond the King and Buckingham. Many aristocrats playing *The Gypsies Metamorphosed* had reason to acknowledge patronage since Arundel "et al owed their places to Buckingham's influence" (McIntyre 1998: 69).

46 Throughout work on gift exchange runs this word, "inexhaustible." To Hyde it is a sign of the property of the gift to regenerate, it cannot be used up; to Derrida it can be both a desired attribute and a threatening muchness promising only *ennui*. Like Dyer's examination of the musical as an abundant form, moments in performance which celebrate the possibility of the inexhaustible are often utopian.

47 A more pressing political reading than that based on gift exchange could see this scene as a satire upon a ruler who orchestrates a performance of largesse that is indeed only the ostentatious return of the little the subject had at the beginning. At a masque performed in James' court, with a monarch notorious for large promises made on a little substance, his subjects had a choice of interpretations to hand when they watched these scenes.

2 Predominantly still

1 See Demaray, *Milton and the Masque Tradition* (1968), Diekhoff, *A Maske at Ludlow* (1968), and Creaser, " 'The present aid of this occasion:' The setting of *Comus*" in *The Court Masque* (1984) for three different, imaginative, and contentious interpretations of how *A Maske* was performed. The scene I consider central in *A Maske*, Diekhoff moves through in a paragraph, returning as quickly as possible to the story which only "races on" when the brothers return (1968: 13).

2 Demaray suggests the chair might have been on a slant in order for the audience to see Comus and the Lady conversing, but I think it is as likely that the audience might have seen Lady Alice being encircled in her chair by the mobile Comus.

3 The critical interpretation of a masque includes the question of whether it is a masque (Barber 1968), a Puritan masque (McGuire 1983), a kid's Sunday outing (Diekhoff 1968), or a reformation of all masques before or to come (Norbrook 1984).

4 I am persuaded by John Creaser's suggestions regarding the varieties of political belief, royal leanings, and Welsh complexities represented in the audience at the performance of *A Maske*, despite some reservations I have about his hyperbole regarding the young poet's talents and virtues (1984). In the delicate task of assessing how an audience might have received a performance, no supposition seems so tenuous as one about the current political climate and the personal views of the participants. As much in process as any unfixed phenomenon, a Royalist's sentiments, a Puritan's beliefs undergo changes according to the behavior (in the last few days, months) of monarch and leaders, and the influence of recent speeches and books.

5 William Riley Parker figures Milton's choice for anonymity as one of an entrance onto the stage of "public life," albeit one from the "side door of anonymity" (1969: 12).

6 For a lovely facsimile of the transformation of the manuscript into printed version of *A Maske*, see S.E. Sprott, editor (1973) *A Maske:The Earlier Versions*. Each page records three versions of the work: the Trinity Manuscript, the Bridgewater Manuscript, and the version of *A Maske* published in 1637. Sprott's introduction conveys the complications and confusions inevitable in dating and attributing handwritten or anonymously published works.

7 Authors who write in other genres and adapt their work for the stage often reveal their opinions about performance in the process. Henry James, for example, seemed to believe the theatre audience incapable of any subtlety. In his adaptation of *The American*, he not only fills in the nuances, he uses mortar and brick. Lest we mistake this for contempt, James wrote of his early love of theatre and his wish to be successful as a playwright.

8 Many readers of Milton find him too wordy to be called theatrical or dramatic; as Christopher Kendrick notes in "Milton and Sexuality: a Symptomatic Reading of *Comus*," Milton "textualizes the spectacle" when I in fact suggest he auralizes and spectacularizes the text (Kendrick 1988: 55). Yet what twentieth-century audiences may receive as "wordy," could very well be an enhanced score of language designed to make meaning in sound as well as print.

9 Though Queens spoke in Jonson's masques, they more often danced than they spoke, and when they did speak, the tone of the poetry usually confirmed the divinity of the speaker. Also see Barbara Breasted concerning the particular reasons for Lady Alice's compromised position, "*Comus* and the Castlehaven Scandal" (1971). As a poet agonizing about his own rights of passage, poetic and sexual, Milton, I suspect, would have risen to the challenge of the sordid

past by subsuming it in his purification, as he sought to do with the rest of the jaded elements of masquing.

10 See the *Apology for Smectymnuus* in which Milton escalates his vision of chastity into a personal trinity absorbing his own body, his own glory (a.k.a. woman), and the combination of the two, God. Without chastity he sins "both against his own body, which is the perfecter sex, and his own glory which is in the woman, and that which is worst, against the image and glory of God, which is in himself" (Milton 1985: 695). See Christopher Kendrick's "Milton and sexuality: a symptomatic reading of *Comus*" for a "politico-cultural" reading of Milton's "chastity cult" (1988: 43).

11 The citations of line numbers are taken from Merritt Y. Hughes' edition of *The Complete Poems*. The three versions of *A Maske* in Sprott's edition have differing line numbers, and the version of *A Maske* in the facsimile edition of the 1645 *Poems* has no line numbers at all.

12 For a detailed discussion of Proteus and the antitheatricalists, see "Puritans and Proteans" in Barish (1981).

13 Notice in line 146 the Lady's "chaste footing" sets a unique, *uncommon* "pace", alerting the revelers who "break off" their "light fantastic round."

14 According to some Protestant theologians, female susceptibility to divine grace was biological: "the 'openness' of the female body made women natural prophets" (Trubowitz 1992: 119).

15 See Milton's discussion of his College title of "Lady" in Prolusion VI (Hughes 1985: 620).

16 The rare female speaker of soliloquies generally establishes her evil purposes to the audience in her solo. Ponderous thinking and figuring belong to men's soliloquies, often establishing their dignity, their lack of resolve or both. Margaret Ferguson has suggested to me that Milton might have known Elizabeth Cary's *The Tragedy of Mariam* (1613), the heroine of which speaks ethically complex soliloquies. The Lady shares her form, as noted earlier, with fictional noblewomen, Duchesses (Malfi) and Queens. In fact, it is tempting to consider the Lady's own self-possession and unmoving body in the light of the resolved and enigmatic line from Webster: "I am the Duchess of Malfi still." It is very possible given dates of performances and Milton's biography that he saw Webster's play performed or that he read the 1623 printed edition.

17 When I refer to the printed editions of *A Maske*, I refer to both the 1637 edition and to the edition published in Milton's 1645 *Poems* and will distinguish between the two only when there are line differences. The dates for several versions of the Trinity Manuscript make it too variable for me to use as an instance of a published version (Milton 1973: 3–13).

18 Literary critics might argue that this is simply the poet becoming better at his craft, but what Milton concentrates on in many of his additions are the areas of the masque the reader cannot see as a spectator might.

19 A sensuous distance between seeing the masque performance or reading the text occurs again at the end of the text where on the page only a few centimeters separate the final song and "dances ended, the Spirit epilogizes." In performance there could have been up to two hours worth of dancing and music between that song and the undoing of the evening through the final verse.

20 There is an anxiety for Milton about ravishment of males as well as females, though the orifice at risk is likely to be the ear. In *A Maske* and other works he worries about the question of how to keep chaste ears while seductive aural spectacle threatens to steal the senses, and how to create seductive language and spectacle that aids the reader/spectator in remaining intact.

21 In the Greek tradition of single question, single answer, the characters also danced, the motion embedded in the call and response made overtly physical by the bodies moving back and forth across the stage (Wiles 2000).

22 From Northbrooke's antitheatrical dialogue between Age and Youth to Comenius' popular schoolbook on the alphabet – that harbinger of printed learning – makers of works in print found the trope of dialogue a useful didactic tool. Dialogue, Socratic question and answer posed as an active debate, let an audience play the accustomed role of spectator and auditor where learning took place in listening to oral presentation and committing the spoken word to memory. As in the narration of Gospel events, miracles, and meetings, "sacred conversations" (*sacra conversazione*) when 'witnessed' by the reader became allegorical tools for Christian living.

23 The Lady articulates one aspect of the performance-print dilemma itself: where courtesy is named is not necessarily where it is practiced. The court in charge of naming often fails to give its audience the experience of the thing named, so courtesy though defined at Court is not known and learned by being at Court. Here is a very minute and simple reminder of comprehension and apprehension: while a name tells the reader what something is, the understanding of meaning comes by apprehension, the epiphanic recognition that *this* is what was meant by *that* word or explanation.

24 An entr'acte occurs between the exit of the Lady and Comus and their reappearence in Comus' domain; a protracted discussion first between her two brothers and then in another exchange between the brothers and Thyrsis. As audience and critics sense from the beginning of the masque, the Lady and Comus are the main characters. The brothers and Spirit play an odd echo to the linguistic "action" of the seducer and his difficult prey. Providing extended commentary on what might happen to the sister they "lost," the brothers speculate on the pregnable possibilities in her virgin "armor." Impractical and abstract, the philosophical debate about the Lady, already witnessed and listened to by the audience, occurs as commentary on the scene about to take place between Comus and the Lady.

As if upping the danger ante, Milton brings in his Attendant Spirit to acquaint the brothers with the here and now of their sister in the woods. In the guise of their father's shepherd Thyrsis, Henry Lawes informs them and us that he too played interloper to the talk between the Lady and Comus, "that damn'd wizard hid in sly disguise" (l. 571). One wonders whether in performance Lawes would have appeared for a few moments during the scene, making the audience aware of other forces looking out for the Lady. Armed with a flower to undo Comus' enchantment, this is after all a wood and one needs must arm oneself with drugs and antidotes, Thyrsis awakens the passive brothers to their duty as saviors. When the scene reopens in Comus' palace, the seducer stands unmasked, and the visible condition of the Lady dispels the fictional traps the brothers imagine for her.

25 As Eve does in *Paradise Lost*, the Lady in *A Maske* fuels the action of her author's story, but these fictional women make trouble for their author when (even) their (imagined) bodies intervene. In Book Four, Eve contemplates self-reflexive pools in which "herself herself" beholds (to borrow Shakespeare's mimetic terms from "Venus and Adonis") and "herself herself" prefers, causing God the correcting author to encourage her to see better and attend to Adam (*Paradise Lost*, IV. 460–70).

26 Continuing in the mode of his earlier disguised interrogation, Comus demands to know the Lady's reasons for what she does, much as Ibsen's Judge Brack does to Hedda Gabler. Men who are not spouses, parents or siblings may prove to be dangerous predators, but often, paradoxically, they alone actually address

questions to women and expect answers. Neither her brothers nor the Attendant Spirit will bother to address the Lady when they "save" her.

27 See Sharon Achinstein (1994), Chapter 4 for a discussion of how Milton theorizes seeing and perspective in *Eikonoklastes*.

28 In added lines in the published versions of 1637 and 1645 Comus taunts the Lady about her attachment to abstract ideals. A word, an idea named "Virginity" can "cozen" or delude a girl, he argues, and lead to the stillness of fidelity as against natural movement, the exchange of beauty's currency (ll. 736–7). As in Milton's other printed addition, Comus takes pains to acquaint the reading audience with a reminder of the young girl's allure, "vermeil-tinctur'd lip," her "love-darting eyes," her "tresses like the Morn," however exaggerated by Comus' all-licensed desire to possess her (ll. 752–3). Since Comus' manipulative tactics run to the visual, he flatters the Lady with comparison, where the "homely" should stay at "home," the beautiful should adorn public spaces (l. 747). Presumably the Masque audience would not need such exposition to understand the lovely Lady's (nubile) attractions or need further arguments to identify Comus' spectacular nature evidenced on stage before them.

29 John Demaray laments how many discussions of the action of *A Maske* depend upon "either personality conflicts or doctrinal differences" when Milton and Lawes, he argues, "created a masque which . . . turns upon magic" (1968: 88). Even folktales and spectacles, however, tend to weave stories of magic and enchantment according to the susceptibility of the enchanted. That the Lady is finally saved from one sort of magic by another does not detract from Milton's dramatic interventions in which she makes clear her own participation in enchantment and her ability to participate in breaking its hold.

30 Christopher Kendrick poses similar questions in his essay "Milton and Sexuality: *Comus.*" Kendrick, with a layered analysis moving from psychoanalytic to Foucauldian to a "politico-cultural" reading, assesses Milton's sexuality as filtered through the Lady. While illustrating some remarkable points regarding *A Maske*, masques and drama, Kendrick seems to imitate his psychoanalytic progenitor by hardly dwelling on what words Milton assigns the Lady herself. A reader searches for the Lady in much the way one searches for Dora, wondering how these intricate theories about her came about almost without her (1987).

31 See *Milton and Sex* where Edward le Comte discusses the awkwardness Milton left behind in his "gums of glutinous heat" (1977: 1–4).

32 Margaret Ferguson suggests that because Milton's Echo is "translated to the skies," she gains a more heavenly aspect than Ovid's creation, and thus becomes an apt precursor to Sabrina.

33 As with most of the meeting points of stillness and motion, the river in its flowing past can be both perpetual movement and, as Philip Schwyzer (1997) notes about the geographic locations in *A Maske*, a boundary marker employed for its fixity between one side and another.

34 Oral tradition and drama rely on circulation of stories and texts through storytelling and performance; the stories live because they move and are seen in performance. In her essay "Two Masques of Ceres and Proserpine: *Comus* and *The Tempest*," Mary Loeffelholz alludes to the "persistent power of Ovidian metamorphoses," or in theatrical terms protean change, throughout *A Maske* (1987: 33). In her reading Sabrina "incorporates the threat of metamorphoses and transforms it into a cure" (33). Oddly Sabrina's moisture by cleansing the Lady effectively returns her to the everyday exchange of words, of potential marriage. Embodied fluidity, Sabrina pulls the Lady back into the flow of movement. The Lady's engaged conversing threatened to take her out of the

chaste circulation because she would belong to Comus, be his sexually and be lost (not visible) to her family and her community.

3 Theatrically pressed

1 Lois Potter (1989), Dale Randall (1995) and Susan Wiseman (1998) are three of the scholars who are exceptions to this rule; I rely on their work in this chapter. Martin Butler first called scholarly attention to the period just before the Interregnum in his *Theatre and Crisis* (1984).

2 "Often in studies of Renaissance and Restoration drama and theatre [the gap between 1642 and 1660] *replaces* discussion of the period standing by synecdoche for eighteen years of largely unacknowledged and uninvestigated but immensely diverse dramatic, and some theatrical, activity" (Wiseman 1998: 1).

3 Fox reminds us that when material was "posted up in public places" there would be at "least one reader in the crowd who could speak up for all to hear . . . Even if people could not read themselves, they brought printed texts and books in the expectation that they would be read aloud to them when the opportunity arose. The Bible was the supreme example of this" (2000: 37, 38).

4 "New insights into the role of print as a medium for the articulation of controversial views asks us to see a sphere of public expression that preceded and in some ways enabled" later "conversational settings" like the coffeehouses (Bruster 2000: 63). Bruster suggests the "playfulness" of pamphlets at the turn of the seventeenth century gestured toward "arenas of celebrity and public discourse that were the public playhouses" (65).

5 "In earlier times the reader interiorized the text; he made his voice the body of the other; he was its actor. Today, the text no longer imposes its own rhythm on the subject, it no longer manifests itself through the reader's voice" (de Certeau 1984: 175–6).

6 Of course this period saw the development of private reading as well. In Derek Hirst's description former playgoers were being encouraged to become collectors of previously ephemeral experience: "As the English Revolution ran its course, would-be playgoers were translated into private consumers of the literary collections which poured from the press" (1995: 245). My insistence on remembering the revolution as one of oral performance as well as private reading is in response to the critical work that is very good at imagining the impact of print on private lives but less so at figuring the movement between oral reception and private reading which still existed during this century. Nigel Smith acknowledges "the Leveller tracts are very easy for us to read because they look like modern journalistic prose, although they would have seemed quite difficult and obscure to contemporaries who were educated to expect very different (and to *us* difficult) pieces of writing" (1993: 236). But I wonder again whether this does mark a distinction between a "style" of prose expected to be received in some part orally versus one expected to be produced for educated readers. Whatever the import, Smith makes an important intervention to remind us to query our own habits of reception. In *Oral and Literate Culture, 1500–1700* Adam Fox changes the way we understand print and its oral reception in the period; his is an invaluable intervention (2000).

7 "The civil war pamphleteers' tools of wit, inflated language, and scurrility, as well as the folk genres of the letter, the jestbook, the almanac, the ghost-warning piece and the ballad were all forms taken from the vernacular tradition" (Achinstein 1994: 11).

8 Two scholars, Alexandra Halasz and Stuart Sherman effectively use Anderson and Habermas to extend our understanding of sixteenth- and seventeenth-century political and social space, see p. 88.

9 "George Thomason, a publisher and bookseller, decided to make a collection of contemporary publications . . . Thomason collected *all* available publications, without regard either to quality or party line . . . he normally dated each publication on the day he received it" (Potter 1989: 1). In a century where published plays slowly came to be considered more than simply entertaining ephemera, it is fascinating to think of Thomason's intent. What world did he consider himself saving for posterity? What story did he think "books, pamphlets, newsbooks, broadsides, and manuscripts" of the period would tell later generations? The collection of ephemera has no particular monetary value; it is a collection in service of posterity. One might even say this sort of collection participates in a different form of gift exchange, making itself available for use for generations to come. Scholars themselves express their gratitude for the tracts in their acknowledgments, admitting it would be impossible for the work to be done without this bequest from Thomason. Potter directs readers interested in Thomason to Lois Spencer (1958) "The Professional and Literary Connexions of George Thomason."

10 Sharon Achinstein cites the case of the Royalist John Taylor (author of *Crop-earre Curried*): "we have a writer compelled to show readers how to act by reading; the reader must read the enemy argument properly" (1994: 146).

11 Susan Wiseman argues that throughout the period an equation was made between "action," theatrical in its earliest definition, and political action necessary for the people (1998: 81–7).

12 Foucault's discussion of language in *The Order of Things* might be remembered in the light of the changing nature of representation. While Foucault dwells in the proximate relation of meaning to word, a table tells something of itself through the word, he also offers a meditation on "resemblance" through the word 'murmur.' Though nostalgic in his reminiscence, Foucault, I would suggest, furthers our understanding of the way words might be said to be closer to things in representational value in the early modern period through the murmur, the sound that was sense. The nature of the word then might be understood as an aural phenomenon in a period when sound also conveyed a sense of shape.

13 "It is tempting to believe that their playful, sardonic spirit lived on in the blasphemy and scurrility of the Restoration stage and in the profane vigour of British working-class movements of the next two centuries" (Nelson 1992: 71).

14 The theatrical qualities of ephemeral pamphlet exchange and dramatic presentation between the public theatre plays and pamphlet writing had begun to be exploited before the Interregnum. Thomas Middleton practiced the overlapping styles when he lifted much of *A Game of Chess* (1624) from popular pamphlets denouncing Spain and Catholicism. Ben Jonson's play *The Staple of the News* stages the making and receiving of ephemeral literature, in this case news, within the world of public commentary. At the end of each act four "gossips" – four female characters speaking gossip, the ephemeral speech of women – comment upon the action of the play. Jonson invents and controls marketplace public response by scripting it himself, upstaging the responses of the receiving audience.

15 One wonders how this marginalia was read aloud, was there a kind of statement, digression, summation? Did marginalia get performed at all?

16 For details see Potter's survey of "The Plays and the Playwrights: 1642–1660" in *The Revels History of Drama in English*, IV (1975–83), as well as Randall (1995). Susan Wiseman (1998) argues for the drama of the period to be surveyed beyond the customary Royalist works.

17 Not only did playwrights write pamphlets as a means of livelihood during the Interregnum, many actors used their skills. John Harris, the publisher of the

newsbook *Mercurius Militaris*, is accused of being "a rebel and subversive journalist." Because he is an actor, he is a "vagabond," never more so than when the theatres are closed and companies cannot be registered. Harris "'sometimes a Players Boy . . . since the suppression of the Play-houses, hath betaken himself to the Profession of a Printer.'" Nigel Smith notes that Harris uses Shakespeare throughout his work to emphasize the "need to resist tyrants" (1993: 242). The description of Harris as a Players Boy and the association of wandering as an untrustworthy state for the reporting of news, emphasize yet again the 'feminine' of movement to the equation of performance and print. Indeed if Harris was a 'players boy' he might well have played the female roles in the Shakespearean productions he makes use of now in print.

18 What we know of the Ranters we know by the "explosion of anti-Ranter tracts." For information on the critical disagreements about the Ranters, see Gucer (2000: 77–8).

19 In a recent acknowledgment of the dramatic power of published pamphlets from the Interregnum, Caryl Churchill incorporates excerpts from the Putney Debates as dramatic dialogue in her play *Light Shining in Buckinghamshire* (1992).

20 Wiseman makes an important intervention when she asks why scholars of Renaissance drama "working with the insights of Michel Foucault, Clifford Geertz, Victor Turner" have "found little to interest them in a period of great social change [the Interregnum]" (1998: 15). However, Wiseman herself leaves her investigation of performance in the period to a very brief "Interchapter" in which she discusses the meaning of terms rather than the actual spaces and potential for the public sphere of performance she so persuasively argues for in the Introduction.

21 While the influences on Milton's style have been widely studied and revised, the quite plain information about Milton's professional interest in the making of drama has rarely been interpreted in terms of his work. John Demaray has been the most thorough critic in documenting Milton's creation of "puritan theatre" (1968; 1980).

22 Turnabout being fair play in the pamphlet world, Milton has his own theatrical response to a 'bad' player. In *Eikonoklastes* Milton, according to Richard Helgerson, takes "his lead from one of the king's favorite authors"; likening Charles "to the dissembling tyrant of Shakespeare's *Richard III*," Milton claims "to have heard 'the general voice of the people' almost hissing [Charles] and his ill-acted regality off the stage" (1987: 11). Like Overton, Milton seems to accept a certain amount of acting to be part of the public role of leader; thus the subject can also be critic, finding the acting "ill."

23 Such characters, Virtue, Vice, Truth, give spiritual notions "corporeal" immediacy and come from a tradition aligned with rhetoric and theatre, the "theatre memory system" (Yates 1966: 145, 140). As Frances Yates details, rhetoricians practiced the imaginative and pictorial rendering of concepts in the service of memory.

24 The angry response of those who found the tract scandalous and those who took it to be a call for sexual freedom taught Milton that the reader does indeed exercise power and that "reception invents, shifts about, distorts" (Chartier 1994: x).

25 Page citations for Milton's prose are from *Complete Poems and Major Prose*, Merritt Y. Hughes (ed.).

26 It must be said that the pamphlet and tract writers of the century had no reason to think outside of the effect of thinking/receiving upon the body. Whether it be a figuring of an enemy in grotesque, scatological terms, or a rendering of the experience of error or waywardness as one immediately legible upon the body,

the consequences of any form of perception were immediately expressed in language figuring the sensual reception of the body.

27 Of course, behind these imagined monsters and bright angels lies the history of allegory. Readers familiar with Edmund Spenser would certainly remember Una and Duessa, whose bodies – Duessa's seditiously protean – are reported vividly. But the audiences for the pamphletheatre had also changed from the audience for *The Faery Queen* and the vision of the monarch, however complex, offered a singular focus turned multiple for some auditors in the factional arguments of the Interregnum.

28 Nigel Smith suggests Milton relies on Italian history, Paolo Sarpi's "histories of the Council of Trent," to animate his imprimaturs: who "Milton brings to life satirically as the bobbing priests and friars: 'Sometimes 5 *Imprimaaturs* are seen together dialogue-wise in the Piatza of one Title page, complementing and ducking each to other with their shav'n references'" (1990: 111).

29 Later in Milton's life when he switches allegiance about freedom of the press he does not seem to change his ideas about the fluid nature of argument and poetic creation in books so much as his belief that the receivers can be trusted to be fluid themselves. In fact, it is a too literal interpretation of *DDD* that spoils Milton's dream of a fit audience for reception, contemplation, and action.

30 In the history of five-act plays, the third act is the one in which the playwright has the most freedom to surprise the audience and subvert tradition because the fourth and fifth act will come along where all is ordered by resolution or at least by a fashioned ending.

31 M.T. Clanchy writes of the history of the Crier's importance in the legal sessions (1979: 272–75) and Bruce Smith suggests that the Messenger at the beginning of *Everyman* is a figure not unlike the Crier because both "define an auditory circule that encompasses both actors and audience" (1999: 272).

32 Roger Chartier notes that in the Toledo edition of *La Celestina* the "proof-reader" adds a poem to the end where he directs the reader to "deliver asides in a low voice . . . vary his pitch, and impersonate each character in turn" (1989: 104).

33 The tendency to use names to identify the nature of the character may be borrowed from pamphlets earlier in the century where, according to Douglas Bruster, popular literary characters became "public personalities," and the literal nature of names turned "identities into things" (2000: 60).

34 I owe the original idea for this section of the chapter to discussion after a talk given by Nigel Smith at the University of Michigan (1996) in which he encouraged me to pursue the influence of theatrical thinking on Overton's representation of political action.

35 See Achinstein for a discussion of Milton's idealism (1994: 18–19).

4 Decidedly moving

1 A like restriction was imposed onto the theatres: when Charles II licensed only two theatres for playing, he created the atmosphere for rivalry between the two playhouses. In the years before the Interregnum, when there were many theatres, playwrights wrote for a diverse set of players and audiences. After the division of the two houses, the plays were often more pointedly aimed at a particular playhouse style and were often in reaction to a recent play at the "other House."

2 Text and learning appeal to understanding, power in performance appeals to the passions. Falling into theatre gossip, Behn revises herself: "Benjamin was no such Rabbi neither, for I am informed that his Learning was but Grammar high; (sufficient indeed to rob poor Salust of his best orations)" (I, 224). Behn belies

her own pretended lack of learning by knowing what in Jonson constitutes plagiarism from Salust.

3 According to Milhous and Hume in *Producible Interpretation*, Behn's explanation about giving the actor "the part" is not a figure of speech (Summers speculates Angel was the under prepared, overacting culprit in *The Dutch Lover* (I, 220)). "After the play was accepted by the manager the author read it aloud to the actors . . . [probably] roles were assigned by the manager with the advice of the author" (1985: 47–8).

4 Langhans' observation raises the expectations of his reader. Surely such unique attention to detail would mean a full study of the promptbook from a Behn play. Instead Langhans cites only a small section of *Sir Patient Fancy*.

5 Behn herself may not have written all the detailed directions, though the directions do specifically instruct an actor about how the line should be delivered – something of interest both to the author and the theatre manager. For example, in *The Lucky Chance* the stage directions instruct Leticia "who seems to weep" rather than inducing her to weep by referring to her weeping in the lines themselves as earlier authors might have done. The attention to detail for the actors in the italicized instructions in Behn's plays anticipate in miniature the paragraphs of directions that precede each act of a modern play by Ibsen or Pirandello. See Marvin Carlson's "The Status of Stage Directions" for a review of contemporary semiotic attentions to how stage directions function (1991).

6 Though Germaine Greer and other scholars caution against trusting attributions of work to women writers or relying on the authenticity of an edited collection, the irony is that at the time of reading (with the exception of potential cases of total plagiarism) there could be no doubt whose play it was, unless the author was disguising him or herself (Behn 1989). Ours is the problem of attribution, a textual one.

7 Robert Erickson in "Lady Fullbank and the Poet's Dream" identifies what he calls Behn's "gospel of Eros" as representing a "force of spiritual and intellectual renewal beyond the gross delights of the sensual body . . . a life-enhancing, feminized version of sexual libertinism" (1996: 101–2). In the renewal Erickson characterizes I see an analogy in the energy Behn's characters display when engaged in the free choice of exchange.

8 Rosenthal goes on to elucidate Behn's position: "Just as commodification both offers and dispels the possibility of happiness for Imoinda, the circulation of writing as commodity (economic capital) rather than gift (social capital) both advances and undermines Behn's position as author" (1996: 142).

9 In *The Ornament of Action*, Peter Holland finds the "vast majority – eighteen in all" of Behn's "discovery" scenes to be "bedroom scenes" played "upstage" (1979: 41–2). As if he must undertake an unpleasant task – Behn's "positively obsessive" interest in "discoveries" proves so unusual as to "necessitate consideration" – Holland gives Behn an entire paragraph of her own. Holland's important work gives life to many of the productions left to flounder in textual confusion, yet he picks Behn up with linguistic tweezers, only able to stomach the comedies, "I have omitted the farces," and those only long enough to let him enumerate thirty-one discoveries. Fortunately Dawn Lewcock (1996) corrects this oversight by not only pointing out "the sheer professionalism Behn's plays show particularly in the ways in which she understands and uses the potential of the scenic stage," but by theorizing how Behn's use of discoveries offers a "simultaneity" that affects the reception of the audience (1996: 70).

10 The forestage peopled by characters milling about the 'street,' signified by the appropriate London street scenery or country gardens depicted in the inner stage, invited the audience to fancy themselves in familiar settings, free to roam. Perhaps many of the women "of quality" in the audience – accustomed to

moving from coach to door back to coach again in the company of a guardian – saw Behn's female characters cavorting even in the fictional out of doors as too bawdy (the confined movement of women of quality is a practice lamented by Lucretia and Isabella in *Sir Patient Fancy*, Act I). The shocking freedom of movement of the play's young heroines could convey wantonness so swiftly that even the most decorous language could not dispel the visual effect of a woman's "looseness," literally, her being loose.

11 See Todd (1989), Hutner (1993), Diamond (1989), and Boebel (1996).

12 See Skantze (1994) "The Lady Eve; or, Who's on First?" for a discussion about the strikingly rare appearance of women in first scenes, and the theatrical effect of having male characters describe the women who come after them. By the eighteenth century it was commonplace to have the women enter for the first time in Act II.

13 In the seventeenth-century English playhouse looking up and right or up and left was associated with the frequent play between the pit and the boxes. The boxes over the apron stage itself just below Angellica's balcony further incorporated the theatrical world and social world since those in the boxes made up part of the full stage as viewed by those in the pit.

14 Behn often uses actual pictures of women as props in the course of a play that startle the spectator into a visual recognition of woman as ornament and commodity, more manageable/collectible the more she is immobile. In *The Amorous Prince* Curtius adopts the role of pimp advertising by handing out small portraits of his wares: "copies of the most fair originals, not to be bought but hired" (II, 181).

15 Fame entails another conundrum of print, performance, commodification, and circulation. Fame has a shelf-life: if hoarded too closely, kept too long, it spoils for being out of circulation. Yet if too freely spent it becomes common.

16 As this paragraph makes clear, Angellica's position can in other interpretive models be seen as powerful. For an interpretation of Angellica's manipulation of power through a "reversed double gaze," see Heidi Hutner who argues that "Behn utilizes the construction of the sexualized whore to subert the ideology of passive, self controlled and commodified womanhood" (1993: 107). As is clear in this chapter, I see Behn using another female character, Hellena, to contrast Angellica's passivity – one not subverted but corrected – a passivity born in part from her acquiescence to the market world of whore and paying customer.

17 Where the pit had been the province of those who paid the least in the early seventeenth century, in theatres after 1660 "the cheapest places were moved to above and behind the occupants of the pits and boxes" (Langhans 2000: 15).

18 Royalists in Behn's representations play with the impertinent freedom available only to those who loyally and ironically consider themselves subjects. Self-policing, puritanical strictures seem to freeze the reformed into worry and hesitant action, while the cavaliers and the romancing royalists of *The Good Old Cause* break rules with abandon. Since most of Behn's royalists behave like Catholics on holiday, obedient only to God, they provide a tempting, if a bit oversimplified, parallel to Elizabeth Eisenstein's proposed dichotomies of oral tradition and Roman rite with printed culture and Protestant biblical authority (1980). Eisenstein herself complicates the dichotomy in a later essay when she suggests that print could be a weapon in the hands of the Catholic church, one they employed in "anti-Ottoman propaganda of the late 15th century" (1985: 27).

19 Renaming Killigrew's Thomaso Willmore, Behn invites any number of echoes while honoring Shakespeare, whose own play upon his stubborn, licentious name in the sonnets and the plays can be seen in this inherited character. Laura Rosenthal suggests Behn appropriates Killigrew's play in order to chastise him

under cover of his own drama. He merited Behn's resentment both because of his overweening power in the theatre and his abandonment of Behn when she went to prison in Holland after Charles II employed her as a spy at Killigrew's suggestion (1996: 119).

20 See David M. Sullivan "The Female Will in Aphra Behn" (1993).

21 Cornelia may dismiss trees and statues in Ovid, but Behn craftily sets this scene in a garden that is a collector's showcase. Here again is a vivid contrast between the meticulously designed and geometrically fixed garden of the Medici and the characters in Behn's play who circulate in and out of the shutters on which are painted a representation of the garden. In the actual Medici Villa in Rome the design of the wall surrounding the cortile that leads to the gardens incorporated a proscenium façade for the many festivals and spectacles held by the Medicis.

22 In her book *The First English Actresses*, Elizabeth Howe begins to address the remarkable silence about the history of the first actresses on the English stage. Though Katharine Maus' important article appeared in 1979, in general the entrance of actresses onto the stage has had few chroniclers. Unfortunately, Howe posits a strange connection between the actress and her effect on the playwrights: "the actresses caused rape to become for the first time a major feature of English tragedy" (1992: 42–3). In this kind of 'she asked for it' phrasing, the actresses by virtue of being female call forth their own sexual objectification and their own role as victims of violence. In fact, it is clear that before the Restoration boys dressed as women were ready surrogates on stage for the violation of women by men.

23 Though one can push too hard at the multiple resonances of Behn's female characters' names and Shakespeare's famous daughters, wives and mothers, a Cornelia who ironically echoes "like a bird in a cage," and longs to avoid the convent or old men's embraces cannot be completely separate from the other young Cordelia who is invited by an old man to a prison where Lear imagines "we two alone will sing like birds i' the cage" (V. iii. 9).

24 In the Preface Behn suggests women who mask themselves become active pirates "pickeroons that scour for prey . . . pillage ye, then gladly let you go" (III, 286).

25 For an ongoing debate on the scale of the Dorset Garden scenic stage, apron-stage and interior, see Edward Langhans, "A Conjectural Reconstruction of the Dorset Garden Theatre" (1972); John R. Spring, "Platforms and Picture Frames: A Conjectural Reconstruction of the Duke of York's Theatre: A Review of Facts and Problems" (1977); Robert Hume, "The Nature of the Dorset Garden Theatre" (1982); Frans Muller, "Flying Dragons and Dancing Chairs at Dorset Garden" (1993).

26 Since these three characters portray Behn's manipulation of characters from *Commedia dell'Arte*, they are not simply objects, but indeed masks. Like the famous half-leathern mask of Arlecchino or the jowly-cheeked masks of the lazii, the names and the dress of Behn's characters disguise singular features of the actors and reveal stereotypes. Masks indeed allow an actor to emphasize the motion of the body, the fluctuations of the voice while most of the face remains immobile, hidden behind the sign of the character's nature. Depending upon the actor and the audience, some of the masks can surprise, frighten, and delight in the distance played between expected enactment and possible interpretations of the role.

27 In this way Tickletext as a character seems to foreshadow Jeremy Collier, the literal-minded cleric who writes an attack on the stage at the end of the century, see Chapter 5.

28 See Cibber (1889) and Wilson (1958) for accounts of Leigh's talents.

29 Of course in any play written in England, staged in Italy, the terms of Protestant and Catholic are at work in the representation of even pretend bishops and

foolish pastors. To complicate matters, the scandal of the false Popish Plot had broken in the year before *The Feigned Courtesans* was performed, making any mention of Catholic rapacity subject to comparison with the contemporary trials of "conspirators."

5 Perpetually stilled

1 According to Robert Hume Collier's regulating desire did not result in regulation: "What is truly important about 'the Collier crisis' is not his impact on the drama (or lack thereof), but rather the failure of the authorities to set the moribund censorship mechanism back in working order" (1999: 496). Hume ties Collier's failure to the coming of the 1737 Licensing Act and its stifling of English drama. My interest in Collier's tract is not so much what it made happen or didn't make happen in the theatre as how the way he goes about arguing for reform involves the same terms – women, stillness, silence, chastity, male authority – we have seen used to give and adjust value for print and performance throughout the century.

2 Stuart Sherman in *Telling Time* enriches the discussion of an audience created by periodicals by navigating the Scylla of Jurgen Habermas and the Charybdis of Benedict Anderson: "each is most revealing where the other is least exact. Habermas ignores the true timing of the [news]paper he discusses, while Anderson overlooks the complex traffic that they facilitated among silence, print, and speech" (1996: 113). *The Spectator*, Sherman argues, incorporated the "Habermasian imaging [of the public sphere]" and the Andersonian "clocking [the calendar of the newspaper creating a community joined in time] of the readership" into a "new correspondence with its readers, as both a communication (corresponding with them) and a mirroring (corresponding to them)" (114).

3 In *Imagined Communities* Benedict Anderson neglects an area full of potential for theorizing the making of nation in the imagination, the world of the familial and domestic (1991). There have been interventions about gender and nation in the early modern period (see Howard and Rackin 1997), but the world one generally knows best, the family, offers many opportunities for comparisons between an identity based on relations, kin, and an identity based on fealty to one's national kin. See Susan Staves (1990) for a lucid examination of the late seventeenth-century commentary on the relation of monarch to people made in the domestic representation of the relation between husband and wife. See also Backsheider (1993).

4 Collier's pamphlets elicited many responses, from Vanbrugh himself (see p. 147), and from John Dennis who styles his rebuttal: "The usefulness of the stage to the happiness of mankind, to government, and to religion" (1698).

5 Both Robert Hume (1976) and David Roberts question the category of "the Ladies" and wonder about the existence of a "Ladies" faction. Roberts acknowledges the "disappointingly thin collection of recent guesses at what women expected of the Restoration playhouses and how they behaved when they went to them" (1989: 1). The playwrights of the 1680s and 1690s might simply have had more information by witnessing the women in the audience – no doubt overhearing or conversing with women outside the playhouse. Still the term "Ladies" as if all agreed and all were the same cannot be used without qualification or at least must be held gingerly in quotation marks. Having questioned the authority of the "Ladies," Hume replaces the "male" and "female" into their traditional roles when he comments: "The Ladies presumably objected to *what* was shown, the men of the pit probably objected

to the negative *way* it was shown" (1976: 390, emphasis mine). Like Ben Jonson, Hume assumes women to be impressionable by sight and prone to shock at the simple display, while the men would think about the conditions of the representation, analyze the process of the show.

6 Conservative, reforming forces, have historically assumed a collective voice for the "gentler sex," a voice attributed to women but frequently invented for them. This political crossdressing, a high-toned, high-pitched ventriloquism, allows several self-interested groups to shelter themselves under the skirts of an unassailable womanhood and conversely offer the "Ladies" masculine protection. See the Epilogue for Defoe's importation of the need to defend the book, which he figures as an unprotected, ravishable text.

7 While Milton also hopes to cleanse the tradition of the masque in his *A Maske* by the creation of his chaste Lady, the Lady's proof of virtue lies in her method of *speech*, though compromised in performance by the attendant confusion and discrepancies between chastity and theatrical seduction. See Chapter 2.

8 Mary Saunderson and Anne Bracegirdle at Lincoln's Inn Fields actually became shareholders not only of onstage talk, but of offstage company profits in 1695 (Maus 1979: 600).

9 Indiana represents the collectible not only in her desire to be known as the property of her lord, but also because she is emblematic of the trade in rare commodities brought from the 'islands' to England to be sold. Like her male counterpart Belcour in Richard Cumberland's *The West Indian*, she is Englishand foreign; her nationality is concealed from her at birth since she is raised in a colony.

10 A shopgirl quoted in (created by) *The Spectator* succinctly states these terms by speaking of her customers as "ready to interpret my looks and gestures according to their own Imaginations" (Ketcham 1985: 30).

11 Some of Collier's diffidence cloaks the dangerous practice of repeating filth to abolish filth. At one point, as if he can no longer withstand the power of these salacious texts, Collier anticipates the argument of those who accuse him in his naughty catalogue; rather than be titillated by his project, he insists he finds this "fight indeed" "horrible" (80). "I am quite tired with these wretched sentences . . . almost unwilling to shew it" (1698: 80).

12 Vanbrugh sends his Loveless to the playhouse where he watches a play in which a rake barely overcomes his desire to "relapse." Loveless comes home to describe the affecting scene later to his own wife (soon to be tormented by her husband's relapse, his unfaithfulness with her cousin Berintha). All this occurs in a play called *The Relapse*. The audience recognized Vanbrugh's reference to Colley Cibber's *Love's Last Shift*. Vanbrugh amends Cibber's story, unable to believe in the rake's spotless repentance. Throughout the play almost every character is cuckolded or cuckolding using disguise and relying upon the ingenuity of old lovers.

13 "After the Glorious Revolution had effectively declared the relationship between sovereigns and subjects contractual instead of divine, Bishop Gilbert Burnet, one of the revolution's most enthusiastic supporters, had no trouble remembering the *Reformatio Legum* and found it easy to declare that marriage was not a sacrament and that its supposed indissolubility rested on misapprehending it as a sacrament instead of a contract" (Staves 1979: 116). See Staves (1990) for a description of the complicated legal terms for married women's property.

14 While the wedded two who were supposed to become one bifurcated into disagreements and unmanageable separation on stage, the playhouses themselves suffered a kind of marriage and divorce during the last two decades of the century. Having split the playgoing populace between them in the years after the Restoration, the Duke's and King's Companies united in 1682. To a

great extent oral culture thrives on multiplicity and variety, on collaboration and anonymity, and the famed liveliness and proliferation of pre-Revolutionary drama owed its fecundity in part to the numbers (still debatable) of theatres extant. The oral quality of the earlier theatre after the Restoration (1660s to 1682 thereabouts) fomented in the dual/duet of the two playhouses. When the companies united in 1682, the number of plays by proportion dwindled, the variety of genre, of types and counter-types conjured out of the often jocular competition between the two houses ended.

15 In *The Lucky Chance* Sir Cautious fears that the 'news' of his wife's infidelity, engineered by him, would cause him to be "put in print at Snowhill," i.e., ridiculed in a ballad broadside (III, 276).

16 For a more tangible notion of how an actress might call forth a certain part created for her by her author, one might think of the actresses Carole Lombard and Jean Arthur. Both women had comedic, knowing turns of intonation and a way of playing at playing the 'woman' which would powerfully affect not only the writing for, but the reception of the actress. I imagine from the roles Barry played she was an intelligent comic who could move in her own doubled space of past and present and take her audience with her.

17 See Charles Gildon's *The Life of Mr Thomas Betterton* and Milhous and Hume (1985: 59–69).

18 At this point I must give the certain march of my own narrative an interrupting corrective: it behooves us to remember that performance like literature, like life, tends to give the lie to relentlessly demarcated evolutionary theories. For example, there is some reason to claim that eighteenth-century plays represent a shift that signals a move from theatrical, oral performance to the influential increase of the public reception of news of the world and characters in action in print, as Julie Stone Peters suggests. However, the nineteenth century in England, despite rising figures of public literacy, has a stage marked by its own kind of orality. An "actor's" theatre, the profusion of melodrama and burlesque seems to harken back to a world made by the ear through improvisation.

19 Change could still occur without the printed legal agreement substantiating the oral understanding. "Though the Civil Marriage Act itself was repudiated, the Protestant desire to recognize marriage as a civil contract rather than a sacramental union continued to affect ideas about marriage and eventually won out" (Staves 1979: 116).

20 Hume sees the playwrights' response to Collier as a sign of the diminished "cultural position of drama at the end of the seventeenth century." As drama "was a negligible presence in the print culture world of the time," Hume suggests the playwrights were defensive about their craft, its reception and its importance (1999: 494).

21 The term "complexity of thought" signals a late twentieth-century critical value given to texts that work like novels with "elaborate self examination" and the representation of complex thinking. Such complexity is rarely attached to the "somatic intelligence" Melrose describes as part of theatregoing. Complexity is a word to be aware of: it is often a way of distinguishing print culture as an inevitable advance on oral tradition (see Finnegan 1994).

22 In other instances on the stage, *Richard II* for example, one character 'hands' a word to his/her playing partner, which can set up a staged improvisational exchange, the words acting as catalyst for making up (see Skantze 2000). Here, however, the break in Constant's soliloquy as well as the setness of the language inhibit the sense of staged improvisation.

23 Of course Mirabelle 'farms out' his trickery to his servant.

24 The distinction is not between Shakespeare as a "better" or more "persuasive" playwright than Vanbrugh; Congreve's universally acclaimed speeches contain matching prisms and matching distance.

Epilogue

1 Theatre historians will forgive me I hope for this broad statement. Much as theatrical history has produced excellent and nuanced arguments (upon which I draw) about the slow change in theatrical design, the majority of writing about the difference between the stage before and after the proscenium does collapse the late seventeenth and all of the eighteenth century into late nineteenth-century conventions.

2 According to Richmond Barbour Jonson initiates the conception of the property book and the definition of the self, though it will take a century before an author's ownership was law: "By so tenaciously insisting upon his agency – in a single volume, under his name, repossessing his scattered and immensely various work – Jonson made a decisive cultural improvisation. He became England's first great advertiser of the proprietary self" (1998: 510–11). It seems no accident that Barbour sees Jonson's act as one of cultural *improvisation*, even here in the midst of his laying claim to his property in print, Jonson must use the tools of performance to advertise himself.

3 For a discussion of the evolution of box seats in the theatre, see Marvin Carlson's *Places of Performance* (1989). Carlson remains an inspiring exemplar of performance studies at its kinetic best; in this book he shows the intersection of architecture, place, and social ritual in the buildings and monuments and cities that are sites of performance.

4 See Petrucci (1995), Saenger (1997), and Coleman (1996). For a voluble increase in our understanding of the presence of sound and its power in the early modern period, see Bruce Smith (1999).

5 Easy as it is to forget the world of sound when writing and reading, one need only remember an occasion – a play, a children's performance, a reading – when the voice of the performer dropped to a whisper, not a performed whisper but an inaudible one. The bodies of those in the audience strain to make out the words, supplying possible phrases which would complete the sense of the imperfectly heard. The tension of trying to apprehend the meaning fills the room.

6 One can see the history of the changing value of forms of production in this small example. Now a handwritten note looks less 'official' than a formally printed document.

7 Susan Stewart sees a change in the purpose of collecting during this period: the "motives of antiquarianism" change from the late sixteenth to the late seventeenth century. In the late sixteenth century the "collection of antiquities was generally politically supported and politically motivated" and such collections were used to "authenticate the history of kingdoms." However, by the end of the seventeenth century the motives of antiquarians might be investigative, Henry Bourne's collection of "pagan and papist relics" used to expose the remnants of superstition "surviving among the common people," or elegiac, John Aubrey's collection of antiquities "symbolic of a dying English past" (1993: 141).

Bibliography

Achinstein, Sharon (1994) *Milton and the Revolutionary Reader*, Princeton: Princeton University Press.

Agnew, Jean-Christophe (1986) *Worlds Apart: the Market and the Theatre in Anglo-American Thought 1550–1750*, New York: Cambridge University Press.

Alciati, Andrea (1531 reprint) *Emblemas*, Madrid.

Altaba-Artal, Dolors (1995) "Aphra Behn's *The Feign'd Curtezans; or, A Night's Intrigue* from Calderon's Casa con dos puertas mala es de guardar," *Restoration and 18th Century Theatre Research*, 10 (1): 29–43.

Anderson, Benedict (1991) *Imagined Communities*, revised edition, London: Verso.

Arendt, Hannah (1958) *The Human Condition*, Chicago: University of Chicago Press.

Artuad, Antonin (1958) *The Theater and Its Double*, New York: Grove Press.

Bach, Rebecca Ann (1995) "'Ty Good Shubshects': The Jacobean Masque as Colonial Discourse", *Medieval and Renaissance Drama in England*, 7: 206–23.

Backsheider, Paula (1993) *Spectacular Politics: Theatrical Power and Mass Culture in Early Modern England*, Baltimore: Johns Hopkins University Press.

Bacon, Jon Lance (1991) "Wives, Widows and Writings in Restoration Comedy," *Studies in English Literature, 1500–1900*, 31 (3): 427–44.

Barber, C.L. (1968) "*A Maske Presented at Ludlow Castle*: The Masque as a Masque," in John Diekhoff (ed.) *A Maske at Ludlow*, Cleveland: Case Western Reserve University, 188–206.

Barbour, Richmond (1992) "The Elizabethan Jonson in Print", *Criticism*, Summer, 34: 317–26.

—— (1998) "Jonson and the Motives of Print," *Criticism*, Fall, 40 (4): 499–517.

Barilli, Renato (1989) *Rhetoric*, Minneapolis: University of Minnesota.

Barish, Jonas (1981) *The Antitheatrical Prejudice*, Berkeley: University of California Press.

Barroll, Leeds (1996) "Theatre as Text: the Case of Queen Anna and the Jacobean Court Masque," in A.L. Magnusson and C.E. McGee (eds) *The Elizabethan Theatre*, XIV: 175–93.

Bassnett, Susan (1989) "Struggling With the Past: Women's Theater in Search of a History", *New Theatre Quarterly* 5 (18): 107–12.

——, Michael Booth, and John Stokes (1988) *Bernhardt, Terry and Duse: the Actress in Her Time*, New York: Cambridge University Press.

Bataille, Georges (1988) *The Accursed Share: An Essay on General Economy*, trans. Robert Hurley, New York: Zone Books.

Baxandall, Michael (1972) *Painting and Experience in Fifteenth-Century Italy*, New York, Oxford: Clarendon Press.

Behn, Aphra (1915) *The Works of Aphra Behn*, M. Summers (ed.), 6 vols, London.

—— (1967) *The Rover*, Frederick M. Link (ed.), Lincoln: University of Nebraska Press.

—— (1986) *The Rover*, Simon Trussler (ed.), London: Swan Theater Plays.

—— (1989) *The Uncollected Verse of Aphra Behn*, Germaine Greer (ed.), Stumps Cross, Essex: Stumps Cross Books.

—— (1992) *The Works of Aphra Behn*, Janet Todd (ed.), Columbus: University of Ohio.

Belsey, Catherine (1988) *John Milton: Language, Gender, Power*, Oxford: Oxford University Press.

Bennett, Susan (1990) *Theatre Audiences: A Theory of Production and Reception*, London, New York: Routledge.

Berg, Sara van den (1991) "Ben Jonson and the Ideology of Authorship," in Jennifer Brady and W.H. Herendeen (eds) *Ben Jonson's 1616 Folio*, Newark: University of Delaware Press, 111–37.

Berger, John (1972) *Ways of Seeing*, New York: Viking.

Bevington, David (ed.) (1995) *The Theatrical City: Culture, Theatre, and Politics in London 1576–1649*, Cambridge: Cambridge University Press.

Bhabha, Homi K. (1997) "The Other Question: the Stereotype and Colonial Discourse," in K.M. Newton (ed.) *Twentieth-Century Literary Theory: A Reader*, New York: St. Martin's Press, 293–301.

Blum, Abbe (1988) "The Author's Authority: *Areopagitica* and the Labour of Licensing," in Mary Nyquist and Margaret W. Ferguson (eds) *Re-membering Milton*, New York: Methuen, 74–96.

Boaz, David (1997) *The Libertarian Reader: Classic and Contemporary Readings from Lao-tzu to Milton Friedman*, New York: Free Press.

Boebel, Dagny (1996) "In the Carnival World of Adam's Garden: Roving and Rape in Behn's *The Rover*," in Katherine M. Quinsey (ed.) *Broken Boundaries: Women and Feminism in Restoration Drama*, Lexington: University of Kentucky Press, 54–70.

Bogart, Anne (2001) *A Director Prepares*, London: Routledge.

Bourdieu, Pierre (1990) *The Logic of Practice*, trans. Richard Nice, Cambridge: Polity Press.

Brady, Jennifer (1991) "'Noe Fault, but Life': Jonson's Folio as Monument and Barrier," in Jennifer Brady and W.H. Herendeen (eds) *Ben Jonson's 1616 Folio*, Newark, London: University of Delaware Press, 192–216.

—— and Herendeen, W.H. (eds) (1991) *Ben Jonson's 1616 Folio*, Newark, London: University of Delaware Press.

Breasted, Barbara (1971) "*Comus* and the Castlehaven Scandal," *Milton Studies*, 3: 201–24.

Bristol, Michael (1996) *Big-Time Shakespeare*, London: Routledge.

Brook, Peter (1968) *The Empty Space*, New York: Atheneum.

—— (1987) *The Shifting Point*, New York: Harper and Row.

Brown, John Russell (1999) *New Sites for Shakespeare*, London: Routledge.

Brown, Steve (1990) "The Boyhood of Shakespeare's Heroines: Notes on Gender Ambiguity in the Sixteenth Century," *Studies in English Literature*, 30: 243–63.

Bruster, Douglas (2000) "The Structural Transformation of Print in Late Elizabethan England," in Arthur Marotti and Michael Bristol (eds) *Print, Manuscript, and Performance: The Changing Relations of the Media in Early Modern England*, Columbus: Ohio State University Press, 49–89.

Butler, Judith (1990) "Performative Acts and Gender Constitution," in Sue-Ellen Case (ed.) *Performing Feminisms*, Baltimore, London: Johns Hopkins University Press, 270–82.

Butler, Martin (1984) *Theatre and Crisis, 1632–1642*, New York: Cambridge University Press.

—— (1991) "'We Are One Mans All': *The Gipsies Metamorphosed*," *The Yearbook of English Studies*, 21: 253–73.

Burke, Kenneth (1969) *A Rhetoric of Motives*, Berkeley: University of California Press.

Camille, Michael (1992) *Image on the Edge: The Margins of Medieval Art*, Cambridge: Cambridge University Press.

Canfield, J. Douglas (1989) *The Word as Bond in English Literature from the Middle Ages to the Restoration*, Philadelphia: University of Pennsylvania Press.

Carlson, Marvin (1989) *Places of Performance: The Semiotics of Theatre Architecture*. Ithaca: Cornell University Press.

—— (1991) "The Status of Stage Directions," *Studies in the Literary Imagination*, Fall, 24 (2): 37–47.

—— (1994) "Invisible Presences – Performance Intertextuality," *Theatre Research International*, Summer, 19 (2): 111–17.

—— (1996) *Performance*, London: Routledge.

Carruthers, Mary (2001) "Rhetorical *Ductus* or Moving Through Composition," in Mark Franko and Annette Richards (eds) *Acting on the Past: Historical Performances Across the Disciplines*, Hanover and London: Wesleyan University Press, 99–117.

Carson, Anne (1995) *Glass, Irony and God*, New York: New Directions Books.

Carter, Angela (1980) "The Language of Sisterhood," in Michael Leonard and Christopher Ricks (eds) *The State of the Language*, Berkeley, London: University of California Press, 226–34.

—— (1991) *Wise Children*, New York: Farrar, Strauss and Giroux.

Case, Sue-Ellen (1988) *Feminism and Theater*, New York: Methuen.

—— (1990) *Performing Feminisms*, Baltimore, London: Johns Hopkins University Press.

—— and Janelle Reinelt (eds) (1991) *The Performance of Power: Theatrical Discourse and Politics*, Iowa: University of Iowa Press.

Centlivre, Susanna (1714) *The Wonder! A Woman Keeps a Secret*, London.

de Certeau, Michel (1984) *The Practice of Everyday Life*, trans. Steven F. Rendall, Berkeley: University of California Press.

Chartier, Roger (ed.) (1987) *The Culture of Print*, Princeton: Princeton University Press.

—— (1989) "Leisure and Sociability: Reading Aloud in Early Modern Europe," in Susan Zimmerman and Ronald F.E. Weissman (eds) *Urban Life in the Renaissance*, Newark: University of Delaware Press, 105–20.

—— (1992) "The World of the Text, the World of the Reader," Talk given at the Modern Language Association Conference in New York.

—— (1994) *The Order of Books*, trans. Lydia G. Cochrane, Stanford: Stanford University Press.

—— (1995) *Forms and Meanings: Text, Performance, and Audience from Codex to Computer*, Philadelphia: University of Pennsylvania Press.

Chaudhuri, Una (1993) "The Spectator in Drama/Drama in the Spectator: Peter Schaffer's *Equus*," in Hersh Zeifman (ed.) *Contemporary British Drama*, Toronto: University of Toronto Press, 41–61.

Cibber, Colley (1889) *An Apology for the Life of Mr. Colley Cibber*, 2 vols, London: J.C. Nimmo.

Cixous, Hélène (1976) "The Laugh of the Medusa," *Signs*, 1, 875–93.

Clanchy, M.T. (1979) *From Memory to Written Record*, Cambridge, MA: Harvard University Press.

Clark, Sandra (1983) *The Elizabethan Pamphleteers*, Rutherford, NJ: Fairleigh Dickinson University.

Coleman, Joyce (1996) *Public Reading and the Reading Public in Late Medieval England and France*, New York: Cambridge University Press.

Collier, Jeremy (1698 reprint; 1972) *A Short View of the Immorality and Profaneness of the English Stage*, New York: .

le Comte, Edward (1977) *Milton and Sex*, New York: Columbia University Press.

Cordner, Michael (1990) "Marriage Comedy after the 1688 Revolution: Southerne to Vanbrugh," *The Modern Language Review*, April, 85: 273–89.

Cox, James (1926) *The Rise of Sentimental Comedy*, Folcroft, PA: Folcroft Press.

Creaser, John (1984) "'The Present Aid of this Occasion': The Setting of *Comus*," David Linley (ed.) *The Court Masque*, Manchester: Manchester University Press, 111–34.

Danchin, Pierre (ed.) (1981) *The Prologues and the Epilogues of the Restoration, 1660–1700*. vol. i, Nancy: Université Nancy II.

Darnton, Robert and Daniel Roche (eds) (1989) *Revolution in Print*, Berkeley: University of California Press.

Davies, Marie Therese Jones (1967) *Inigo Jones, Ben Jonson et le masque*, Paris: M. Didier.

Davis, Natalie Zemon (1975) *Society and Culture in Early Modern France*, Stanford: Stanford University Press.

Dawson, Anthony (1996) "Performance and Participation: Desdemona, Foucault, and the Actors Body," in James C. Bulman (ed.) *Shakespeare, Theory and Performance*, London: Routledge, 29–45.

Dekker, Thomas and Thomas Middleton (1987 reprint) *The Roaring Girl*, Paul Mulholland (ed.), Manchester: Manchester University Press.

Demaray, John (1968) *Milton and the Masque Tradition*, Cambridge, MA: Harvard University Press.

—— (1980) *Milton's Theatrical Epic: The Invention and Design of Paradise Lost*, Cambridge, MA: Harvard University Press.

Derrida, Jacques (1992) *Given Time. I, Counterfeit Money*, Chicago: University of Chicago Press.

Diamond, Elin (1989) "Gestus and the Signature in Aphra Behn's *The Rover*," *ELH*, Fall, 56 (3): 519–41.

—— (1996) *Performance and Cultural Politics*, London: Routledge.

Diekhoff, John S. (ed.) (1968) *A Maske at Ludlow*, Cleveland: Press of Case Western Reserve University.

—— (1968) "A Masque at Ludlow," in John S. Diekhoff (ed.), *A Maske at Ludlow*, Cleveland: Press of Case Western Reserve University, 1–16.

DiGangi, Mario (1995) "'Asses and Wits' The Homoerotics of Mastery in Satiric Comedy," *ELR*, Spring, 25 (2): 179–208.

Dolan, Jill (1989) "In Defense of the Discourse: Materialist Feminism, Postmodernism, Poststructuralism . . . and Theory," *TDR*, 33: 58–71.

Dollimore, Jonathan (1989) *Radical Tragedy: Religion, Ideology, and Power in the Drama of Shakespeare and his Contemporaries*, New York: Harvester Wheatsheaf.

Dryden, John (1912) *Dramatic Essays by John Dryden*, New York.

Dutton, Richard (1997) "The Birth of the Author," in Cedric C. Brown and Arthur F. Marotti (eds) *Texts and Cultural Change in Early Modern England*, New York: St. Martin's Press, 153–78.

Dyer, Richard (1992) *Only Entertainment*, London: Routledge.

Eisenstein, Elizabeth L. (1980) *The Printing Press as an Agent of Change*, Cambridge: Cambridge University Press.

—— (1985) "On the Printing Press as an Agent of Change," in Olson, David R. *et al.* (eds) *Literacy, Language, and Learning: The Nature and Consequences of Reading and Writing*, Cambridge: Cambridge University Press, 19–33.

Elsky, Martin (1989) *Authorizing Words: Speech, Writing, and Print in the English Renaissance*, Ithaca: Cornell University Press.

Erickson, Robert (1996) "Lady Fulbank and the Poet's Dream in Behn's *Lucky Chance*," in Katherine M. Quinsey (ed.) *Broken Boundaries: Women & Feminism in Restoration Drama*, Lexington: University of Kentucky Press, 89–110.

Etherege, George (1927) *The Dramatic Works of Sir George Etherege*, Oxford: B. Blackwell.

Evelyn, John (1959) *The Diary of John Evelyn*, E.S. de Beer (ed.), 6 vols, Oxford: Oxford University Press.

Fabian, Johannes (1990) *Power and Performance: Ethnographic Explorations through Proverbial Wisdom and Theatre in Shaba, Zaire*, Madison: University of Wisconsin Press.

Ferguson, Francis (1949) *The Idea of a Theater*, Princeton: Princeton University Press.

Ferguson, Margaret W. (1991) "Juggling the Categories of Race, Class and Gender: Aphra Behn's *Oroonoko*," *Women's Studies*, 19: 159–81.

Ferris, Lesley (1990) *Acting Women*, New York: New York University Press.

Findlen, Paula (1994) *Possessing Nature: Museums, Collecting and Scientific Culture in Early Modern Italy*, Berkeley: University of California Press.

Finke, Laurie A. (1990) "Painting Women: Images of Femininity in Jacobean Tragedy," in Sue-Ellen Case (ed.), *Performing Feminisms*, Baltimore: Johns Hopkins University Press, 223–36.

Finnegan, Ruth (1994) "Literacy as Mythical Charter," in Deborah Keller-Cohen (ed.) *Literacy: Interdisciplinary Conversations*, Cresskill, NJ: Hampton Press, 31–43.

Fish, Stanley (1984) "Authors-Readers: Jonson's Community of the Same," *Representations*, Summer, 7: 26–58.

Foster, Susan Leigh (1995) *Choreographing History*, Bloomington: University of Indiana Press.

—— (1998) "Choreographies of Gender," *Signs* 24, (1): 1–34.

Foucault, Michel (1970) *The Order of Things*, New York: Pantheon Books.

—— (1977) *Language, Counter-Memory, Practice*, Donald F. Bouchard (ed.) Ithaca: Cornell University.

Fox, Adam (1996) "Popular Verses in the Early Seventeeth Century," in James Raven, Helen Small, and Naomi Tadmor (eds) *The Practice and Representation of Reading in England*, Cambridge: Cambridge University Press, 125–37.

—— (2000) *Oral and Literate Culture, 1500–1700*, Oxford: Oxford University Press.

Franko, Mark (1993) *Dance as Text: Ideologies of the Baroque Body*, Cambridge, New York: Cambridge University Press.

—— and Annette Richards (eds) (2000) *Acting on the Past: Historical Performances Across the Disciplines*, Hanover and London: Wesleyan University Press.

Gallagher, Catherine (1988) "Who Was That Masked Woman? The Prostitute and the Playwright in the Comedies of Aphra Behn," *Women's Studies*, 19: 23–42.

Garber, Marjorie (1992) *Vested Interests*, New York: Routledge.

Gilder, Rosamond (1931) *Enter the Actress*, Boston: Houghton Mifflin.

Gildon, Charles (1710) *The Life of Mr. Thomas Betterton*, London: R. Gosling.

Girard, Rene (1965) *Deceit, Desire and the Novel: Self and Other in Literary Structure*, Baltimore: Johns Hopkins University Press.

Gordon, D.J. (1949) "Poet and Architect: The Intellectual Setting of the Quarrel between Ben Jonson and Inigo Jones," *Journal of the Warburg and Courtauld Institutes*, 12: 152–78.

Gossett, Suzanne (1988) "'Man-Maid, Begone!': Women in Masques," in Kirby Farrell, Elizabeth Hageman, and Arthur F. Kinney (eds) *Women in the Renaissance*, Amherst: University of Massachusetts, 118–35.

De Grazia, Margreta (1991) *Shakespeare Verbatim*, Oxford, New York: Oxford University Press.

—— (1995) "Soliloquies and Wages in the Age of Emergent Consciousness," *Textual Practice*, 9 (1): 67–92.

—— Maureen Quilliga, and Peter Stallybrass (eds) (1996) *Subject and Object in Renaissance Culture*, Cambridge: Cambridge University Press.

Greenblatt, Stephen (1988) *Shakespearean Negotiations*, Berkeley: University of California Press.

—— (1995) "Language of Motion: Reflections on a Seventeenth-Century Muscleman," in Susan Leigh Foster (ed.) *Choreographing History*, Bloomington: Indiana University Press.

Gucer, Kathryn (2000) "'Not Heretofore Extant in Print': Where the Mad Ranters Are," *Journal of the History of Ideas*, 61 (1): 75–95.

Gurr, Andrew (1987) *Playgoers in Shakespeare's London*, Cambridge: Cambridge University Press.

Halasz, Alexandra (1997) *The Marketplace of Print*, Cambridge: Cambridge University Press.

Hall, Kim F. (1991) "Sexual Politics and Cultural Identity in *The Masque of Blackness*," in Sue-Ellen Case and Janelle Reinelt (eds) *The Performance of Power*, Iowa: University of Iowa Press, 3–18.

Halpern, Richard (1986) "Puritanism and Maenadism in *A Mask*," Margaret Ferguson, Maureen Quilligan, and Nancy J. Vickers (eds) *Rewriting the Renaissance*, Chicago: University of Chicago Press, 88–105.

Harline, Craig E. (1987) *Pamphlets, Printing and Political Culture in the Early Dutch Republic*, Dordecht: Martinus Nijhoff Publishers.

Heinemann, Margot (1978) "Popular Drama and Leveller Style: Richard Overton and John Harris," in Maurice Comforth (ed.) *Rebels and Their Causes*, London: Lawrence and Wishart, 62–92.

Helgerson, Richard (1987) "Milton Reads the King's Book: Print, Performance and the Making of a Bourgeois Idol," *Criticism*, Winter, 29 (1): 1–25.

Hirst, Derek (1995) "John Milton's *Eikonoklastes*," in David Bevington (ed.) *The Theatrical City*, Cambridge: Cambridge University Press, 245–59.

Hobbes, Thomas (1996) *Leviathan*, Oxford: Oxford University Press.

Holland, Peter (1979) *The Ornament of Action*, Cambridge: Cambridge University Press.

—— (1991) "Reading to the Company," in Peter Holland (ed.) *Reading Plays: Interpretation and Reception*, Cambridge: Cambridge University Press, 8–29.

Holtsun, James (ed.) (1992) *Pamphlet Wars: Prose in the English Revolution*, London, Portland, OR: Frank Cass.

Howard, Jean (1987) "Renaissance Antitheatricality and the Politics of Gender and Rank in *Much Ado About Nothing*," in Jean E. Howard and Marion F. O'Connor (eds) *Shakespeare Reproduced: The Text in History and Ideology*, New York: Methuen, 163–87.

—— (1988) "Crossdressing, the Theater and Gender Struggle in Early Modern England," *Shakespeare Quarterly*, Winter, 39 (4): 418–40.

—— and Katherine E. Maus (eds) *Engendering a Nation: A Feminist Account of Shakespeare's English Histories*, New York: Routledge.

Howard, Skiles (1998) *The Politics of Courtly Dancing in Early Modern England*, Amherst: University of Massachusetts.

Howe, Elizabeth (1992) *The First English Actresses*, Cambridge: Cambridge University Press.

Howell, W.S. (1956) *Logic and Rhetoric in England: 1500–1700*, Princeton: Princeton University Press.

Hughes, Derek (2001) *The Theatre of Aphra Behn*, New York: Palgrave.

Hume, Robert D. (1976) *The Development of English Drama in the Late Seventeenth Century*, Oxford: Oxford University Press.

—— (ed.) (1980) *The London Theatre World 1600–1800*, Carbondale: University of Illinois.

—— (1982) "The Nature of the Dorset Garden Theatre," *Theatre Notebook*, 36 (3): 96–105.

—— (1999) "Jeremy Collier and the Future of the London Theater in 1698," *Studies in Philology*, 96 (4): 480–511.

Hutner, Heidi (ed.) (1993) *Rereading Aphra Behn: History, Theory, and Criticism*, Charlottesville: University Press of Virginia.

—— (1993) "Revisioning the Female Body: Aphra Behn's *The Rover, Parts I and 2*," in Heidi Hutner (ed.) *Rereading Aphra Behn: History, Theory, and Criticism*, Charlottesville: University Press of Virginia.

Hyde, Lewis (1979) *The Gift: Imagination and the Erotic Life of Property*, New York: Random House.

Hyland, Peter (1987) "A 'Kind of Woman': The Elizabethan Boy-Actor and the Kabuki Onnagata," *Theater Research Institute*, Spring, 12 (1): 1–8.

de Jean, Joan (1984) "Lafayette's Ellipses: The Privileges of Anonymity," *PMLA* 99, October: 884–902.

Johns, Adrian. "The Physiology of Reading in Restoration England" in *The Practice and Representation of Reading in England*, James Raven, Helen Small, and Naomi Tadmor (eds), Cambridge: Cambridge University Press, 138–61.

Jonson, Ben (1692 Folio edition) *The Complete Works*, London.

—— (1890) *Masques and Entertainments*, Henry Morley (ed.), London.

—— (1927–53) *Ben Jonson*, C.H. Herford and Percy and Evelyn Simpson (eds), 11 vols, Oxford: Clarendon Press.

—— (1966) *Epicoene; or, the Silent Woman*, L.A. Beaurline (ed.), Lincoln: University of Nebraska Press.

—— (1969) *The Complete Masques*, Stephen Orgel (ed.), New Haven: Yale University Press.

—— (1975) *The Complete Poems*, George Parfitt (ed.), New Haven: Yale University Press.

Kastan, David and John D. Cox (eds) (1997) *A New History of Early English Drama*, New York: Columbia University Press.

Kendrick, Christopher (1988) "Milton and Sexuality: a Symptomatic Reading of *Comus*," in Mary Nyquist and Margaret W. Ferguson (eds) *Re-membering Milton*, New York, London: Methuen, 43–73.

Kernan, Alvin (1987) *Printing Technology, Letters and Samuel Johnson*, Princeton: Princeton University Press.

Ketcham, Michael G. (1985) *Transparent Designs: Reading, Performance and Form in "The Spectator,"* Athens, GA: University of Georgia Press.

Killigrew, Thomas (1664 reprint; 1967) *Comedies and Tragedies*, New York: B. Blom.

King, Thomas (1992) "'As If (She) Were Made on Purpose to Put the Whole World Into Good Humour': Reconstructing the First English Actresses," *TDR*, 36 (3): 78–102.

Kreis-Schinck, Annette (2001) *Women, Writing, and the Theater in the Early Modern Period: The Plays of Aphra Behn and Suzanne Centlivre*, Fairleigh, NJ: Fairleigh Dickinson University Press.

Langhans, Edward A. (1972) "A Conjectural Reconstruction of the Dorset Garden Theatre," *Theatre Survey*, 13: 74–93.

—— (1981) (ed.) *Restoration Promptbooks*, Carbondale: Southern Illinois University Press.

—— (2000) "The Theatre" in Deborah Payne Fisk (ed.) *The Cambridge Companion to English Restoration Theatre*, Cambridge: Cambridge University Press, 1–18.

Lanier, Henry Wysham (1930) *The First English Actresses*, New York: The Players.

Laquer, Thomas (1992) *Making Sex: Body and Gender from the Greeks to Freud*, Cambridge, MA: Harvard University Press.

de Lauretis, Teresa (1987) *Technologies of Gender*, Bloomington: Indiana University Press.

Leacroft, Richard (1973) *The Development of the English Playhouse*, Ithaca: Cornell University Press.

Lepecki, Andre (1996) "Embracing the Stain: Notes on the Time of Dance," *Performance Research International*, 4.

Levine, Laura (1986) "Men in Women's Clothing: Antitheatricality and Effeminization from 1579 to 1642," *Criticism*, Spring, 28: 121–43.

Levi-Strauss, Claude (1969) *The Elementary Structures of Kinship*, trans. James Bell *et al.*, Boston: Beacon Press.

Levy, F.J. (2000) "Staging the News," in Arthur Marotti and Michael Bristol (eds) *Print, Manuscript, and Performance: the Changing Relations of the Media in Early Modern England*, Columbus: Ohio State University Press, 252–78.

Lewcock, Dawn (1996) "More For Seeing Than Hearing: Behn and the Uses of Theatre," in Janet Todd (ed.) *Aphra Behn Studies*, Cambridge: Cambridge University Press, 66–83.

Lindley, David (ed.) (1984) *The Court Masque*, Manchester: University of Manchester Press.

Linklater, Kristin (1992) *Freeing Shakespeare's Voice*, New York: Theatre Communications Group.

Loeffelholz, Mary (1987) "Two Masques of Ceres and Proserpine: *Comus* and *The Tempest*," in Mary Nyquist and Margaret W. Ferguson (eds) *Re-membering Milton*, New York, London: Methuen, 25–42.

Loewenstein, Joseph (1985) "The Script in the Marketplace," *Representations*, 12: 101–14.

—— (1991) "Printing and the 'Multitudinous Presse': The Contentious Texts of Jonson's Masques," in Jennifer Brady and W.H. Herendeen (eds) *Ben Jonson's 1616 Folio*, Newark, London: University of Delaware Press, 168–91.

Lussier, Mark (1991) "'The Vile Merchandize of Fortune': Women, Economy, and Desire in Aphra Behn," *Women's Studies*, 18 (4): 379–93.

Lyons, Charles R. (1987) "Silent Women and Shrews: Eroticism and Convention in *Epicoene* and *Measure for Measure*," *Comparative Drama*, Summer, 23 (2): 123–40.

Marcus, Leah (1988) *Puzzling Shakespeare: Local Reading and Its Discontents*, Berkeley: University of California Press.

Marotti, Arthur and Michael Bristol (eds) (2000) *Print, Manuscript, and Performance: the Changing Relations of the Media in Early Modern England*, Columbus: Ohio State University Press.

Marshall, David (1986) *The Figure of Theater*, New York: Columbia University Press.

Masson, David (1881) *The Life of John Milton*, New York: Macmillan & Co.

Masten, Jeffrey (ed.) (1997) *Language Machines*, London: Routledge.

Matson, Wallace I. (1996) "Why Isn't the Mind-Body Problem Ancient?" in P.K. Feyerband and G. Maxwell (eds) *Mind, Matter and Method*, Minneapolis: University of Minnesota.

Maus, Katharine Eisaman (1979) "'Playhouse Flesh and Blood': Sexual Ideology and the Restoration Actress," *ELH*, 46: 595–617.

Mauss, Marcel (1967) *The Gift: Forms and Functions of Exchange in Archaic Societies*, trans. Ian Cunnison, New York: Norton.

Mazio, Carla (ed.) (1997) *The Body in Parts*, London: Routledge.

McGuire, Maryann Cale (1983) *Milton's Puritan Masque*, Athens, GA: University of Georgia Press.

McIntyre, Jean (1998) "Buckingham the Masquer," *Renaissance and Reformation*, 22 (3): 59–81.

McLuskie, Kathleen (1991) "The Poets' Royal Exchange: Patronage and Commerce in Early Modern Drama," *Yearbook of English Studies*, 21: 53–62.

Melrose, Susan *(1994) A Semiotics of the Dramatic Text,* London: St. Martin's Press.

Mendelson, Sara Heller (1987) *The Mental World of Stuart Women*, Brighton, Sussex: Harvester Press.

Merleau-Ponty, Maurice (1964) *Signs,* trans. Richard C. McCleary, Evanston: Northwestern University Press.

Milhous, Judith and Robert D. Hume (1985) *Producible Interpretation*, Carbondale: Southern Illinois University Press.

Miller, D.A. (1989) *The Novel and the Police*, Berkeley: University of California Press.

Milton, John (1645) *Poems of Mr. John Milton*, London.

—— (1973) *A Maske; The Earlier Versions,* S.E. Sprott (ed.), Toronto: University of Toronto Press.

—— (1985) *Complete Poems and Major Prose*, Merritt Y. Hughes (ed.), New York: Macmillan.

Mirabelli, Philip (1989) "Silence, Wit, and Wisdom in *The Silent Woman*," *Studies in English Literature*, 29: 309–36.

Modiano, Raimonda (1989) "Coleridge and Wordsworth: the Ethics of Gift Exchange and Literary Ownership," *The Wordsworth Circle*, 20 (2): 113–20.

Mulvey, Laura (1989) *Visual and Other Pleasures*, Bloomington: University of Indiana Press.

Muller, Frans (1993) "Flying Dragons and Dancing Chairs at Dorset Garden," *Theatre Notebook,* 48: 80–95.

Munns, Jessica (1993) "'Good, Sweet, Honey, Sugar Candied Reader': Aphra Behn's Foreplay in Forewords," in Heidi Hutner (ed.) *Rereading Aphra Behn: History, Theory, and Criticism*, Charlottesville: University Press of Virginia, 44–62.

Murray, Timothy (1987) *Theatrical Legitimation*, New York: Oxford University Press.

Nagler, A.M. (1952) *A Sourcebook in Theatrical History*, New York: Dover Publications.

Nelson, Byron (1992) "The Ranters and the Limits of Language," in James Holtsun (ed.) *Pamphlet Wars,* London, Portland, OR: Frank Cass, 60–75.

Newman, Karen (1989) "City Talk: Women and Commodification in Jonson's *Epicoene*," *ELH*, Fall 56 (3): 503–18.

Neville, Jennifer (1999) "Dance the Garden: Moving and Static Choreography in Renaissance Europe," *Renaissance Quarterly*, Autumn, 52 (3): 805–36.

Nicoll, Allardyce (1952) *A History of English Drama*, 6 vols, Cambridge: Cambridge University Press.

Norbrook, David (1984a) *Poetry and Politics in the English Renaissance*, London: Routledge.

—— (1984b) "The Reformation of the Masque," in David Lindley (ed.) *The Court Masque*, Manchester: Manchester University Press, 94–110.

Northbrooke, John (1845) *A Treatise Against Dicing, Dancing, Plays and Interludes*, London: Shakespeare Society Reprint.

Nyquist, Mary and Margaret Ferguson (eds) (1988) *Re-membering Milton*, New York, London: Methuen.

O'Connell, Michael (1985) "The Idolatrous Eye: Iconoclasm, Anti-theatricalism, and the Image of the Elizabethan Theater," *ELH*, Summer, 52 (2): 279–310.

O'Donnell, Mary Anne (1986) *Aphra Behn: an Annotated Bibliography of Primary and Secondary Sources*, New York: Garland Publishers.

Ong, Walter S.J. (1958) *Ramus, Method, and the Decay of Dialogue*, Cambridge, MA: Harvard University Press.

—— (1967) *The Presence of the Word*, New Haven: Yale University Press.

—— (1971) *Rhetoric, Romance and Technology*, Ithaca: Cornell University Press.

—— (1982) *Orality and Literacy*, London: Methuen.

Orgel, Stephen (1965) *The Jonsonian Masque*, Cambridge, MA: Harvard University Press.

—— (1975) *The Illusion of Power: Political Theatre in the English Renaissance*, Berkeley: University of California Press.

—— (1989) "Nobody's Perfect: Or Why Did the English Stage Take Boys for Women?" *South Atlantic Quarterly*, Winter, 88 (1): 7–30.

—— (1994) "Acting Scripts, Performing Texts," in Randall M. Leod (ed.) *Crisis in Editing: Texts of the English Renaissance*, New York: AMS, 251–94.

Owen, Susan J. (1996) *Restoration Theatre and Crisis*, New York: Oxford University Press.

Parker, William Riley (1969) *Milton's Contemporary Reputation*, Folcroft, PA: Folcroft Press.

Parker, Patricia (1987) *Literary Fat Ladies*, London: Methuen.

—— (1989) "On the Tongue: Cross Gendering, Effeminacy and the Art of Words," *Style*, Fall, 23 (3): 445–65.

—— (1993) "Othello and Hamlet: Dilation, Spying and the 'Secret Place of Woman,'" *Representations*, Fall, 44: 60–95.

Payne, Deborah (1991) "'And Poets Shall By Patron-Princes Live': Aphra Behn and Patronage," in Mary Anne Schofield and Cecilia Macheski (eds) *Curtain Calls*, Athens, GA: University of Georgia Press, 105–19.

—— (1995) "Reified Object or Emergent Professional? Retheorizing the Restoration Actress," in J. Douglas Canfield and Deborah Payne (eds) *Cultural Readings of Restoration and 18th-Century English Theatre*, Athens, GA: University of Georgia Press, 13–38.

Peacock, John (1995) *The Stage Designs of Inigo Jones: the European Context*, Cambridge: Cambridge University Press.

Pearson, Jacqueline (1988) *The Prostituted Muse: Images of Women and Women Dramatists 1642–1737*, New York: Harvester Wheatsheaf.

Pepys, Samuel (1983) *The Diary of Samuel Pepys*, Robert Latham and William Matthews (eds), 11 vols, Berkeley: University of California Press.

Peters, Julie Stone (1987) "'Things Governed By Words': Late 17th-century Comedy and the Reformers," *English Studies*, 2: 142–53.

—— (1990) *Congreve, the Drama and the Printed Word*, Stanford: Stanford University Press.

—— (2000) *The Theatre of the Book, 1480–1880: Print, Text, and Performance in Europe*, Oxford: Oxford University Press.

Petrucci, Armando (1995) *Writers and Readers in Medieval Italy: Studies in the History of Written Culture*, New Haven: Yale University Press.

Postlewait, Thomas and Bruce A. McConachie (eds) (1989) *Interpreting the Theatrical Past*, Iowa: University of Iowa Press.

Potter, Lois (1975–83) "The Plays and the Playwrights: 1642–1660," in Edwards, R. (ed.) *The Revels History of Drama in English, volume IV*, London: Methuen.

—— (1989) *Secret Rites and Secret Writing: Royalist Literature 1641–1660*, Cambridge: Cambridge University Press.

Randall, Dale B.J. (1995) *Winter Fruit: English Drama, 1642–1660*, Lexington: University of Kentucky Press.

Raven, James, Helen Small, and Naomi Tadmor (eds) (1996) *The Practice and Representation of Reading in England*, Cambridge: Cambridge University Press.

Rhodes, Neil and Jonathan Sawday (2000) (eds) *The Renaissance Computer: Knowledge Technology in the First Age of Print*, London: Routledge.

Riggs, David (1989) *Ben Jonson: A Life*, Cambridge, MA: Harvard University Press.

Ripa, Cesare (1618 reprint: 1986) *Iconologia*, Torino: Folgola Editore.

Roach, Joseph (1985) *The Player's Passion*, Newark: University of Delaware Press.

—— (1989) "Power's Body: the Inscription of Morality as Style," in Thomas Postlewait and Bruce A. McConachie (eds) *Interpreting the Theatrical Past*, Iowa: University of Iowa Press, 99–118.

—— (1992) "Mardi Gras Indians and Others: Genealogies of American Performance," *Theatre Journal*, December, 44: 461–83.

—— (1996) *Cities of the Dead: Circum-Atlantic Performance*, New York: Columbia University Press.

Roberts, David (1989) *The Ladies: Female Patronage of Restoration Drama 1660–1700*, Oxford: Oxford University Press.

Rose, Mark (1993) *Authors and Owners: The Invention of Copyright*, Cambridge, MA: Harvard University Press.

Rosenthal, Laura (1996) *Playwrights and Plagiarists in Early Modern England*, Ithaca: Cornell University Press.

Saenger, Paul (1997) *Space Between Words: The Origin of Silent Reading*, Stanford: Stanford University Press.

Sanders, Julie (1996) "'The Day's Sports Devised in the Inn': Jonson's *The New Inn* and Theatrical Politics," *The Modern Language Review*, July 91: 545–60.

Schofield, Mary Anne and Cecilia Macheski (eds) (1991) *Curtain Calls*, Athens, GA: University of Georgia Press.

Schwyzer, Philip (1997) "Purity and Danger on the West Bank of the Severn." *Representations*, Fall 60: 22–48.

Senelick, Laurence (1992) *Gender in Performance: the Presentation of Difference in the Performing Arts*, Hanover: Tufts University/University Press of New England.

Sennett, Richard (1976) *The Fall of Public Man*, New York: W.W. Norton.

Serres, Michel (1982) *Hermes: Literature, Science, Philosophy*, Josue Harari and David F. Bell (eds), Baltimore: Johns Hopkins University Press.

Shakespeare, William (1996) *The Tempest*, John Russell Brown (ed.), New York: Applause Books.

—— (1996) *King Lear*, John Russell Brown (ed.) New York: Applause Books.

—— *The Norton Shakespeare*, Stephen Greenblatt, Walter Cohen, Jean Howard, and Katherine Maus (eds), New York: W. W. Norton.

Shapiro, Susan (1988) "'Yon Plumed Dandebrat': Male 'Effeminacy' in English Satire and Criticism," *Review of English Studies*, 39 (155): 400–12.

Sharp, Ronald A. (1986) "Gift Exchange and the Economies of Spirit in *The Merchant of Venice*," *Modern Philology*, February: 250–65.

—— (1989) "Keats and the Spiritual Economies of Gift Exchange," *Keats-Shelley Journal*, 38: 66–81.

Sherman, Stuart (1996) *Telling Time: Clocks, Diaries, and English Diurnal Form, 1680–1785*, Chicago: University of Chicago Press.

Sherman, William H. (1996) "The Place of Reading in the English Renaissance: John Dee Revisited," in James Raven, Helen Small, and Naomi Tadmor (eds) *The Practice and Representation of Reading in England*, Cambridge: Cambridge University Press, 62–76.

Shershow, Scott Cutler (1994) "'The Mouth of 'hem All': Ben Jonson, Authorship, and the Performing Object," *Theatre Journal*, 46: 187–212.

Shevelow, Kathryn (1989) *Women and Print Culture*, London: Routledge.

Shoaf, R.A. (1990) "'Unwemmed Custance': Circulation, Property, and Incest in the Man of Law's Tale," *Exemplaria*, March, 2 (1): 289–302.

Shuger, Deborah (1997) "'Gums of Gluttinous Heat' and the Streams of Consciousness: the Theology of Milton's *Maske*," *Representations*, Fall, 60: 1–21.

Skantze, P.A. (1994) "The Lady Eve; or, 'Who's on First?'" *Women in Theatre: Occasional Papers*, Warwick: University of Warwick.

—— (2002, 2000 reprint) "Making It Up: Improvisation as Cultural Exchange between Shakespeare and Italy," in Michele Marrapodi (ed.) *Shakespeare and Intertextuality*, Manchester: Manchester University Press.

Smith, Bruce (1999) *The Acoustic World of Early Modern England*, Chicago: University of Chicago Press.

Smith, Nigel (1990) "*Areopagitica*: Voicing Contexts, 1643–5," in David Loewenstein and James Grantham Turner (eds) *Politics, Poetics, and Hermeneutics in Milton's Prose*, Cambridge: Cambridge University Press, 103–22.

—— (1993) "Soapboilers Speak Shakespeare Rudely: Masquerade and Leveller Pamphleteering," *Critical Survey*, 5 (3): 236–43

—— (1994) *Literature and Revolution in England, 1640–1660*, New Haven: Yale University Press.

Spacks, Patricia Meyer (1985) *Gossip*, New York: Knopf.

Spencer, Lois (1958) "The Professional and Literary Connexions of George Thomason," *The Library*, XIII.

Spring, John R. (1977) "Platforms and Picture Frames: a Conjectural Reconstruction of the Duke of York's Theatre: a Review of Facts and Problems," *Theatre Notebook*, 31: 6–19.

Stallybrass, Peter (1999) "Worn Worlds: Clothes, Mourning and the Life of Things," in Dan Ben-Amos and Liliane Weissberg (eds) *Cultural Memory and the Construction of Identity*, Detroit: Wayne State University Press, 27–44.

States, Bert O. (1985) *Great Rekoning in Little Rooms: On the Phenomenology of Theater*, Berkeley: University of California Press.

Stavely, Keith (1975) *The Politics of Milton's Prose Style*, New Haven: Yale University Press.

Staves, Susan (1979) *Players' Scepters: Fictions of Authority in the Restoration*, Lincoln: University of Nebraska Press.

—— (1990) *Married Women's Separate Property in England, 1660–1833*, Cambridge: Cambridge University Press.

Stewart, Susan (1993) *On Longing*, North Carolina: Duke University Press.

Stone, Laurence (1977) *The Family, Sex and Marriage in England 1500–1800*, New York: Harper and Row.

Straker, Stephen M. (1985) "What Is the Histories of Theories of Perception the History Of?" in Richard Westfall, Margaret Osler, and Paul Farber (eds) *Religion, Science and Worldview*, Cambridge: Cambridge University Press, 245–73.

Strong, Roy C. (1984) *Art and Power: Renaissance Festivals, 1450–1650*, Woodbridge, Suffolk: Boydell Press.

Strum Kenney, Shirley (1980) "The Publication of Plays," in Robert Hume and Arthur Scouten (eds) *The London Theatre World 1600–1800*, Carbondale: Southern Illinois University Press.

Styan, J.L. (1986) *Restoration Comedy in Performance*, Cambridge: Cambridge University Press.

Sullivan, David M. (1993) "The Female Will in Aphra Behn," *Women's Studies*, 22: 335–47.

Sutherland, James (1986) *The Restoration Newspaper and Its Development*, Cambridge: Cambridge University Press.

Swann, Marjorie (2001) *Curiosities and Texts: the Culture of Collecting in Early Modern England*, Philadelphia: University of Pennsylvania Press.

Sweeney, III, John Gordon (1985) *Jonson and the Psychology of Public Theater*, Princeton: Princeton University Press.

Todd, Janet (1989) *The Sign of Angellica: Women, Writing and Fiction, 1600–1800*, New York: Columbia University Press.

—— (ed.) (1996) *Aphra Behn Studies*, Cambridge: Cambridge University Press.

Tribble, Evelyn (1993) *Margins and Marginality: the Printed Page in Early Modern England*, Charlottesville: University Press of Virginia.

Trubowitz, Rachel (1992) "Female Preachers and Male Wives: Gender and Authority in Civil War England," in J. Holtsun (ed.) *Pamphlet Wars: Prose in the English Revolution*, London, Portland, OR: Frank Cass.

Trussler, Simon (1994) *The Cambridge Illustrated History of British Theatre*, Cambridge: Cambridge University Press.

Ulmer, Greg (1985) *Applied Grammatology*, Baltimore: Johns Hopkins University Press.

Vanbrugh, Sir John (1698) *A Short Vindication of* The Relapse *and* The Provoked Wife *from Immorality and Profaneness*, London.

—— (1969)*The Provoked Wife*, Curt A. Zimansky (ed.), Lincoln: University of Nebraska Press.

Vickers, Nancy (1981) "Diana Described: Scattered Woman and Scattered Rhyme," *Critical Inquiry*, 8: 265–79.

Voss, Paul J. (2001) *Elizabethan News Pamphlets: Shakespeare, Spenser, Marlowe and the Birth of Journalism*, Pittsburgh, PA: Duquesne University Press.

Wall, Wendy (1993) *The Imprint of Gender: Authorship and Publication in the English Renaissance*, Ithaca: Cornell University Press.

Weimann, Robert (2000) *Author's Pen and Actor's Voice: Playing and Writing in Shakespeare's Theatre*, Cambridge: Cambridge University Press.

West, William N. (1997) "Spaces for Experiment: Theaters and Encyclopedias in Early Modern England," *Dissertation Abstracts International*, 57 (8): 3486–7.

Wickham, G. (1959) *Early English Stages*, London: Routledge.

Wiles, David (2000) *Greek Theatre Performance: an Introduction*, Cambridge: Cambridge University Press.

Williams, David (ed.) (1988) *Peter Brook: A Theatrical Casebook*, London: Methuen.

Williams, Raymond (1954) *Drama in Performance*, Chester, PA: Defour Editions.

Wilson, J.H. (1958) *All the King's Ladies*, Chicago: University of Chicago Press.

Wiseman, Susan (1998) *Drama and Politics in the English Civil War*, Cambridge: Cambridge University Press.

Wollman, Richard (1993) "The 'Press and the Fire': Print and Manuscript Culture in Donne's Circle," *SEL*, 33 (1): 85–97.

Wolfe, Don Marion (ed.) (1994) *Leveller Manifestoes of the Puritan Revolution*, New York and London: T. Nelson and Sons.

Womack, Peter (1986) *Ben Jonson*, New York: B. Blackwell.

Wycherley, William (1967) *The Plain Dealer*, Lincoln: University of Nebraska Press.

Yates, Frances (1966) *The Art of Memory*, Chicago: University of Chicago Press.

—— (1969) *Theatre of the World*, Chicago: University of Chicago Press.

Index